# Knowlton–Pearson Correspondence

Lizzie Andrew Borden, circa 1890.

# The Knowlton-Pearson Correspondence
## 1923 - 1930

UNPUBLISHED LETTERS BETWEEN
FRANK WARREN KNOWLTON
AND EDMUND LESTER PEARSON
ON THE LIZZIE A. BORDEN CASE

Michael Martins
Dennis A. Binette
Stefani Koorey
Editors

FALL RIVER
HISTORICAL SOCIETY
PRESS

Fall River Historical Society Press
451 Rock Street
Fall River, MA, 02720
fallriverhistorical.org
(508) 679-1071

ISBN: 978-0-9641248-9-9

Printed in the United States of America on acid-free paper.

Book and cover design by Stefani Koorey, PearTree Press, Westport, MA.

*In memory of Frank Warren Knowlton Jr.*

*(1912-2002)*

# TABLE OF CONTENTS

# INTRODUCTION

*Dear Knowlton, —It is possible that you remember, but probable that you have forgotten one Edmund Pearson, who sat at your table in Memorial Hall, and used to talk with you about the Borden case.*

So begins the first letter in this collection sent from Edmund Lester Pearson to Frank Warren Knowlton, the son of Hosea Morrill Knowlton, the prosecuting attorney at the famed murder trial. Interested in the study of crime for both its psychological and social aspects, Pearson had always been fascinated by the trial of Lizzie Andrew Borden and wished to include an essay on the case in a volume he was preparing about American murders, "The Borden Case," in *Studies in Murder*, published by The Macmillan Company in 1924.

Edmund Pearson was born in Newburyport, Massachusetts, on February 11, 1880. He obtained his Bachelor of Arts from Harvard University in 1902, after which he left New England for Albany, New York, where he studied library science. He obtained employment in that field in the Washington, D.C. Public Library. In 1914, he began working at the New York Public Library, an institution with which he was to remain for the next thirteen years. He was also employed as a book reviewer for *The Outlook*, and from 1906 to 1920, also prepared the column "The Librarian" for the *Boston Evening Transcript*.

He began his correspondence with Frank W. Knowlton in 1923. At that time, aside from *The Fall River Tragedy* by Edwin Porter and a couple of short essays, there was virtually no other material available to Pearson on the subject. This is what prompted his first letter to Knowlton, one that began a correspondence between the two men that lasted until 1930. Pearson's fascination with his topic is evident from the very beginning, when he confides to Knowlton that it is "plain that Miss Borden is my *prima donna*."

The collection which follows describes how, through their pursuits, the two were able to uncover a considerable number of manuscripts, photographs, and transcripts of testimony. The reader can see first-hand how Pearson persisted, with the assistance of Frank W. Knowlton, until he eventually managed to accumulate a vast body of material from which to draw as he prepared his work. A good portion of the documents referred to are currently part of the Borden archive at the Fall River Historical Society, some of which were published as *The Commonwealth of Massachusetts vs. Lizzie A. Borden: The Knowlton Papers, 1892-1893.* The collection was presented to the museum in 1998 by Frank W. Knowlton Jr., son of the man addressed in this volume.

In order to preserve the integrity of the collection, all of the letters and news clippings were transcribed in their original form, despite errors in content, spelling, and punctuation. We have also retained the author's decisions in crossing out words and phrases.

These letters span over seven years, a period during which the crime writer authored three volumes containing essays on the Borden case: *Studies in Murder* (1924), *Murder at Smutty Nose* (1927), and *Five Murders* (1928). His major work on the case, *The Trial of Lizzie Borden,* was published in 1937 as the first in the series "Notable American Trials." It was the last of Pearson's work published in his lifetime; he died on August 8 of that year of bronchial pneumonia in New York City. He is buried in his native Newburyport.

Frank W. Knowlton was born in New Bedford, Massachusetts on August 1, 1878. He obtained his early education in his native city and subsequently entered Tufts College, graduating from that institution in 1899. Following in his father's footsteps, he pursued a career in law, attending Harvard Law School and graduating *cum laude* in 1902. First employed by the firm of Ropes, Gray, Boyden, and Perkins, in 1904, he became associated with Choate, Hall, and Stewart. Entering the firm as a law clerk, he soon after joined the partnership. In Brookline, Massachusetts, on June 30, 1908, he married Isabelle Grady Rioso. They had three sons.

Active in town affairs in Weston, Massachusetts, where he settled with his family, he was a trustee at Tufts College. He also served as a member of the council of the Boston Bar Association. While appearing in a case before the Board of Tax Appeals in Boston, in February of 1932, he was stricken with a heart attack. His death came the following month.

The fully annotated correspondence in this volume will fascinate not only those interested in the Borden case but any individual who enjoys the investigative process. The Fall River Historical Society is pleased to make available this collection from its archive of Borden-related material.

## The Editors

# THE CORRESPONDENCE

Edmund Lester Pearson, circa 1924.

———o○❀○o———

# The New York Public Library
### Astor, Lenox and Tilden Foundations

**476 FIFTH AVENUE**

*New York,* July 30, 1923

Dear Knowlton, -

It is possible that you remember, but probable that you have forgotten one Edmund Pearson, who sat at your table in Memorial Hall, and used to talk with you about the Borden case. I am that same man, and still interested in that case, - next to the trial of Professor Webster, it is Massachusetts' greatest murder case.

I am writing for The Macmillan Company, which publishes my books, a volume to contain some five or six essays of considerable length about certain extraordinary American murder trials or cases. One of them is finished; on another, the trials of Thomas Bram in Boston, I am now working, and have ~~access to~~ the stenographic reports of both trials, thanks to Mr. Asa French and Mr. Boyd Jones, who were on opposite sides in the second trial. Newspaper reports are not sufficient for my purpose, as I am trying to give a more correct account than they furnish. In short, I am trying to do what is done by British writers on those subjects: to give an authoritative brief history of each case, not deal with them as the average writer for the Sunday newspaper would do. When I say brief, I do not mean a mere sketch; the essays will run to about ten to twelve thousand words apiece, but they are not, of course, complete reports of the trials. I have the only book, so far as I know, ever published on the Borden case; it is by Porter of the Fall River Globe, it is out of print and scarce. I have heard that the Borden estate bought it up and suppressed it, as far as possible. I am also planning to go to Fall River to learn what I can there.

What I wish, of course, is to get reports of the testimony and arguments in the preliminary hearing at Fall River, as well as in the <u>trial itself</u>. If it is possible, and if you feel willing to do this, will you lend me for my use here in New York, such ~~records~~ reports as belong to your Father's estate, from his participation in these trials? If this is not possible, or agreeable to you in any way, can you put me in the way of obtaining the records elsewhere? The case must go in the book; its peculiar nature, the interest it aroused then still exists, I find, in many quarters; the distinguished counsel engaged; the peculiar rulings of the court; all these make it plain that Miss Borden is my <u>prima donna</u>.

I may add that I am a writer of ~~some~~ ten years of experience, with some knowledge of how to work with material like this, and that I am also a librarian (Editor of Publications at this Library) and hence a safe man to be trusted with valuable books. All this is to lead you to take judicial notice of the fact that I am not a yellow journalist.

Any information which you can give me <u>re</u> the Bordens will be most gratefully received. And your Petitioner will ever pray.

Faithfully yours,

Edmund Lester Pearson

**Biographical Note:** Memorial Hall is located in Cambridge, Massachusetts, at Harvard University, built to honor Harvard men who sacrificed their lives in defense of the Union in the Civil War. **Dr. John White Webster** (American professor of chemistry, mineralogy, and geology at Harvard University, his alma mater), 1793-1850; **Asa Palmer French** (American lawyer, US Attorney for the District of Massachusetts from 1906-1914), 1860-1935; **Boyd Bradshaw Jones** (American lawyer, partner in law firm of Hurlburt, Jones & Hall, Boston), 1856-1930; **Edwin H. Porter** (reporter for the *Fall River Daily Globe* and author of *The Fall River Tragedy: A History of the Borden Murders*, Fall River, MA: George R. H. Buffinton, Press of J. D. Munroe, 1893), 1864-1904; **Hosea Morrill Knowlton** (American lawyer, District Attorney for the Commonwealth of Massachusetts from 1879-1893, he led the prosecution against Miss Lizzie A. Borden, and later served as the Attorney General of the Commonwealth from 1894-1902), 1847-1902.

**Case Detail, Dr. Parkman Murder:** Dr. John White Webster aspired to a lifestyle that his modest salary could not support, forcing him to borrow heavily from friends and associates, including Dr. George Parkman, a prominent physician, businessman, and philanthropist, as well as a member of one of Boston's richest

Frank W. Knowlton Sr., circa 1928.

families. On November 23, 1849, as Parkman was attempting to collect payment, Webster struck Parkman on the head with a piece of firewood from the nearby fireplace. The blow fractured Parkman's skull, and Webster's efforts to revive him were unsuccessful. Webster bolted his lab door and dismembered Parkman's body. He burned most of Parkman's body in the lab furnace. There were no eyewitnesses to this event, but Webster's own suspicious behavior led to his arrest on November 30, 1849. His trial began in March of 1850—without the corpus delicti. On March 30, he was found guilty by a jury and hanged in Leverett Street Jail in Boston on August 30, 1850. Webster's trial is notable because it was one of the first murder convictions based on the testimony of medical experts and other forensic evidence to identify a body and establish guilt beyond a reasonable doubt.

The story of this murder appears in Pearson's *Murder at Smutty Nose* (1932) under the title "America's Classic Murder, or The Disappearance of Dr. Parkman."

***Case Detail, Thomas Bram:*** In July 1896, the brigantine *Hebert Fuller* set out from Boston with eleven people on board and loaded with lumber, on a voyage to Rosario, Argentina. After eighteen days at sea, the *Herbert Fuller* turned up in Halifax, Nova Scotia, with only eight people aboard and flying a black distress flag. On the ship's jolly boat, towed behind the brig, were the corpses of three victims— each axed to death. The dead included Captain Charles Nash, his wife Laura, and second mate August Blomberg. They had been murdered on the night of July 13. There were three suspects: Lester Hawthorne Monks, the sole pleasure passenger, whose baggage included whiskey, brandy, and sixty bottles of beer; Justus Leopold Westerberg, a Swedish sailor who often talked to himself; and Thomas M. Bram, the first mate. It was he who discovered the murder weapon and threw it overboard, saying he was protecting the crew from further attack. He also destroyed other evidence by doctoring the ship's logs. Westerberg said he saw Bram striking someone in the cabin where the bodies of the captain and his wife were found. Bram argued that he could not have been seen from where Westerberg stood at the ship's wheel. Bram had a criminal history, having once sold a ship and its contents, later telling the owners that the boat had sunk.

Bram was found guilty and sentenced to hang. Due to a procedural error, a second trial was ordered and he was again found guilty but not given the death sentence. A writer named Mary Roberts Rinehart (1876-1958), known as "America's Agatha Christie," wrote a fictional account of the story in 1914 (*The After House: A Story of Love, Mystery and a Private Yacht* ) and had Westerberg committing the murder instead of Bram. The book became extremely popular and Teddy Roosevelt took an interest in the case, lobbying President Woodrow Wilson to pardon Bram, who was so pardoned in 1919.

Rinehart's *The Circular Staircase* (1908) was a book found in the library of Lizzie A. Borden upon her death.

The story of this murder appears in Pearson's *Studies in Murder* (1924) under the title "Mate Bram!"

## Letter Number 2
## Knowlton to Pearson - August 1, 1923

————∘◦◦❦◦◦∘————

August 1, 1923.

Edmund Lester Pearson, Esq.,
The New York Public Library,
476 Fifth Avenue, New York City.

My dear Pearson:

I do remember you and pleasant companionship of our table in
Memorial Hall. I am very glad to have your letter.

I should be very glad to see an adequate essay treating the Borden
case. It was a remarkable case and ought to be adequately reviewed. I
have been to the Attorney General's office at the State House here in
Boston and I find that they have there the complete stenographic report
of the trial, with all the arguments on the incidental questions of law.
These typewritten reports are bound in two volumes of considerable
size, the whole comprising I should say, about fifteen or sixteen hundred
pages. I talked with Mr. Louis Freeze, Chief Clerk at the office, and as
far as he knows it is the only copy extant. He feels some hesitation in
lending it to me or any individual. He will, if you are in Boston, readily
make it available to you, or if it would better serve your purpose, he tells
me that he would be willing to send it to the New York Public Library,
entrusting it to the care and custody of the Library so that it would be
available for your use. I should rather gather that that would be satisfactory to you.

Incidentally I called up the State Library at the State House and
the Social Law Library, at the Court House, to see whether they had
any publications that might interest you. I find that they both have
Porter's book which you have, and they also have a pamphlet of some
forty-seven pages published in Boston in 1894 by Judge Charles G.
Davis entitled "Conduct of the Law in the Borden Case with Suggestions of Changes in Criminal Law and Practice." This might be interest-

ing to you, if you come on, or perhaps I can induce one of these libraries to send it to the New York Public Library. They looked up in the index to periodicals at the State Library and tell me that in the 27th volume of the American Law Review, at page 819, there is an article by J. H. Wigmore entitled "Borden Case".

I am somewhat in doubt about the report of the testimony and arguments in the preliminary hearing at Fall River. I have written to New Bedford and to Fall River to see if I can locate a copy, without any sanguine hope of success. Unfortunately, my father never kept any private files of his official cases, but left all the files, records, reports of testimony and everything in the custody of his successors in office, and I have written to the present District Attorney for the Southern District to learn whether he has in his files a copy of the inquest testimony. I will later let you know what I hear from these sources.

Somewhere at home I am quite sure that I have the original photographs which were used as exhibits at the trial of the case. They are gruesome affairs, showing the bodies of Andrew Borden and of his wife, as they were discovered, with all their terrible hatchet wounds, taken rather inartistically and somewhat poorly focused so as to make them even more grotesque than they need be. How I got them I do not know, and I haven't seen them for a few years, but I think I know where they are at home, and if you would like to have them to use or to refer to as you read the testimony, I should be very glad to lend them to you.

Let me know if you would like to have these matters sent on to you at the New York Library by the Attorney General's office, or one of the libraries I mentioned, and I will arrange it.

It was a remarkable trial. All of the counsel on both sides are now dead. All of the judges who presided at the case, there were three in number, are dead. The old sheriff in whose care she was has died and almost the only characters now living who had important parts are Lizzie Borden and her sister, Emma Borden. You may be perhaps interested to know that within a few months Lizzie Borden has launched litigation against her sister, Emma, seeking a partition of the real estate left by her father. This litigation was undoubtedly brought about by a disagreement between them.

There are a great many stories of Lizzie Borden going about, and perhaps the old police officers in Fall River can tell you quite a bit about her. She has lived comparatively quietly, except for the incidents of which the police would know, and except for one rather curious thing. About ten or fifteen years ago there was much in vogue around these parts an emotial tragedienne called Nance O'Neil, who played in heartrending melodramas and who was supposed to be about the most intensely emotional actress at that time. Lizzie Borden apparently formed a tremendous admiration for Nance O'Neil, and when Nance O'Neil was involved in litigation with her managers and creditors, which resulted in extended hearings in the equity session at the court at Boston, Lizzie Borden emerged from her retirement and became an almost daily spectator at the trial. I mention this simply as throwing some light on the probability that beneath her traditional cool and stolid Yankee exterior she seems to have had quite a depth of emotional power.

If you go to Fall River do not fail to see John W. Cummings, one of the older lawyers there, who was a great friend and confidant of my fathers and advised with him a great deal. He perhaps can give you more help there than anybody else, although I daresay Milton Reed of that city also could give you a great deal of the contemporaneous atmosphere. Judge Braley of our Supreme Court could doubtless tell you some things of interest, as he was, I think, at that time a practicing lawyer in Fall River.

I wonder if you have ever considered what I have always been lead to believe was one of our outstanding capital cases of Massachusetts, the case of Commonwealth v. Knapp, a case in which John Francis Knapp, Joseph Jenkins Knapp, George Crowninshield and Richard Crowninshield were indicted for the murder of Joseph White of Salem, and in which one of the alleged principals, Richard Crowninshield, committed suicide before the trial. This case is reported in 9 Pickering, 496 and 10 Pickering, 477. It was a case of such tremendous public interest at that time that Daniel Webster, although not holding office, was obtained to assist the Attorney General in prosecuting the case, and he obtained the convictions of the persons charged. I have always believed that that case was in the matter of public interest, particularly for days when there were no general newspaper reports, a case which aroused the Commonwealth perhaps more than any other case has before, or with one or two exceptions, since. As the murder was committed nearly one hundred years ago, it may be hard to get much contemporaneous material. I should rather suppose that the Law Libraries here would have a good deal upon the subject, as at that time there were a great many pamphlets published and sold which purported to give all the testimony.

With best regards, and hoping to see you if you come on this way, I am

Very truly yours,

FWK:ED

**Biographical Note:** Memorial Hall is located in Cambridge, Massachusetts, at Harvard University, built to honor Harvard men who sacrificed their lives in defense of the Union in the Civil War. **Louis Freeze** (Chief Clerk at the office of the Attorney General of the Commonwealth of Massachusetts), 1866-1956; **Charles Gideon Davis** (American lawyer, District Court Judge, Massachusetts, author of "The conduct of the law in the Borden case, with suggestions of changes in criminal law and practice," in *A Collection of Articles Concerning the Borden Case, Boston Daily Advertiser*, 1894), 1820-1903; **John Henry Wigmore** (American lawyer and legal scholar, known for his expertise in the law of evidence, author of "The Borden Case," *American Law Review* 17, November/December, 1893, 819-45), 1863-1943; **Hosea Morrill Knowlton** (American lawyer, District Attorney for the Commonwealth of Massachusetts from 1879-1893, he led the prosecution against Miss Lizzie A. Borden, and later served as the Attorney General of the Commonwealth from 1894-1902), 1847-1902; **Nance O'Neil** (American stage and film actress, one time friend of Lizzie A. Borden), 1874-1965; **John William Cummings** (American lawyer and politician, 14th and 16th mayor of Fall River, Massachusetts), 1855-1929; **Milton Reed** (American lawyer and politician, 13th mayor of Fall River), 1848-1932; **Henry King Braley** (12th mayor of Fall River, Associate Justice of the Massachusetts Supreme Judicial Court), 1850-1929; **Daniel Webster** (American lawyer and statesman, US. Secretary of State under Presidents William Henry Harrison, John Tyler, and Millard Fillmore), 1782-1852.

*Case detail, Commonwealth v. Knapp:* On April 6, 1830, eighty-two-year-old retired Captain Joseph White, who made his fortune as a shipmaster and trader in Salem, Massachusetts, was killed in his bed by a blow to the head and thirteen stab wounds. White lived with his niece, Mary Beckford, Lydia Kimball, a domestic servant, and Benjamin White, a distant relative who worked as the house handyman. Beckford's daughter Mary was married to Joseph Jenkins Knapp Jr., and the couple lived on a farm seven miles away in Wenham, Massachusetts. Initial suspects included the servants and Benjamin White. Since nothing of value

# The New York Public Library
### Astor, Lenox and Tilden Foundations

476 FIFTH AVENUE
*New York,* July 30, 1923

Dear Knowlton,- It is possible that you remember, but probable that you have forgotten one Edmund Pearson, who sat at your table in Memorial Hall, and used to talk with you about the Borden case. I am that same man, and still interested in that case,-next to the trial of Professor Webster, it is Massachusetts' greatest murder case.

I am writing for The Macmillan Company, which publishes my books, a volume to contain some five or six essays of considerable length about certain extraordinary American murder trials or cases. One of them is finished; on another, the trials of Thomas Bram in Boston, I am now working, and have access to the stenographic reports of both trials, thanks to Mr. Asa French and Mr. Boyd Jones, who were on opposite sides in the second trial. Newspaper reports are not sufficient for my purpose, as I am trying to give a more correct account than they furnish. In short, I am trying to do what is done by British writers on these subjects: to give an authoritative brief history of each case, not deal with them as the average writer for the Sunday newspaper would do. When I say brief, I do not mean a mere sketch; the essays will run to about ten to twelve thousand words apiece, but they are not, of course, complete reports of the trials. I have the only book, so far as I know, ever published on the Borden case; it is by Porter of the Fall River Globe, it is out of print and scarce. I have heard that the Borden estate bought it up and suppressed it, as far as possible. I am also planning to go to Fall River to learn what I can there.

What I wish, of course, is to get reports of the testimony and arguments in the preliminary hearing at Fall River, as well as in the trial itself. If it is possible, and if you feel willing to do this, will you lend me for my use here in New York, such records *reports* as belong to your Father's estate, from his participation in these trials? If this is not possible, or agreable to you in any way, can

First letter in the correspondence from Pearson to Knowlton.

was stolen and none of the footprints matched anyone who lived in the house, they were finally excluded.

Knapp and his brother John Francis were arrested after a long investigation and after Joseph confessed to his role in the plot, which included the hiring of Richard Crowninshield to carry out the actual attack. The motive was financial, with Knapp attempting to destroy White's will that favored White's nephew Stephen, because he believed that if he died without one, the estate would be divided among his close relatives, giving his mother-in-law a considerable fortune.

While Knapp was on trial, Crowninshield committed suicide by hanging himself in his jail cell. The first trial was declared a mistrial and the second trial brought the debate over forensic evidence to the fore. The prosecutor was the great Daniel Webster, and his summation was later "deemed a masterpiece of oratory." Both brothers were convicted. John Francis Knapp was hanged before a crowd of thousands in front of Salem Gaol on September 28, 1830. Joseph met that same fate three months later.

The case inspired Edgar Allan Poe to write "The Tell-Tale Heart" and Nathaniel Hawthorne to write *The Scarlett Letter.*

## Letter Number 3
## Knowlton to Otis S. Cook, Esq. - July 31, 1923

————•–o◦❀❀◦o–•————

July 31, 1923.

Otis S. Cook, Esq.,
Box 323,
Nantucket, Mass.

Dear Otis:

Do you know whether in the New Bedford Office there are any papers left referring to the old Lizzie Borden case? There is an author friend of mine who is working on a volume of essays about famous cases and he has asked my help about this case and is very anxious to obtain the stenographic report of the testimony and arguments at the preliminary hearing, the inquest. I hardly know where to put my hand on it for him and it occurred to me that possibly it might be still in the New Bedford office.

Yours very truly,

FWK:ED


*Biographical Note:* **Otis Seabury Cook** (American lawyer, partner in the firm of Knowlton, Perry & Cook, and later partner in the firm of Cook, Brownell & Taber), 1873-1939.

## Letter Number 4
## Knowlton to Michael J. Orpen, Esq. - August 1, 1923

———∘∘❀❀❀❀∘∘————

August 1, 1923.

Michael J. Orpen, Esq.,
Clerk, Second District Court of Bristol,
Fall River, Massachusetts.

Dear Mr. Orpen:

An author friend of mine is preparing an essay to be published by Macmillan on the famous Borden case. He has been writing to me for material and he is very anxious to see the testimony and arguments at the inquest. You may perhaps know or recall that Lizzie Borden's testimony at the inquest was offered in the trial in the Superior Court and occasioned a famous legal controversy. I haven't any idea where to tell him that this can be found, unless it is filed in the records of your court where the inquest was held.

I should be very glad, if it is not troubling you too much, to have you tell me whether it is filed away there, so that I can write to Mr. Pearson in New York, and if it is there he undoubtedly would like to come on to Fall River and inspect it. Any help that you may be able to give me, I should be very grateful for.

Yours very truly,

FWK:ED

*Biographical Note:* **Michael James Orpen** (Clerk of the Second District Court of Bristol County, Massachusetts), 1881-1935.

## Letter Number 5
## Knowlton to Stanley P. Hall, Esq. - August 1, 1923

———••○○❦○○••———

August 1, 1923.

Stanley P. Hall, Esq.,
District Attorney, Southern District,
Taunton, Massachusetts.

My dear Stanley:

At the trial of the case of Commonwealth v. Lizzie A. Borden, in 1893, a considerable controversy was waged at the time over the admissibility of testimony offered by Lizzie Borden at the inquest before the District Court at Fall River. A New York friend of mine, an author, is preparing an essay on this case and is very anxious to see the report of the testimony and arguments at the inquest. I have made it possible for him to see the report of the trial in the Superior Court, but he would like to inspect the testimony at the inquest and the arguments there. I haven't any idea where it would be, but it occurred to me that perhaps in the files of the District Attorney's office there would be some papers on this famous case, and that perhaps in those files would be the material that he would like to see.

I am sorry to trouble you about the matter, but if you could at your convenience tell me whether or not there are extant any of the original files of this case in the District Attorney's office, I should be very glad to inform my friend in New York and he doubtless, if you are willing, would come on from New York to see them in connection with the preparation of his work.

With best regards, I am

Yours very truly,

FWK:ED

*Biographical Note:* **Stanley Perkins Hall** (American lawyer, District Attorney of Southern District, Taunton, Massachusetts), 1889-1926.

## Letter Number 6
### Pearson to Knowlton - August 3, 1923

# The New York Public Library
### Astor, Lenox and Tilden Foundations

**475 FIFTH AVENUE**

*New York,* August 3, 1923

My dear Knowlton, -

I am indeed grateful for your long and interesting letter, for the offers you make of help in getting me information, and for the trouble you have already taken.

The offer of Mr. Freeze to send the report of the trial to the Library here, for my use, is quite satisfactory. It had better not come yet, however, as I suppose there is a limit to the time they would like to have it absent, and I shall not need it until I get back from a vacation. I am going away about the 13th, to be back around the 1st of September. Then I will write to him, or have the Library do so, and make the arrangements.

The pamphlet by Judge Davis is new to me, and it is possible that I can see it in the Bar Association Library here. I will find out.

The article by Dean Wigmore on the Borden Case I have already seen, and made notes from. That is a valuable one to me, as it contains the frank comments and criticisms of a lawyer upon the Court's exclusion of testimony, and almost amounts to saying that the trial resulted in a miscarriage of justice. I believe it did, but would rather have these criticisms come from a lawyer. I am on rather delicate ground in dealing with this case, since it resulted in an acquittal, and the accused still lives. But I read, in a Boston paper, about 1912, an article which said that the Fall River Globe had published annually, on the anniversary of the murder (which was <u>August 4th</u>-- , by the way) articles pointing strongly at "the poor girl", - as some people called

~ 14 ~

her. I think that Bobby Dean wrote me that the Globe ceased this after Porter's death.

It is especially kind of you to try to get the report of the hearing at Fall River. That was extraordinarily long - three or four days - about all of the counsel who were at the final trial were present (except Governor Robinson, - and, I guess, W.H. Moody) and she testified herself. If you do not get it, I shall have to rely on Porter, who is fairly full here, but of course not absolutely reliable for accuracy. He took an enormous interest in the case, and was apparently astounded and almost crushed at the final decision.

If you find the photographs you mention, and care to lend them to me, I would like to have them for my own consultation. They would be too gruesome for reproduction in my book, I am certain, but I might wish to have them copied by the photostat man here in the library, and keep them among my memoranda of the case, and of other cases. But I will not do even this, if you object. I will be glad to see them, however. I recall a rather ghastly story you once told me, concerning, I think, the skulls of that poor old couple.

I have clippings from the Boston papers about Miss Borden's recent litigation. I tried to run down, last summer, a rumor I had heard of her marriage, but could find nothing definite until the newspapers discussed this law-suit, and spoke of her as still unmarried. I have ~~head~~ heard one or two strange stories of her, but the Nance O'Neil one is new to me, and most interesting. I have heard that she used, in Boston, to stay at the Bellevue, which was formerly a favorite of mine.

Thanks also for the mention of people in Fall River who might be willing to give me information. I shall go over there in September or October, as I wish to see the house, if it is standing, and any other places connected with the event, as well as to talk with various folk. There is a druggist named, I think, Eli Bence, whom I wish to see; the jurymen all come from other towns, and probably few of them are alive today.

I have thought a little of the White murder in Salem, and have friends there who have urged it upon me. I had thought that perhaps it had been written up too much (like the Parkman case) but I am not sure that the present generation knows much about it. I must beware of too much New England in my book. My present cases are the Nathan murder in New York in 1870; the two trials of Bram before a U.S. Circuit Court in Boston, for the murders on the barkentine Herbert Fuller (you will

October 9, 1923.

Mr. Edmund L. Pearson,
　　The New York Public Library,
　　　　476 Fifth Avenue,
　　　　　　New York, New York.

Dear Pearson:

I am sending you today by express a considerable assortment of papers in the matter of Commonwealth v. Lizzie A. Borden. A great deal of these will be of no particular use to you as I have not attempted to go through them and sort them out.

Of course you appreciate that these files have been kept more or less confidential and while I do not know that there is anything in them which is of particularly private nature, I have not been through them enough to have any judgment on it. If there is anything which seems to you to be more or less private and confidential, I am going to ask you to exercise your discretion in the matter and preserve the confidence. Ultimately, when you have entirely finished with them I should, of course, be glad to have them back, but not until you have wholly finished with them.

I hope you have been successful in getting the record of the trial from Mr. Freeze.

Yours very truly,

FWK:ED

remember this, in 1896 - 98) in which I fortunately found the chief government witness living on the next street to me in New York; and an old New York State case the Boorn murder. I may also take up a Kansas case, and had thought of two other New England cases - the Tucker and the Mrs Rogers, because of the extraordinary popular agitation for commutation of sentence. They both present difficulties; in fact difficulties bristle everywhere, in making choice of subjects.

It is rather a strange thing to get a respectable American publishing house to agree to such a book, anyway. The topic is usually treated, in this country, merely in a sensational manner. If you are familiar with the Notable British Trials series, and have read the introductions to some of the best of those (Burke and Hare, and George Joseph Smith, for examples) you will know what I am trying to do, - without, of course, printing the complete report of the trial.

I can still remember, vividly, the afternoon (thirty years ago ~~tomorrow~~ last June - sorrow and alas!) when I saw put out on a small blackboard at the door of the Newburyport Herald, the legend:

Lizzie Borden Not Guilty.

I hope to be in Newburyport and Boston before cold weather comes, and shall certainly try to come in long enough to thank you personally.

Sincerely yours

Edmund L. Pearson

*Biographical Note:* **Louis Freeze** (Chief Clerk at the office of the Attorney General of the Commonwealth of Massachusetts), 1866-1956; **Charles Gideon Davis** (American lawyer, District Court Judge, Massachusetts, author of "The conduct of the law in the Borden case, with suggestions of changes in criminal law and practice," in *A Collection of Articles Concerning the Borden Case, Boston Daily Advertiser,* 1894), 1820-1903; **John Henry Wigmore** (American lawyer and legal scholar, known for his expertise in the law of evidence, author of "The Borden Case," *American Law Review* 17, November/December, 1893, 819-45), 1863-1943; **Robert Augustus Dean** (American lawyer, practicing in Fall River), 1881-1924; **Edwin H. Porter** (reporter for the *Fall River Daily Globe* and author of *The Fall River Tragedy: A History of the Borden Murders,* Fall River, MA: George R. H. Buffinton, Press of J. D. Munroe, 1893), 1864-1904; **George Dexter Robinson** (American lawyer, Governor of Massachusetts from 1883-1886 and principal attorney for the defense in the Commonwealth of Massachusetts vs. Lizzie A. Borden), 1834-1896; **William Henry Moody** (American lawyer, assisted Hosea Knowlton in the prosecution of Lizzie A. Borden, Secretary of the Navy and Attorney General under President Theodore Roosevelt, and justice of the Supreme Court), 1853-1917; **Nance O'Neil** (American stage and film actress, one time friend of Lizzie A. Borden), 1874-1965; **Eli Bence** (druggist at D.R. Smith's in Fall River and witness to Lizzie Borden's attempt to purchase prussic acid on the day before the murders, his testimony was excluded at the trial), 1865-1915.

***Case Detail, Commonwealth vs. Knapp (referred to here as the White murder):*** See Letter #2 for information.

***Case Detail, Dr. Parkman Murder:*** See Letter #1 for information.

***Case Detail, Nathan Murder:*** On July 28, 1870, fifty-six-year-old Benjamin Nathan, one of New York's most prominent citizens, former vice president of the New York Stock Exchange, past president of Congregation Shearith Israel, the oldest Jewish congregation in the United States, and a founder of the Jews' Hospital, later known as Mount Sinai, was brutally beaten to death. The murder weapon was a heavy iron bar, called a carpenter's dog, that was eighteen inches long with ends that turned at right angles. One end was covered in blood and caked with gray hairs. The only other two people in the home that night were two of Nathan's nine children: Frederick, 25, and Washington, 23. The rest of the family were at their country home in Morristown, New Jersey. Son Washington, a reputed ne'er do well who often argued with his father was the prime suspect, but he had an alibi. After the inquest, rewards were offered and many theories were discussed in the nation's newspapers, but no one was ever charged with the crime and it remains unsolved. The story of this murder appears in Pearson's *Studies in Murder* (1924) under the title "The Twenty-Third Street Murder."

***Case Detail, Thomas Bram:*** See Letter #1 for information.

***Case Detail, Jesse and Stephen Boorn:*** On May 10, 1812, in Manchester, Vermont, Russell Colvin was supposedly clubbed to death. Colvin had recently lost his Vermont farm and had to move his wife Sally and their six children to the home of his in-laws. It was not a hospitable arrangement. Jesse and Stephen Boorn, Sally's brothers, resented their many mouths to feed. In addition, Colvin was a "wanderer" and would often take a walk and not return for months at a time. On the date in question there was a day-long argument that ended in violence, with Stephen (according to Colvin's son Lewis, who was present) hitting Colvin with a stick and then a tree limb to knock him to the ground. Stephen then hit him again. Lewis ran away so there was no witness to the outcome of this act. Colvin disappeared and it was assumed it was his usual wandering habit. After several years, foul play was suspected.

Sally, in the meantime, became pregnant. She needed her husband to be dead in order to "swear the child" —name the father and compel him to provide child support. Stephen supposedly told her she could swear the child because he knew that Colvin was dead.

In 1819, seven years after Colvin's disappearance, the uncle of Stephen and Jesse had a dream that Colvin's ghost came to him and said he was murdered and buried in an old cellar hole. A few small items belonging to Colvin were found at this location and a court of inquiry was formed. Stephen had moved to New York, so Jesse Boorn was arrested. He was pressured to confess and did so, naming Stephen as the killer. He then led them to where they had buried the body, but only a few charred bone fragments were found.

Stephen was brought back from New York and the brothers were charged with murder. Jesse recanted his confession, but the State's Attorney ignored the recantation because more witnesses came forward to swear that they had heard Stephen and Jesse threaten Colvin's life.

Stephen then confessed, but claimed he had acted in self-defense. The trial was held on October 27, 1819. The principal evidence consisted of the confessions, as there was no body, and the eyewitness accounts of the arguments. The jury found them both guilty of murder. Jesse was given life in prison and Stephen was sentenced to death.

Stephen placed an ad in the newspapers asking for information about the whereabouts of Russell Colvin, asserting he was still alive. A man was found in Dover, New Jersey, who called himself Russell Colvin, and brought to Manchester, Vermont. The man recognized many of the neighbors, calling them by name, and was able to identify locations and buildings related to Colvin's life there.

It was agreed that Russell Colvin was indeed still alive and the brothers were granted a new trial, which the prosecution responded *nolle prosequi*, indicating that they would not pursue the case.

With one last twist, Jesse changed his name to Jesse Bowen and was a counterfeiter in a ring in Cleveland, Ohio. He admitted to a man that he and his brother had killed a man and had been released from jail when an impostor they hired to play the dead man had convinced the court that he had not died.

The story of this murder appears in Pearson's *Studies in Murder* (1924) under the title "Uncle Amos has a Dream."

**Case Detail, Charles Lewis Tucker:** On March 31, 1904, in Weston, Massachusetts, forty-one-year-old Miss Mabel Page was stabbed to death in the home of her widowed father, Edward Page. She had been alone in the house as Edward's son Harold was at work in Boston, and the housekeeper, Amy Roberts, was away for the day running errands. The elder Page set off about 9:30 in the morning for a "ramble," which took him to the post office at Auburndale, the public library there, and to visit friends. He returned to a quiet home about 2:00 in the afternoon, had a snack, and then went in search of his daughter. He found her murdered in her room with her throat cut. The medical examiner noted upon his inspection of the body that day that she had been stabbed in the back as well, with the wound of five inches piercing her heart.

A forty-eight-year-old unemployed man by the name of Charles Lewis Tucker was ultimately arrested for the crime. He had a knife with a bloody five-inch blade that he destroyed into fragments after the murder for fear, he said, of being accused. In the same pocket as the broken knife, the police discovered a small pin with a Canadian emblem that the Page housekeeper said belonged to Mable. In addition, Mable's purse had been robbed of twelve dollars, money found on the person of Tucker.

Tucker denied the charge against him but stood trial and was found guilty on wholly circumstantial evidence. He was sentenced to be hanged. A great public outpouring ensued to commute his sentence to life in prison, with 100,000 residents of the state signing a petition, but the governor of the Commonwealth (Curtis Guild Jr., 1860-1915), after a lengthy re-examination of the facts of the case, declined to commute the sentence. Charles Lewis Tucker was electrocuted for his crime on June 12, 1906.

***Case Detail, Mrs. Mary Mable Rogers:*** Mary Mable Rogers (1883-1905) was the last woman legally executed in the state of Vermont. She was hanged for the 1902 murder of her husband, Marcus Rogers.

Mary grew up in a troubled home. Both of her parents were drunks and her father had twice tried to kill her. She married Marcus Rogers at the age of fifteen, he being ten years her senior. The couple had a child in 1901, but the child died when Mary claimed she dropped the baby and he hit his head. In 1902, Marcus moved to live with his brothers to work on their farm and Mary moved to Bennington, Vermont. Mary publicly dated and slept with several men during her husband's absence, including Morris Knapp and the brothers Levi and Leon Perham. Mary asked Levi to kill Marcus, but he refused. Leon, still a teenager, agreed to help.

Mary was known for her outrageous behavior and invited her husband to visit her. On August 9, 1902, she and Leon invited him to play a game where they would tie his hands and he would have to escape the binds. With his hands tied behind his back, Mary forced him to breathe chloroform while Leon held him down. Unconscious, he was tossed in the nearby river where he drowned. Mary attached a forged suicide note to her husband's hat and took his life insurance police book from his pocket.

Leon confessed to the crime in exchange for a lesser sentence. The jury found Mary guilty and was sentenced to hang. Only one other woman had been hanged in Vermont, and the public was stunned by the harshness of the sentence against the nineteen year old. There was talk of commuting the sentence and evidence was presented of her mental incompetence. Supporters for her commutation from around the country contributed money to hire lawyers and publicize her case.

In November 1905, the US Supreme Court rejected her final request for a new trial. On December 8, Mary's execution took place, but was botched. The rope used was too long and her feet kept hitting the ground underneath the gallows. In the end, her neck did not break from the fall but, instead, she strangled to death, a process that took some fourteen minutes. The story of this murder appears in Pearson's *Studies in Murder* (1924) under the title "The Hunting Knife."

***Case Detail, Burke & Hare:*** Encouraged by the ease with which William Burke and William Hare made money robbing graves and selling the cadavers to the medical school at Edinburgh University in 1827 in Scotland, the duo decided to take matters in their own hands and assist people to their deaths. Their favored method of execution was suffocation after plying their victims with whiskey—it left the body unmarked and undamaged, a much better subject for dissection. In the aftermath of their killing spree, this kind of murder became known as "Burking."

The pair selected their victims from those who would be less likely to be missed. In total, they murdered at least sixteen people and sold their bodies for between seven to ten pounds a piece. William Hare was offered immunity in return for testifying against his partner.

Their trial began on Christmas Eve 1828 and Burke was found guilty of the murder of Marjory Docherty, Mary Patterson, and James Wilson. He was hanged at Lawnmarket in front of a crowd of over 25,000 on January 28, 1829. His body was put on public display and then donated to medical science for dissection.

Burke's skin was used to bind books and card holders and his skeleton is still on display at Surgeon's Hall in Edinburgh, next to his death mask and a life mask of Hare's face.

***Case Detail, George Joseph Smith:*** This case is known as "The Brides in the Bath" murders. George Joseph Smith (1872-1915, alias Oliver George Love, Charles Oliver James, Henry Williams, and John Lloyd) was convicted of the murders of Bessie Williams, Alice Burnham, and Margaret Elizabeth Lofty. Life insurance benefits was the motive, as in each case, the victims had taken out a policy in the days and weeks before their deaths.

At first, each case was treated as an accident. Divisional Detective Inspector Arthur Neil and the famed pathologist Dr. Bernard Spilsbury opined that it was impossible for anyone to accidentally drown in any of the baths in question. Later, after an exhumation of Margaret Lloyd, Spilsbury noted not only the bruise on her elbow that he had seen before, but also two microscopic marks. Spilsbury proposed an experiment whereby they would test the actual bathtubs with a live woman to see how it might be possible to drown someone. It was then that he realized that if the women had been seized by the feet and suddenly pulled them up toward himself at the head of the tub, sliding the upper part of the body under the water. This sudden flood of water into the nose and the throat might cause loss of consciousness and would explain the absence of major injuries.

George Joseph Smith was tried for the murders on June 22, 1915, found guilty and sentenced to death. He was hanged on August 13, 1915, in Maidstone Prison.

## Letter Number 7
## Michael J. Orpen to Knowlton - August 4, 1923

———— ·-°-◦◦❊❊◦◦-°-· ————

## Commonwealth of Massachusetts
### Second District Court of Bristol
### Fall River

EDWARD F. HAFINY, JUSTICE
MICHAEL J. ORPEN, CLERK
ANNIE H. BIRD, ASSISTANT CLERK

August 4, 1923.

Frank W. Knowlton, Esq.,
30 State Street,
Boston, Mass.

Dear Mr. Knowlton:

I have examined the old documents in the Clerk's Office and find no trace of inquest of Lizzie Borden.

Under the law the Magistrate sitting at the inquest, files his findings with the Clerk of the Superior Court. I might suggest that the testimony of Lizzie Borden at the inquest may be filed in the archives of District Attorney, as I understand it was offered at the trial at Superior Court, said trial being conducted by none other than the Honorable Hosea M. Knowlton himself.

If your friend cares to come to Fall River, he may search the records of the different newspapers at the Library. I understand they have an extended report of the proceedings in the Borden Murder Case.

I remember reading the history of the Borden Murder in a book published by one "Porter" who was a reporter at that time. Seems to me I borrowed the same from the chief of Police of Fall River, (Martin Feeney) and I suggest that you write to him for the loan of the same, I think he would gladly comply with your request, as I have talked the matter with him.

Very truly yours,
Michael J. Orpen, Clerk

MJO/ACO

*Biographical Note:* **Michael James Orpen** (Clerk of the Second District Court of Bristol County, Massachusetts), 1881-1935; **Edward F. Hanify** (American lawyer, Justice of the Massachusetts Superior Court from 1829 to 1954), 1881-1954; **Annie H. Bird** (Assistant Clerk of the Second District Court of Bristol County, Massachusetts), 1869-1933; **Hosea Morrill Knowlton** (American lawyer, District Attorney for the Commonwealth of Massachusetts from 1879-1893, he led the prosecution against Miss Lizzie A. Borden, and later served as the Attorney General of the Commonwealth from 1894-1902), 1847-1902; **Edwin H. Porter** (reporter for the *Fall River Daily Globe* and author of *The Fall River Tragedy: A History of the Borden Murders*, Fall River, MA: George R. H. Buffinton, Press of J. D. Munroe, 1893), 1864-1904; **Martin Feeney** (Chief of Police of Fall River from 1917-1931), 1862-1937.

## Letter Number 8
## Stanley P. Hall to Knowlton – August 4, 1923

————·◦○§⧉§◦○·————

THE COMMONWEALTH OF MASSACHUSETTS
Office of the
DISTRICT ATTORNEY
Southern District

Stanley P. Hall
District Attorney

Assistants
  Edward T. Murphy, Fall River
  Joseph A. Gauthier, New Bedford

Taunton, Massachusetts

August 4, 1923

Frank W. Knowlton, Esq.,

    Boston, Mass.,

My dear Frank:

I have your letter of Aug. 1st in reference to the report at the inquest in the Lizzie A. Borden case. The records that were turned over to me when I took office did not go back as far as 1893, but I am writing to Mr. Kenney to see if he can give any clue. Mr. Borden, the clerk, is out of town today, but I will also inquire of him.

I should like to find the same because I should be very much interested in reading them myself as well as letting your friend inspect them. I will let you know the result of what Mr. Kenney and Mr. Borden say.

Very truly yours,

Stanley P. Hall

*Biographical Note:* **Stanley Perkins Hall** (District Attorney of Southern District, Taunton, Massachusetts), 1889-1926, **Edward T. Murphy** (Assistant District Attorney, Southern District, Fall River, Commonwealth of Massachusetts), 1889-1975; **Joseph Arthur Gauthier** (Assistant District Attorney, Southern District, New Bedford, Commonwealth of Massachusetts), b. 1878; **Simeon Borden Jr.** (Clerk of the Court, Bristol County, Massachusetts), 1860-1924; **Joseph Thomas Kenney** (American lawyer, District Attorney of Southern District, New Bedford, Massachusetts, president of E. Anthony & Sons, Inc., publisher of New Bedford *Standard-Mercury*), 1877-1936.

## Letter Number 9
## Otis S. Cook to Knowlton – August 6, 1923

OTIS SEABURY COOK
MORRIS R. BROWNELL
FREDERIC H. TABER

COOK, BROWNELL & TABER
COUNSELORS AT LAW
MASONIC BUILDING
NEW BEDFORD, MASS.

August 6, 1923.

Frank W. Knowlton, Esq.,

30 State street,

Boston.

Dear Frank: -

Such papers as I have found in the Lizzie Borden case perhaps will not be useful for the purpose of your friend who is writing up cases, but I am going to send you the whole bunch by express. You may as well keep them or destroy them as you think best. I do not seem to find any court papers or testimony transcribed. There are a number of letters from theorists.

I have also the photographs showing the Borden house and the ruins of Mr. and Mrs. Borden with the marks of the hatchet, etc. If you want these, I shall send them at another time.

I guess that these are all the papers that we have had. I don't remember seeing any others.

These papers were in a tin box by themselves and have been there for years stowed away in our old files.

I hope that you are having a pleasant summer and getting a chance to take some rest and exercise which will be beneficial. I hope that you won't overdo. Perhaps you know how to take care of yourself and don't need my advice.

Your mother was in the office a few days ago and said that you had played eighteen holes. I think that I haven't played so many as that all together since John died. He and I used to practice a little in the old days, and I still miss him in a good many ways.

Please give my regards to Mr. Choate.

Faithfully yours,

O.S. Cook

OSC/ELJ

*Biographical Note:* **Otis Seabury Cook** (American lawyer, partner in the firm of Knowlton, Perry & Cook, and later partner in the firm of Cook, Brownell & Taber, New Bedford), 1873-1939; **Morris Ruggles Brownell** (American lawyer, partner in the firm of Cook, Brownell & Taber, New Bedford), 1881-1957; **Frederic Howland Taber** (American lawyer, partner in the firm of Cook, Brownell & Taber, New Bedford), 1883-1970; **Mrs. Hosea Morrill Knowlton** (Sylvia Bassett Almy of New Bedford, married Hosea M. Knowlton in 1873), 1852-1937; **Charles F. Choate Jr.** (American lawyer, partner in the firm of Choate, Hall & Stewart, Boston), 1866-1927.

## Letter Number 10:
## Knowlton to Pearson - August 16, 1923

————⊶◦⊶⊱✸⊰⊶◦⊶————

August 16, 1923.

Edmund L. Pearson, Esq.,
The New York Public Library,
476 Fifth Avenue,
New York City.

My dear Pearson:

Your letter of the 3d came while I was on a vacation and from which I have just returned for simply a day. I have not yet put my hand on the inquest testimony. I am still following trails which may lead to it. I have, however, received a large bunch of files consisting principally of correspondence passing among the prosecuting attorneys and hundreds of letters from cranks and others which are rather amusing and interesting. The only thing of importance that I have seen among them yet is a memorandum in William H. Moody's handwriting with the pages cited of the points valuable for the prosecution which they had relied upon to prove by the inquest testimony and without which they would not be able to establish. If we get the inquest testimony, this may be of some interest to you to show the importance placed upon it by the prosecuting attorneys.

I judge from your letter that you are not going to start active work until around the first of September. I shall be back then and will see if I have anything more by that time.

Yours very truly,

FWK:ED

*Biographical Note:* **William Henry Moody** (American lawyer, assisted Hosea Knowlton in the prosecution of Lizzie A. Borden, Secretary of the Navy and Attorney General under President Theodore Roosevelt, and justice of the Supreme Court), 1853-1917.

## Letter Number 11:
## Knowlton to Michael J. Orpen - August 16, 1893

———o·o @𝕏@ o·o———

**August 16, 1923.**

Michael J. Orpen, Esq.,
Clerk, 2d District Court of Bristol,
Fall River, Mass.

Dear Mr. Orpen:

Your letter of August 4 came while I was on my vacation and it has just come to my attention.

Thank you very much indeed for your suggestion. I have written to Mr. Kenney to find out about the old files and I shall write to Mr. Borden to see whether it may be filed in the Superior Court.

I have Porter's book and so has my friend. I also have access to the original stenographic report of the trial itself at the office of the Attorney General.

However, I thank you very much for your interest in the matter and your very kind letter.

Yours very truly,

FWK:ED

*Biographical Note:* **Michael James Orpen** (Clerk of the Second District Court of Bristol County, Massachusetts), 1881-1935; **Joseph Thomas Kenney** (American lawyer, District Attorney of Southern District, New Bedford, Massachusetts, president of E. Anthony & Sons, Inc., publisher of New Bedford *Standard-Mercury*), 1877-1936; **Simeon Borden Jr.** (Clerk of the Court, Bristol County, Massachusetts), 1860-1924; **Edwin H. Porter** (reporter for the *Fall River Daily Globe* and author of *The Fall River Tragedy: A History of the Borden Murders*, Fall River, MA: George R. H. Buffinton, Press of J. D. Munroe, 1893), 1864-1904.

## Letter Number 12:
## Knowlton to Stanley P. Hall - August 16, 1923

August 16, 1923.

Stanley P. Hall, Esq.,
District Attorney, Southern District,
Taunton, Massachusetts.

Dear Mr. Hall:

Thank you very much for your kind letter of August 4, which came while I was on my vacation and which I have just seen.

I think Mr. Kenney is at present on a vacation, but if you get any clues to the old files I should be very glad to know of them.

I shall write to Simeon Borden myself so that you need not bother with that source.

Yours very truly,

FWK:ED

*Biographical Note:* **Stanley Perkins Hall** (District Attorney of Southern District, Taunton, Massachusetts), 1889-1926; **Joseph Thomas Kenney** (American lawyer, District Attorney of Southern District, New Bedford, Massachusetts, president of E. Anthony & Sons, Inc., publisher of New Bedford *Standard-Mercury*), 1877-1936; **Simeon Borden Jr.** (Clerk of the Court, Bristol County, Massachusetts), 1860-1924.

## Letter Number 13:
## Knowlton to Simeon Borden - August 16, 1923

————∘◦○§◎§○◦∘————

August 16, 1923.

Simeon Borden, Esq.,
Clerk of Courts,
Taunton, Mass.

Dear Sim:

An author friend of mine who is making a study of the Lizzie A. Borden case has inquired of me where he can see the original inquest testimony which was offered in the Superior Court and excluded. Can you give me any light as to where I might be able to get hold of it? Possibly it may have gotten into your old files. Any help that you can give me I shall be very glad to have.

Yours very truly,

FWK:ED

*Biographical Note:* **Simeon Borden Jr.** (Clerk of the Court, Bristol County, Massachusetts), 1860-1924.

## Letter Number 14:
## Stanley P. Hall to Knowlton - August 17, 1923

THE COMMONWEALTH OF MASSACHUSETTS
OFFICE OF THE
DISTRICT ATTORNEY
SOUTHERN DISTRICT

STANLEY P. HALL
DISTRICT ATTORNEY

ASSISTANTS
EDWARD T. MURPHY, FALL RIVER
JOSEPH A. GAUTHIER, NEW BEDFORD

**TAUNTON**     August 17th
1923

Frank Knowlton, Esq.,
30 State Street,
Boston, Mass.

Dear Mr. Knowlton:

Mr. Kenney has written me he has no record of any sort, or any papers, in the Lizzie Borden case. I saw Mr. Borden to-day, who has just written you. I regret that I have not been able to help you more on this matter.

Yours very truly,
Stanley P. Hall

SPH:AW

*Biographical Note:* **Stanley Perkins Hall** (District Attorney of Southern District, Taunton, Massachusetts), 1889-1926, **Edward T. Murphy** (Assistant District Attorney, Southern District, Fall River, Commonwealth of Massachusetts),1889-1975; **Joseph Arthur Gauthier** (Assistant District Attorney, Southern District, New Bedford, Commonwealth of Massachusetts), b. 1878; **Joseph Thomas Kenney** (American lawyer, District Attorney of Southern District, New Bedford, Massachusetts, president of E. Anthony & Sons, Inc., publisher of New Bedford *Standard-Mercury*), 1877-1936; **Simeon Borden Jr.** (Clerk of the Court, Bristol County, Massachusetts), 1860-1924.

## Letter Number 15:
## Simeon Borden to Knowlton - August 17, 1923

---

# Commonwealth of Massachusetts.
### Bristol County.
### Office of Clerk of the Courts.

*Taunton,*      August 17, 1923

Frank W. Knowlton, Esq.,
    Attorney at Law,
        Boston, Mass.

Dear Frank: -

We have made careful search in the files and in several other places for the testimony taken at the inquest in the Elizabeth Borden case, and are unable to find the same. It was probably in the hands of the Commonwealth at the time of the trial, and I would suggest that you write to the Police Department of Fall River. If there is anything more we can do relative to getting track of thistestimony [*sic*], please let us know.

I expect to see you with us, next month.

Yours truly,
Simeon Borden
Clerk.

*Biographical Note:* **Simeon Borden Jr.** (Clerk of the Court, Bristol County, Massachusetts), 1860-1924.

## Letter Number 16:
## Handwritten - Pearson to Knowlton - August 18, 1923

———·∘◦⊛◦∘·———

**MARTHA TRACY, M.D.**
**DIRECTOR**

### ROCKY POND CAMP
*in the foothills of the Adirondacks*
**CLEMONS, N.Y.**

August 18 [1923]

Dear Knowlton:

Some of these letters from "cranks and others" sound interest-ing. I wish to reconstruct the public feeling at the time, so far as possible. Shall return to N.Y. about September 4.

Sincerely,
E.L. Pearson

*Biographical Note:* **Dr. Martha Tracy** (Dean of the Woman's Medical College, The Woman's Medical College of Pennsylvania, Philadelphia), 1876-1942; **Rocky Pond Camp**, located in Clemens, New York, in the Adirondacks, four miles from Lake George. The recreational camp offered a "comfortable camp for men & women. Private lake, swimming, hiking, canoeing, good food," June to September. It was run by Dr. Martha Tracy, a public health physician.

# Letter Number 17:
## Knowlton to Simeon Borden – August 22, 1923

—·-∘-⚬❀❀⚬-∘-·—

August 22, 1923.

Simeon Borden, Esq.,
Clerk of the Courts,
Taunton, Mass.

Dear Simeon:

Thank you for your letter of August 17th.

Since writing you I have received an intimation that very possibly my father, after the trial in the Superior Court, promised that he would not make public the inquest testimony and as the testimony had been excluded in the Superior Court, put the file beyond the reach of the ordinary searcher. If that is so, I think that it would be impossible to dig it up at this time. Thank you, however, for your letter.

I expect to see you next months but the recent shocking accident to Mrs. Clarence Cook at Mt. Washington suggests to me that we may very possibly have to reckon on a later trial -- it is too early yet to tell.

Very truly yours,

FWK/BW

*Biographical Note:* **Simeon Borden Jr.** (Clerk of the Court, Bristol County, Massachusetts), 1860-1924, **Hosea Morrill Knowlton** (American lawyer, District Attorney for the Commonwealth of Massachusetts from 1879-1893, he led the prosecution against Miss Lizzie A. Borden, and later served as the Attorney General of the Commonwealth from 1894-1902), 1847-1902.

*Case Detail, Mrs. Clarence Cook:* On August 20, 1923, Mrs. Clarence Cook of New Bedford, Massachusetts, was killed in an elevator accident at the Mount Washington Hotel at Breton Woods, New Hampshire. She was crushed between the elevator and the wall when the car started as she was about to enter or leave it. The elevator boy was held for questioning. She was the widow of Clarence A. Cook, a prominent New Bedford businessman.

## Letter Number 18a:
## B. B. Jones to Knowlton – September 17, 1923

---

HURLBURT, JONES & HALL
530 EXCHANGE BUILDING
53 STATE STREET

TELEPHONE MAIN 6447

HENRY F HURLBURT
BOYD B JONES
DAMON E HALL
HENRY F HURLBURT JR
PHILIP N JONES
FRANCIS P GARLAND
GOLDMANN EDMUNDS
ALBERT W ROCKWOOD
HERBERT U SMITH
FRANK D HEALY
ARTHUR B TYLER
GORDON W PHELPS
BENJAMIN C PERKINS

BOSTON   Sept. 17, 1923

Frank W. Knowlton, Esq.,
30 State St.
Boston, Mass.

My dear Mr. Knowlton:

I enclose herewith letter from Judge Carleton [*sic*] which is self-explanatory.

Yours truly,
B.B. Jones

(Enclosure)

*Biographical Note:* **Boyd Bradshaw Jones** (American lawyer, partner in law firm of Hurlburt, Jones & Hall, Boston), 1856-1930; **Henry Francis Hurlburt** (American lawyer, former District Attorney of Essex County, Massachusetts, partner in law firm of Hurlburt, Jones & Hall, Boston), 1856-1924; **Damon E. Hall** (American lawyer, former Assistant Attorney General, partner in the law firm of Hurlburt, Jones & Hall, Boston), 1875-1953; **Henry Francis Hurlburt Jr.** (American lawyer, member of law firm of Hurlburt, Jones & Hall, Boston), b. 1880; **Philip Nelson Jones** (American lawyer, member of law firm of Hurlburt, Jones & Hall, Boston), 1880-1949; **Francis P. Garland** (American lawyer, authority on libel law, member of law firm of Hurlburt, Jones & Hall, Boston), 1875-1953; **Goldmann Edmunds** (American lawyer, member of law firm of Hurlburt, Jones & Hall, Boston), 1873-1950; **Albert W. Rockwood** (American lawyer, member of law firm of Hurlburt, Jones & Hall, Boston), 1892-1980; **Herbert Urban Smith** (American lawyer, member of law firm of Hurlburt, Jones & Hall, Boston), 1887-1971; **Frank Dale Healy** (American lawyer, member of law firm of Hurlburt, Jones & Hall, Boston), 1896-1963; **Arthur Blaisdell Tyler** (American lawyer, member of law firm of Hurlburt, Jones & Hall, Boston), 1869-1926; **Gordon Winfield Phelps** (American lawyer, member of law firm of Hurlburt, Jones & Hall, Boston), 1898-2000; **Benjamin Chute Perkins** (American lawyer, member of law firm of Hurlburt, Jones & Hall, Boston), 1897-1965; **Otis Johnson Carlton** (Justice of Central District Court of Northern Essex County, Massachusetts), 1876-1932.

## Letter Number 18b:
## Otis J. Carlton to B. B. Jones - September 15, 1923

————·∘·⊚⊛⊚·∘·————

September 15, 1923

**OTIS J. CARLTON**
83 MERRIMACK STREET
HAVERHILL, MASS.

Boyd B. Jones, Esq.,
530 Exchange Bldg.,
53 State St.
Boston.

Dear Mr. Jones:

I have your favor of the 14th and shall be very glad to look over the Moody papers in an endeavor to find the testimony of Lizzie Borden before the coroner for the use of Mr. Knowlton. Mr. Moody's papers are in eight or ten large wooden boxes so Mr. Knowlton will appreciate that it will require some time to go through them but you can assure him that I will attend to the matter as promptly as possible.

Very truly yours,
Otis J. Carlton

*Biographical Note:* **Otis Johnson Carlton** (Justice of Central District Court of Northern Essex County, Massachusetts), 1876-1932; **Boyd Bradshaw Jones** (American lawyer, partner in law firm of Hurlburt, Jones & Hall, Boston), 1856-1930; **William Henry Moody** (American lawyer, assisted Hosea Knowlton in the prosecution of Lizzie A. Borden, Secretary of the Navy and Attorney General under President Theodore Roosevelt, and justice of the Supreme Court), 1853-1917.

## Letter Number 19:
## Knowlton to B.B. Jones - September 18, 1923

—·◦○❊○◦·—

September 18, 1923.

Boyd B. Jones, Esq.,
530 Exchange Building,
53 State Street, Boston, Mass.

My dear Mr. Jones:

Thank you very much for your letter from Judge Carlton. I have written to him directly.

Yours very truly,

FWK:ED

*Biographical Note:* **Boyd Bradshaw Jones** (American lawyer, partner in law firm of Hurlburt, Jones & Hall, Boston), 1856-1930; **Otis Johnson Carlton** (Justice of Central District Court of Northern Essex County, Massachusetts), 1876-1932.

## Letter Number 20:
## Knowlton to Otis J. Carlton - September 19, 1923

September 18, 1923.

Hon. Otis J. Carlton,
83 Merrimack Street,
Haverhill, Mass.

Dear Judge Carlton:

Mr. Jones has forwarded to me your very kind letter of September 15.

I hesitate very much to ask you to go through Mr. Moody's papers unless they happen to be so segregated in envelopes or folders as to make it comparatively simple. Please do not go to too much trouble about this, although for the sake of posterity I think that some day the inquest testimony ought to be located.

I have gone through all my father's papers and I do not find it. I do find, however, in his papers six or eight sheets of foolscap in Mr. Moody's handwriting in which he has summarized the inquest testimony very briefly, with the page numbers of the stenographic report against the references in an endeavor to stipulate the points which the prosecuting officer had relied upon the inquest evidence to prove and which would be lost if it were not admitted. It is this paper largely and the care that Mr. Moody took in summarizing it which makes me think it might possibly be among his papers. If, without too much trouble, you can make a brief search, I should be very glad.

Yours very truly,

FWK:ED

*Biographical Note:* **Otis Johnson Carlton** (Justice of Central District Court of Northern Essex County, Massachusetts), 1876-1932; **Boyd Bradshaw Jones** (American lawyer, partner in law firm of Hurlburt, Jones & Hall, Boston), 1856-1930; **William Henry Moody** (American lawyer, assisted Hosea Knowlton in the prosecution of Lizzie A. Borden, Secretary of the Navy and Attorney General under President Theodore Roosevelt, and justice of the Supreme Court), 1853-1917.

## Letter Number 21:
## Pearson to Knowlton - October 3, 1923

———··o○❦○o··———

# The New York Public Library
### Astor, Lenox and Tilden Foundations

**476 Fifth Avenue**

*New York,* October 3, 1923

Frank W. Knowlton, Esq.
   c/o Choate, Hall and Stewart
    30 State Street
    Boston, Mass.

Dear Knowlton:

I am writing to-day to Mr. Louis Freeze to arrange about borrowing the report of the Borden trial, as a result of your kindness in interviewing him on the subject.

Owing to a great deal of other work, I have not been able yet to get the Bram case finished, but I need the Borden record now so that I can read it over and familiarize myself again with its points before I go over to Fall River. I intend to go there sometime in the last two weeks of this month, but am not sure of the date yet.

If you have any of those files of correspondence or records or photographs which you are willing to let me use, I shall be glad to have them as soon as convenient to yourself. I may also ask you before I go to Fall River if you will kindly give me letters to Messrs. John W. Cummings and Milton Reed,whom you mention as advisable to see.

I appreciate the fact that I am putting you to a good deal of trouble and that you have already been most kind in this matter. I shall come in to thank you personally and have a talk on my way through Boston to Newburyport.

With best wishes,

Sincerely yours,
Edmund L. Pearson

HW

*Biographical Note:* **Charles F. Choate Jr.** (American lawyer, partner in the firm of Choate, Hall & Stewart, Boston), 1866-1927; **Damon E. Hall** (American lawyer, former Assistant Attorney General, partner in the law firm of Hurlburt, Jones & Hall, Boston), 1875-1953; **Ralph A. Stewart** (American lawyer, former Assistant Attorney General of Massachusetts under Herbert Parker, partner in the firm of Choate, Hall & Stewart, partner in the firm Stewart & Chase), 1870-1926; **Louis Freeze** (Chief Clerk at the office of the Attorney General of the Commonwealth of Massachusetts), 1866-1956; **John William Cummings** (American lawyer and politician, 14th and 16th mayor of Fall River, Massachusetts), 1855-1929; **Milton Reed** (American lawyer and politician, 13th mayor of Fall River), 1848-1932.

*Case Detail, Thomas Bram:* See Letter #1 for information.

## Letter Number 22:
## Knowlton to Pearson - October 3, 1923

October 3, 1923.

Mr. Edmund L. Pearson,
New York Public Library,
476 Fifth Avenue,
New York City.

My dear Pearson:

I am glad to enclose the letters to Mr. Cummings and Mr. Reed.

The correspondence and photographs are at home. I have got them together and will send them to you in the course of a few days - as soon as I get the time to do them up.

I am sorry to tell you that my efforts to locate the inquest testimony are futile. I am coming to believe that it was either purposely delivered to Miss Borden's counsel or destroyed so that it would not become public. However, in Fall River at the Public Library you will find a complete file of the Fall River papers as far back as the time of the inquest, and I am told by Fall River people that doubtless it will be reported there almost stenographically. You will also find among the papers which I am going to send to you five or six sheets of foolscap, in Mr. Moody's handwriting, in which he has enumerated the important points established by Lizzie Borden's testimony at the inquest, upon which a great deal depended and which they lost the benefit of when the evidence was excluded, and with some notes in my father's handwriting of how they could still establish a few of the points in spite of the exclusion.

If you have any difficulty about getting the record from Mr. Freeze, let me know.

Yours very truly,

FWK:ED

*Biographical Note:* **John William Cummings** (American lawyer and politician, 14th and 16th mayor of Fall River, Massachusetts), 1855-1929; **Milton Reed** (American lawyer and politician, 13th mayor of Fall River), 1848-1932; **William Henry Moody** (American lawyer, assisted Hosea Knowlton in the prosecution of Lizzie A. Borden, Secretary of the Navy and Attorney General under President Theodore Roosevelt, and justice of the Supreme Court), 1853-1917; **Louis Freeze** (Chief Clerk at the office of the Attorney General of the Commonwealth of Massachusetts), 1866-1956.

## Letter Number 23:
## Knowlton to John W. Cummings - October 4, 1923

———•∘∘🙥🙣∘∘•———

October 4, 1923.

John W. Cummings, Esq.,
56 North Main Street,
Fall River, Mass.

Dear Mr. Cummings:

I am glad to introduce to you by this letter my friend, Edmund L. Pearson of New York.

Mr. Pearson is engaged in a task that I envy him very much - that of making a study of the famous case of Commonwealth v. Lizzie A. Borden and preparing for publication an essay on the case.

I have told Mr. Pearson that I knew you would be glad to give him any assistance that you could and I am so interested in his work that I shall personally feel grateful to you for any assistance you can give to Mr. Pearson.

Yours very truly,

FWK:ED

[handwritten notation]
*This letter sent to Milton Reed, Esq., Fall River, Mass.*

*Biographical Note:* **John William Cummings** (American lawyer and politician, 14th and 16th mayor of Fall River, Massachusetts), 1855-1929; **Milton Reed** (American lawyer and politician, 13th mayor of Fall River), 1848-1932.

## Letter Number 24:
## Knowlton to Pearson - October 9, 1923

———·◦◦❈❈❈◦◦·———

October 9, 1923.

Mr. Edmund L. Pearson,
  The New York Public Library,
   476 Fifth Avenue,
    New York, New York.

Dear Pearson:

  I am sending you today by express a considerable assortment of papers in the matter of Commonwealth v. Lizzie A. Borden. A great deal of these will be of no particular use to you as I have not attempted to go through them and sort them out.

  Of course you appreciate that these files have been kept more or less confidential and while I do not know that there is anything in them which is of particularly private nature, I have not been through them enough to have any judgment on it. If there is anything which seems to you to be more or less private and confidential, I am going to ask you to exercise your discretion in the matter and preserve the confidence. Ultimately, when you have entirely finished with them I should, of course, be glad to have them back, but not until you have wholly finished with them.

  I hope you have been successful in getting the record of the trial from Mr. Freeze.

      Yours very truly,

FWK:ED

*Biographical Note:* **Louis Freeze** (Chief Clerk at the office of the Attorney General of the Commonwealth of Massachusetts), 1866-1956.

## Letter Number 25:
## Pearson to Knowlton - October 10, 1923

———•◦○❀❀❀❀◦○○•○————

# The New York Public Library
### Astor, Lenox and Tilden Foundations

**476 FIFTH AVENUE**

*New York,* October 10 [1923]

Dear Knowlton: -

The package came O.K. today, and I shall take it home tonight, and revel - and wallow - in its contents. Thank you. I will take great care about its use in any public way, and consult you where there seems to be the slightest doubt of its advisability.

I have not heard from Mr. Freeze yet, in any way, but I think it probable that this means that the books are on the way. If I do not hear in a few days, I may write you, and ask if you would think it wise to call him up by 'phone ~~ans~~ and see if there is any hitch.

Sincerely yours
E.L. Pearson

***Biographical Note:*** **Louis Freeze** (Chief Clerk at the office of the Attorney General of the Commonwealth of Massachusetts), 1866-1956.

## Letter Number 26:
## Knowlton to Pearson - October 11, 1923

---

October 11, 1923.

Mr. Edmund L. Pearson,
The New York Public Library,
476 Fifth Avenue,
New York, New York.


My dear Pearson:

I called Mr. Freeze on the telephone this morning. He told me that he had taken the matter up with the Attorney General and had obtained his permission to send the testimony to you and that as soon as he could get it adequately packed he would ship it on. He moves rather slowly, although you can rely on him, but if you do not receive the testimony in the course of a week, let me know and I will prod him again.

Yours very truly,

FWK:ED


*Biographical Note:* **Louis Freeze** (Chief Clerk at the office of the Attorney General of the Commonwealth of Massachusetts), 1866-1956; **Jay R. Benton** (Attorney General for the Commonwealth of Massachusetts from 1923-1927), 1885-1953.

## Letter Number 27:
## Post Card from Pearson to Knowlton – October, 1923

THE NEW YORK PUBLIC LIBRARY
476 FIFTH AVENUE

I have received the books from Mr Freeze. Thanks for your help.
E.L.P.
Oct. 15

*Biographical Note:* **Louis Freeze** (Chief Clerk at the office of the Attorney General of the Commonwealth of Massachusetts), 1866-1956.

## Letter Number 28:
## Pearson to Knowlton – November 22, 1923

—————·○◦✄◦○·—————

# The New York Public Library
### Astor, Lenox and Tilden Foundations

**476 FIFTH AVENUE**

New York,November 22, 1923

Mr. Frank W. Knowlton
30 State Street
Boston, Mass.

Dear Knowlton:

Thanks to your introduction, Mr. Cummings saw me as soon as I arrived in Fall River, and gave me a long interview. He was most kind and very interesting in his conversation. He gave me several hints which I found well worth while following up. I made three attempts to see Mr. Milton Reed, but could not locate him. They said, in Mr. Cummings' office, that he was in poor health a good deal of the time, and others told me that he might be out of town, so in the end I had to leave without seeing him. I talked with a good many other people, including the Chief of Police, and visited, to my great delight, several places connected with the event. I waited for about half an hour in front of the present home of the lady who calls herself, in the telephone directory, <u>Lizbeth</u> A. Borden, and although I had little hope of seeing her, I was more disappointed than I was many years ago when I waited one and one-half hours in Hyde Park but failed in the end to see the Queen of England. Since then I have seen a Queen or two, but I am afraid now that I shall die without ever having seen this famous citizen of Fall River. I was rebuked by a young woman in a picture postcard shop for asking why they didn't have a postcard with the picture of the Borden house on Second Street, and was told that only "outsiders" take any interest in the case.

On the whole, however, of the dozen or more people with whom I talked about the case, I found very little sentiment which would have been agreeable to the Reverends Buck and Jubb. The prediction made by the Providence Journal at the time of the acquittal that many persons would disagree with the result of the trial, seems to have been amply fulfilled. I spent two or three hours in the Public Library searching over old files of the Fall River Globe. What they used to say every year on the anniversary of the murder was certainly a plenty! I wonder if the other papers or any of the pro-Lizzie forces ever replied.

My visit to Fall River was very interesting and useful to me and I am grateful to you for helping to make it so. I will send you, in a short time, the letter about which we spoke so that you can consult with Mr. Pillsbury about it.

Sincerely yours,
Edmund L. Pearson

HW

*Biographical Note:* **John William Cummings** (American lawyer and politician, 14th and 16th mayor of Fall River, Massachusetts), 1855-1929; **Milton Reed** (American lawyer and politician, 13th mayor of Fall River), 1848-1932, **Martin Feeney** (Chief of Police of Fall River from 1917-1931), 1862-1937; **Reverend Edwin Augustus Buck** (missionary for the City Missionary Society with the Central Congregational Church in Fall River), 1824-1903; **Reverend William Walker Jubb** (pastor of Central Congregational Church in Fall River from 1891-1896), 1837-1904; **Albert Enoch Pillsbury** (American lawyer, Attorney General, Commonwealth of Massachusetts from 1891-1893), 1849-1930.

## Letter Number 29:
## Knowlton to Pearson – November 23, 1923

———··○◦§◦○··———

November 23, 1923.

Mr. Edmund L. Pearson,
476 Fifth Avenue,
New York City.

Dear Mr. Pearson:

Thank you very much for your very interesting letter of November 22.

I am glad that you had such a satisfactory visit at Fall River and to know that it will probably be productive of results.

Yours very truly,

FWK: ED

## Letter Number 30:
## Knowlton to Pearson - December 8, 1923

————∘∘◦❦◦∘∘————

December 8, 1923.

Mr. Edmund L. Pearson,
   The New York Public Library,
     476 Fifth Avenue,
      New York City.

My dear Pearson:

     I happened to find in my desk today the enclosed clipping from the Providence Journal under date of June 25, 1893, which is rather interesting. A duplicate of it may be in the files which I sent to you, but I rather think not.

     You were going to send me, you may remember, a copy of the letter to Mr. Pillsbury, of which we spoke.

               Very truly yours,

FWK: ED

Enc.

*Biographical Note:* **Albert Enoch Pillsbury** (American lawyer, Attorney General, Commonwealth of Massachusetts from 1891-1893), 1849-1930.

*The Providence Journal*, Sunday, June 25, 1893

The Borden Case

How Public Opinion in
Boston Regards the Verdict

Mrs. Mary A. Livermore
Rises to the Occasion

A Nice Derangement of Epitaphs.
Some of the Mysteries of the Case
Which Remain Unexplained.
An Alluring Picture of New England Life.

Boston, June 24: Possibly you have heard enough and more than enough about the Borden case by this time, but it has been discussed so freely and so frequently here during the present week that is naturally enough the first topic that comes to one's mind when one sits down to write. No trial in late years has aroused so much discussion or engendered so much bitterness among the disputants. The comments of the newspapers only faintly echo the talk which one hears in private. It would be difficult to say to which side the balance of sentiment leans. Those who have all along believed Miss Borden to be innocent are naturally making the most noise just at present. But there is, nevertheless, a very large number of persons to whom the verdict has given little satisfaction. I do not mean by this, of course, that they wish the Prisoner had been proved guilty. The crime was too revolting to make such an outcome anything but horrible. And yet they cannot feel that Andrew Borden's daughter has been really vindicated. The jury say not guilty. But there remains the evidence which justified the arrest, and this has not been explained away. They wait to hear the story from Miss Borden's own lips, which she can tell fully and freely now that no one can use it against her, and which she surely will tell, since she is innocent. She must have some coherent and reasonable account to give of her movements on that fatal morning; and there must be some means of corroborating it, at least sufficiently to set at rest- the cruel suspicions which the doubting Thomases still cherish.

I have said that the zealous advocates of Miss Borden's innocence have been heard from with emphasis. This, however, is understating the case. They have done more than give utterance to their joy at the verdict. They have insulted and maligned the law officers of the Commonwealth, the Fall River police, the newspapers that discussed the case cautiously and with dignity, and everybody who ventured to say that there was any reason whatever for believing that Miss Borden was the real criminal. Now they are asking why Miss Borden can't sue the Commonwealth for the damage which it has inflicted upon her money and reputation. Yes, they ask this question seriously, and a public journal sends out to interview the legal authorities upon the point thus raised. Of course the answer is a decided negative. If such a thing were possible the administration of Justice would soon be at an end. There would be no arrests unless conviction were an certainty; and who could vouch for that? But women like Mrs. Mary A. Livermore, who have been denouncing Mr. Knowlton and his associates with much bitterness from the outset, do not let any little technical objection like that obstruct the torrent of their wrath. "Atrocity" is about the mildest word which she uses in a long screed addressed to Miss Borden's chief newspaper counsel. She also alludes with feminine archness to "repulsive bullying," "mountainous iniquity," "vicious practices" and "mendacious officials." Odd, isn't it when all Miss Borden's friends ought to rejoice at the outcome of a trial which has completely vindicated her, as they say, from suspicions which the failure to arrest her would not have diminished. She has had just what every person accused of crime is supposed to long for - a full and fair trial; and she has been acquitted. What more can her friends ask and why abuse the prosecution when it has failed to convict? That is another of the mysteries of this mysterious case.

How much popular sympathy Mrs. Livermore and the rest expect to win I do not pretend to say. I have talked with many women about this case, and almost all of them agree that the accusation was by no means incredible. "Of course a woman could have done it!" - that is their opinion. Whether or not they are mistaken as to the capacities of their sex let others decide. I think, on the whole, that the public here have experienced a feeling of relief at the verdict. Few go to such lengths as Mrs. Livermore. But even those who suspected Miss Borden all along see that the evidence is not conclusive. These criticise the rulings of the Court; no doubt unjustly and foolishly. With such high matters the lay (person?) cannot meddle. The belief that Miss Borden herself ought not to rest content with the verdict is, however, well nigh universal. Although the jury could not see their way clear to render any other (verdict), on the evidence submitted, the importance of finding the real criminal is not diminished. Perhaps this would be a useful outlet for the energies of Mrs. Livermore and her friends. It would be better than forming a Society for the Admiration of Lizzie Borden, which is the usual Boston way, for we have many pleas of our own, and much zeal., in proclaiming them, and we invariably scold those who don't agree with us - gregariously and under the protection of some formidable title if we can.

A striking feature of this now celebrated case is the picture which it gives of life in the Borden household, and presumably in other households in Fall River and elsewhere. I dare say this life is so familiar to many people that they are unable to appreciate the meanness and sordidness of it. Money-grubbing and no more - what a subject of contemplation! Andrew Borden was man worth all the way from $300,000 to $500,000. No one seems to know the exact amount, for he had a way of keeping his own counsel which his daughters have inherited along with the money. But he lived in about the style of a laborer earning $2 a day. His house may have been fairly comfortable, but it was a mean one for a man in his position to occupy. His table was scantily supplied, and the other household expenses were cut down to the lowest limit. He grudged his wife and daughters everything, even the attendance of a private physician when they were ill. How could he expect to be loved, or even respected, by them? If Lizzie had committed the crime with which she was charged, the explanation would not have been difficult. A method of living like this might drive any one to desperation. Yet, so we are told, thousands of well-to-do people in New England live. No wonder that we are a gloomy and discontented race.

The vicious and unjust attacks upon the District Attorney must not be taken as representing thoughtful public opinion here. Among men whose praise is worthwhile you near his zeal and ability highly commended. There can be no doubt of Mr. Knowlton's firm belief in Lizzie Borden's guilt. Naturally enough, he did his utmost to secure her conviction; he would have been false to his trust if he had done less. His argument is regarded as a masterly piece of work, far better than that of Gov. Robinson, who has come out of the case, on the whole, with [*covered?*] laurels. There was no comparison, either in eloquence or in logic, between the speeches of the two men. Some of the people who are now snarling at Mr. Knowlton's heels will feel ashamed of themselves bye and bye and do him justice. But he does not need their approval. His legal brethren know how difficult his task was and how well he acquitted himself in it. And most of us, like Hosea Knowlton, "do like a man that ain't a-feared," since courage is a far rarer quality than we are usually willing to admit.

The Attorney General, Mr. Pillsbury, has not escaped criticism for withdrawing from the case. It has been said that he was well enough to undertake it and that he did not do so because he thought that it might intefere with his political ambitions. No charge could be more absurd. Mr. Pillsbury is courageous enough, too and he is the last man in the world to consult political expediency when duty is in question. He might have been more popular with the Republican managers if he had been less outspoken. The fact is that although he has recovered sufficiently to attend to his ordinary duties, he was by no means able to endure the stress and strain of such a trial as that at. New Bedford. It is easy for those who have no idea of the burdens imposed by that trial to carp and grumble. Nor is it strange that one newspaper in this city went to the length of setting spies upon Mr. Pillsbury in order to work up a story about the amount of work which he was able to do at his office. Such methods will not discredit him with the public. Neither he nor Mr. Knowlton need worry over the attacks to which they are being subjected. Perhaps it is needless to add that they do not worry.

EDWARD FULLER

## Letter Number 31a:
## Pearson to Knowlton - January 23, 1924

———o○o🙖🙖○o○——

# The New York Public Library
### Astor, Lenox and Tilden Foundations

**476 FIFTH AVENUE**

*New York,* January 23, 1924

Dear Knowlton:

I have been interrupted in my work on the Borden case for the past few weeks, but I enclose the letter to Mr. Pillsbury, about which we spoke. I have kept a copy of it, and will abide by your wishes as to whether I shall quote it, or merely refer to its contents, or be silent about it.

Sincerely yours
Edmund Pearson

*Biographical Note:* **Albert Enoch Pillsbury** (American lawyer, Attorney General, Commonwealth of Massachusetts from 1891-1893), 1849-1930.

# Letter Number 31b:
# Copy of letter from Hosea M. Knowlton to Pillsbury dated April 24, 1893

————— ◦○◦ 🎴 ○○◦ —————

### *HOSEA M. KNOWLTON. ARTHUR E. PERRY.*
### *COUNSELLORS AT LAW.*
### *OFFICE:*
### *38 NORTH WATER STREET.*

{Dictated}.

NEW BEDFORD, MASS. April 24, 1893.

Hon. A. E. Pillsbury, Attorney General:

My Dear Sir:-

I have thought more about the Lizzie Borden case since I talked with you, and think perhaps it may be well to write you, as I shall not be able to meet you probably until Thursday, possibly Wednesday afternoon.

Personally I would like very much to get rid of the trial of the case, and fear that my own feelings in that direction may have influenced my better judgment. I feel this all the more upon your not unexpected announcement that the burden of the trial would come upon me.

I confess, however, I cannot see my way clear to any disposition of the case other than a trial. Should it result in disagreement of the jury there would be no difficulty then in disposing of the case by admitting the defendent [sic] to bail: but a verdict either way would render such a course unnecessary. The case has proceeded so far and an indictment has been found by the grand inquest of the county that it does not seem to me that we ought to take the responsibility of discharging her without trial, even though there is every reasonable expectation of a verdict of not guilty. I am unable to concur fully in your views as to the probable result. I think it may well be that the jury might disagree upon the case. But even in my most sanguine moments I have scarcely expected a verdict of guilty.

The situation is this: nothing has developed which satisfies either of us that she is innocent, neither of us can escape the conclusion that she must have had some knowledge of the occurrence. She has been presented for trial by a jury which, to say the least, was not influenced by anything said by the government in the favor of the indictment.

Without discussing the matter more fully in this letter I will only say as above indicated that I cannot see how any other course than setting the case down for trial, and trying it will satisfy that portion of the public sentiment whether favorable to her or not, which is worthy of being respected.

June seems to be the most satisfactory month, all things considered. I will write more fully as to the admission of her confession after I have looked the matter up.

Yours Truly,
H M Knowlton

*Biographical Note:* **Arthur Ebenezer Perry** (American lawyer, partner in the firm of Knowlton & Perry and later Knowlton, Perry & Cook), 1857-1909; **Albert Enoch Pillsbury** (American lawyer, Attorney General, Commonwealth of Massachusetts from 1891-1893), 1849-1930; **Hosea Morrill Knowlton** (American lawyer, District Attorney for the Commonwealth of Massachusetts from 1879-1893, he led the prosecution against Miss Lizzie A. Borden, and later served as the Attorney General of the Commonwealth from 1894-1902), 1847-1902.

## Letter Number 32:
## Knowlton to Pearson - January 25, 1924

————•○○§❈§○•○•————

January 25, 1924.

Mr. Edmund Pearson,
    476 Fifth Avenue,
      New York City.

My dear Pearson:

    I have your letter of January 23 enclosing the letter from my father to the Attorney General on April 24, 1893.

    I saw Mr. Pillsbury yesterday. He is quite a cranky old fellow and it was a little hard to get an expression from him. At first he seemed to think the letter too unimportant to be of interest to anybody, and then upon re-reading it I think he saw that it was a little more than an ordinary letter, and finally said that whether he would feel any reluctance towards its use would depend largely upon the use that was to be made of it. He thought that if you could tell us in what way you intended to make use of the letter or let us see perhaps the first draft of your manuscript in which you refer to it, he could then tell whether it should be made public. Perhaps it is not important enough for you to go this far, but I feel a little sense of responsibility about it and I should be very glad to hear your reaction as to what he suggests.

Yours very truly,

FWK:ED

*Biographical Note:* **Albert Enoch Pillsbury** (American lawyer, Attorney General, Commonwealth of Massachusetts from 1891-1893), 1849-1930; **Hosea Morrill Knowlton** (American lawyer, District Attorney for the Commonwealth of Massachusetts from 1879-1893, he led the prosecution against Miss Lizzie A. Borden, and later served as the Attorney General of the Commonwealth from 1894-1902), 1847-1902.

## Letter Number 33:
## Pearson to Knowlton - January 26, 1924

———•◦○❦○◦•———

# The New York Public Library
### Astor, Lenox and Tilden Foundations

**476 FIFTH AVENUE**

*New York,* January 26, 1924

Dear Knowlton, -

What I wish to do is either to quote the letter in whole or in part, or else to refer to the fact that the District Attorney, at that point in the history of the case, held the opinions which are expressed in it. It puts very clearly his sense of duty in going on with the prosecution - and I expect to make clear that he was justified in feeling this way - and it also predicts the ultimate outcome. It is new and unpublished material, and therefore of especial interest; it may be all that I shall have of this sort. Here was the chief law officer of the County, after the indictment had been found, but three months before the trial, absolutely convinced that it would be wrong to fail to proceed with the prosecution, and yet realizing that a conviction was practically too much to hope for.

I am going to describe, from the newspaper accounts and from Porter's book, the events at the time of the murders, and immediately subsequent to them, and then give a history of the trial in which all these events were elaborated. I want to use the letter as one of the few bits of light which can be thrown upon the intermediate period; of course, I could leave out Mr. Pillsbury's name and the fact that the letter was addressed to him, but I would rather not do that.

Sincerely yours,
Edmund L. Pearson

***Biographical Note:*** **Hosea Morrill Knowlton** (American lawyer, District Attorney for the Commonwealth of Massachusetts from 1879-1893, he led the prosecution against Miss Lizzie A. Borden, and later served as the Attorney General of the Commonwealth from 1894-1902), 1847-1902; **Albert Enoch Pillsbury** (American lawyer, Attorney General, Commonwealth of Massachusetts from 1891-1893), 1849-1930; **Edwin H. Porter** (reporter for the *Fall River Daily Globe* and author of *The Fall River Tragedy: A History of the Borden Murders*, Fall River, MA: George R. H. Buffinton, Press of J. D. Munroe, 1893), 1864-1904.

## Letter Number 34a:
## Knowlton to Pillsbury - January 28, 1924

—·-·○◦❀❁❀◦○·-·—

January 28, 1924.

Hon. Albert E. Pillsbury,
  6 Beacon Street,
    Boston, Mass.

Dear Mr. Pillsbury:

I enclose a copy of a letter that I have received from Mr. Edmund L. Pearson about the proposed publication of his account of the Borden trial. I think I gave you enough outline of the situation last week so that I can add nothing to the letter. I shall be glad to know how you feel about it.

Yours very truly,

FWK:ED
Enc.

*Biographical Note:* **Albert Enoch Pillsbury** (American lawyer, Attorney General, Commonwealth of Massachusetts from 1891-1893), 1849-1930.

## Letter Number 34b:
## Enclosure Pillsbury to Knowlton - January 29, 1924

———·∘-∘❈∘-∘·———

### THE NEW YORK PUBLIC LIBRARY
Astor, Lenox and Tilden Foundations

476 Fifth Avenue

New York  January 26, 1924.

Dear Knowlton, -

What I wish to do is either to quote the letter in whole or in part, or else to refer to the fact that the District Attorney, at that point in the history of the case, held the opinions which are expressed in it. It puts very clearly his sense of duty in going on with the prosecution - and I expect to make clear that he was justified in feeling this way - and it also predicts the ultimate outcome. It is new and unpublished material, and therefore of especial interest; it may be all that I shall have of this sort. Here was the chief law officer of the County, after the indictment had been found, but three months before the trial, absolutely convinced that it would be wrong to fail to proceed with the prosecution, and yet realizing that a conviction was practically too much to hope for.

I am going to describe, from the newspaper accounts and from Porter's book, the events at the time of the murders, and immediately subsequent to them, and then give a history of the trial in which all these events were elaborated. I want to use the letter as one of the few bits of light which can be thrown upon the intermediate period; of course, I could leave out Mr. Pillsbury's name and the fact that the letter was addressed to him, but I would rather not do that.

Sincerely yours,
/s/ Edmund L. Pearson/

*Biographical Note:* **Hosea Morrill Knowlton** (American lawyer, District Attorney for the Commonwealth of Massachusetts from 1879-1893, he led the prosecution against Miss Lizzie A. Borden, and later served as the Attorney General of the Commonwealth from 1894-1902), 1847-1902; **Edwin H. Porter** (reporter for the *Fall River Daily Globe* and author of *The Fall River Tragedy: A History of the Borden Murders*, Fall River, MA: George R. H. Buffinton, Press of J. D. Munroe, 1893), 1864-1904; **Albert Enoch Pillsbury** (American lawyer, Attorney General, Commonwealth of Massachusetts from 1891-1893), 1849-1930.

## Letter Number 35a:
## Knowlton to Pearson - January 31, 1924

————◦◦❀❀◦◦◦————

January 31, 1924.

My dear Pearson:

    I sent Mr. Pillsbury a copy of your letter and I have the enclosed reply from him.

    He is an old crank and the letter is about what I expected it to be. I should say that you better go along with the matter and if you care to show him the galley proof or any part of the manuscript, doubtless you would find him acquiescent. However, he seems to have no decided objection.

Yours very truly,

FWK:ED
Enc.

Edmund L. Pearson, Esq.
476 Fifth Avenue,
New York City.

**Biographical Note:** **Albert Enoch Pillsbury** (American lawyer, Attorney General, Commonwealth of Massachusetts from 1891-1893), 1849-1930.

# Letter Number 35b:
## Enclosure: Pillsbury to Knowlton – January 29, 1924

**ALBERT E. PILLSBURY**
**6 BEACON STREET**
**BOSTON, MASS.**

29 Jan. 1924.

Dear Frank: - -

This letter really adds nothing to the previous statement. If the matter were of any consequence I should like to see, when the time comes, a proof of the passage or passages in connection with which the letter is introduced, which is what I intended to suggest the other day. If this is too much trouble, you may do whatever you like in the premises. Personally I care nothing about it, one way or another. Thank you for calling my attention to it.

Very truly yours,

A.E. Pillsbury

Frank W. Knowlton, Esq.,

30 State street

*Biographical Note:* **Albert Enoch Pillsbury** (American lawyer, Attorney General, Commonwealth of Massachusetts from 1891-1893), 1849-1930.

## Letter Number 36:
## Pearson to Knowlton – March 3, 1924

————•∘◦❀❀◦∘•————

# The New York Public Library
### Astor, Lenox and Tilden Foundations

**476 Fifth Avenue**

New York,......March 3, 1924

Dear Knowlton, -

Here is an announcement of the murder book, which will be out, at the earliest, in May. The Borden case is the leading one, and will probably exceed all the others in length, as you have helped me to get so much interesting material about it.

I may send you a few inquiries in the course of the next week or two. Here are some now: was not that preliminary hearing in Fall River, before Judge Blaisdell, unusual in length, if not unprecedented? I have said something to that effect, but could perhaps make what I have said more definite. I suppose such a preliminary hearing before a magistrate is usual, before the evidence is presented to the Grand Jury, but this lasted six days. I never heard of one as long as that; have you?

Sincerely yours
Edmund L. Pearson

*Biographical Note:* **Josiah Coleman Blaisdell** (District Court Judge of Bristol County, Massachusetts, from 1874-1893, presiding judge at the inquest and preliminary hearing in the Lizzie Borden case), 1820-1900.

## Letter Number 37:
## Knowlton to Pearson - March 4, 1924

———•○○❦○○•———

March 4, 1924.

My dear Pearson:

Thank you very much for your letter of March 3 with the announcement of the book "Studies in Murder". You have whetted my appetite.

My offhand impression is that the preliminary hearing before Judge Blaisdell, which was an inquest, was not unusual at that time. This was not in the nature of a preliminary hearing to determine the guilt or probable cause for holding for the Jury of a defendant charged with murder, in which case a very cursory hearing was usually had, but rather a proceeding under our laws which provides for an Inquest to be held where the Medical Examiner certifies that upon a review and autopsy death has been caused by the act of another and at which the District Attorney may attend and examine the witnesses. My feeling is that while inquests of six days in length are not usual they are not so unusual as to be extraordinary, particularly where the inquiry into the crime discloses rather baffling circumstances. However, I am asking some of my friends among the District Attorneys to let me know about this and I shall tell you what they say.

Yours Sincerely,

Mr. Edmund L. Pearson
    The New York Public Library,
        476 Fifth Avenue,
           New York City.

FWK:ED

*Biographical Note:* **Josiah Coleman Blaisdell** (American lawyer, District Court Judge of Bristol County, Massachusetts, from 1874-1893, presiding judge at the inquest and preliminary hearing in the Lizzie Borden case), 1820-1900.

## Letter Number 38:
## Knowlton to Hon. Herbert Parker- March 4, 1924

March 4, 1924.

Honorable Herbert Parker,
    11 Pemberton Square,
      Boston, Mass.

Dear Mr. Parker:

A friend of mine, an author, in New York, is preparing a book for Macmillan, the publishers, entitled "Studies in Murder", in which he is treating various important trials with an effort at accuracy.

He is writing of the famous "Lizzie Borden" case and asks me whether the preliminary hearing in Fall River before Judge Blaisdell was not unusual in length, if not unprecedented. This was, I understand, an inquest, although the defendant was not arrested until after the inquest was concluded, and lasted six days, at which my father examined all the witnesses and at which Miss Borden testified. The evidence at the inquest was excluded but offered by the Government, as you may remember.

My lacking acquaintance with criminal cases makes me doubtful as to what to tell my friend, the author, although I have written him that I thought that such a hearing while not common was not so unusual as to be extraordinary. It certainly was not unprecedented. I should be glad if you would let me know how you would answer the question.

Yours very truly,

FWK:ED

This letter sent to:

| | |
|---|---|
| Asa P. French, | 45 Milk St., Boston, |
| Hon. James M. Swift, | 82 Devonshire St., Boston |
| Michael J. Sughrue | 20 Pemberton Square, Boston |
| Frederick H. Chase, | 6 Beacon St., Boston. |
| Hon. Robt. O. Harris, | 85 Devonshire St., Boston, |
| Hon. Geo. A. Sanderson, | J. Sup. Ct., Court House, Boston, |
| Hon. John C. Hammond, | 59 Main St., Northampton, Mass. |

*Biographical Note:* **Herbert Parker** (American lawyer, District Attorney for Middle District of Massachusetts from 1896-1899, Attorney General of the Commonwealth of Massachusetts from 1902-1906), 1856-1939; **Josiah Coleman Blaisdell** (American lawyer, District Court Judge of Bristol County, Massachusetts, from 1874-1893, presiding judge at the inquest and preliminary hearing in the Lizzie Borden case), 1820-1900; **Asa Palmer French** (American lawyer, US Attorney for the District of Massachusetts from 1906-1914), 1860-1935; **James Marcus Swift** (American lawyer, District Attorney for Southern District of Massachusetts, Attorney General of the Commonwealth of Massachusetts from 1911-1914), 1873-1946; **Michael J. Sughrue** (American lawyer, District Attorney for Suffolk County in 1905), 1857-1926; **Frederic Hathaway Chase** (American lawyer, partner in the firm of Stewart & Chase, and Stewart, Chase & Baldwin, Assistant District Attorney for Suffolk County, Massachusetts), 1870-1948; **Robert Orr Harris** (American lawyer, Representative from Massachusetts from 1911-1913, US Attorney for District of Massachusetts from 1921-1924), 1854-1926; **George Augustus Sanderson** (American lawyer, Justice of the Superior Court of Massachusetts from 1907-1924, Associate Justice of the Massachusetts Supreme Court from 1924-1932), 1863-1932; **John Chester Hammond** (American lawyer, Northwestern District Attorney of Massachusetts from 1897-1903, partner in firm of Hammond & Hammond), 1842-1926.

## Letter Number 39:
## Handwritten letter from Pearson to Knowlton – March 5, 1924

⸺ ∘∘◦❀◦∘∘ ⸺

# The New York Public Library
### Astor, Lenox and Tilden Foundations

**476 FIFTH AVENUE**

*New York,* March 5, 1924

Dear Knowlton,

Is it possible that you are confusing the inquest with the preliminary trial?

According to Porter's book on the Borden case, the inquest was held before Judge Blaisdell, August 10 - 12, 1892. On the last date Miss Borden was arrested and arraigned in the District Court, before the same Justice, August 13. Mr. Jennings protested at Judge Blaisdell sitting in what he called this "double capacity"; whereupon the District Attorney pointed out that the inquest, which was in itself an action against no one, was still proceeding, and that it had no bearing on the present hearing. The Court overruled Mr. Jennings' action and sustained the District Attorney's demurrer. Both lawyers then agreed on August 22 for the preliminary hearing, which does not seem to be referred to as an inquest. It was afterwards adjourned until August 25, when it began and lasted for <u>six days</u>. It seems to have been a trial in everything except the presence of a jury. Cross-examinations by counsel, and arguments by them, in closing, at any rate. This was the proceeding which I thought might have been unusual, at least in length.

Sincerely yours,
E.L. Pearson

*Biographical Note:* **Edwin H. Porter** (reporter for the *Fall River Daily Globe* and author of *The Fall River Tragedy: A History of the Borden Murders*, Fall River, MA: George R. H. Buffinton, Press of J. D. Munroe, 1893), 1864-1904; **Josiah Coleman Blaisdell** (American lawyer, District Court Judge of Bristol County, Massachusetts, from 1874-1893, presiding judge at the inquest and preliminary hearing in the Lizzie Borden case), 1820-1900; **Andrew Jackson Jennings** (American lawyer, partner in firm of Jennings & Brayton in Fall River, and a member of the legal team that represented Lizzie A. Borden at her trial), 1849-1923.

## Letter Number 40a:
## Knowlton to Pearson - March 7, 1924

———·◦◦❀◦◦·———

March 7, 1924.

My Dear Pearson:

Thank you for your letter of March 5. I am afraid that I did not understand clearly just what took place before Judge Blaisdell. Time has dimmed my memory of the events. I shall make some further inquiries and let you know.

In the meantime I am enclosing three letters which I have received. Mr. Herbert Parker, who was my father's successor as Attorney General, was District Attorney of the Worcester District and he, himself, prosecuted some of the famous murder cases of his time, notably the Tucker case, for the murder of Mabel Page, and the Angles Snell case, a murder which took place on a remote and desolate beach in New Bedford. Asa P. French you know, and James M. Swift was for a while District Attorney for the Fall River District and later Attorney General. He also handled several murder cases.

Yours sincerely,

FWK:ED

Encs.

Mr. Edmund Pearson
    476 Fifth Avenue,
        New York City.

*Biographical Note:* **Josiah Coleman Blaisdell** (American lawyer, District Court Judge of Bristol County, Massachusetts, from 1874-1893, presiding judge at the inquest and preliminary hearing in the Lizzie Borden case), 1820-1900; **Herbert Parker** (American lawyer, District Attorney for Middle District of Massachusetts from 1896-1899, Attorney General of the Commonwealth of Massachusetts from 1902-1906), 1856-1939; **Hosea Morrill Knowlton** (American lawyer, District Attorney for the Commonwealth of Massachusetts from 1879-1893, he led the prosecution against Miss Lizzie A. Borden, and later served as the Attorney General of the Commonwealth from 1894-1902), 1847-1902; **Asa Palmer French** (American lawyer, US Attorney for the District of Massachusetts from 1906-1914), 1860-1935; **James Marcus Swift** (American lawyer, District Attorney for Southern District of Massachusetts, Attorney General of the Commonwealth of Massachusetts from 1911-1914), 1873-1946.

*Case Detail, Charles Lewis Tucker:* See Letter # 6 for information.

*Case Detail, Angles Snell:* On February 11, 1902, seventy-year-old Peleg Cornell of Little Compton, Rhode Island, was bludgeoned to death. A small amount of money was missing when the body was discovered. The case remained unsolved until 1910, when Angles Snell confessed to five murders before his death in the Massachusetts State Prison. Snell was incarcerated for the murder of Tillinghast Kirby, who was found with a fractured skull on a boat near Westport, Massachusetts, on September 9, 1903. He was sentenced to death by electrocution and his death date was set for the week of December 10, 1905. On November 22, 1905, Governor William L. Douglas commuted the death sentence to life imprisonment. Snell dropped dead in the Massachusetts State Prison in Charlestown on March 15, 1910 at the age of sixty-nine, of "sclerosis of coronary arteries." He revealed to his jailers that he had committed five murders in all, with robbery as the sole motive. He admitted to killing Killinghast Kirby, Peleg Cornell, two strangers who came to Westport on a vacation trip, and an unknown Portuguese who paid Snell to guide him to an adjourning town.

## Letter Number 40b:
## Enclosed letter from Herbert Parker to Knowlton
## - March 6, 1924

————— ·-o-ᘓᘓ-o-· —————

LAW OFFICES OF
Herbert Parker
. . . . . . .
. . . . . . .

910-919 Barristers Hall

Boston, March 6, 1924.

Frank W. Knowlton, Esq.,
  Messrs. Choate, Hall & Stewart,
   30 State Street
    Boston, Massachusetts

My dear Mr. Knowlton:

    I am delighted to have your letter bringing to my attention incidents associated with my much loved friend, your father.

    You, of course know, that I had no official or professional relations with the Lizzie Borden case. From time to time, however, I did talk with your father and with Mr. Moody on certain phases of it both before it came to trial and during the trial. The proceedings at and of the inquest were, so far as I can remember, of no especial significance, except because of Miss Borden's having been summoned for attendance there and, as I remember it, she did so appear, but I do not now remember whether she did or did not, expressly waive any claim of immunity. The question of admissibility of her testimony at the inquest was, as you doubtless remember, one of the critical incidents at the trial. Her testimony, as was, I think expected by the prosecutors, excluded.

    The inquest, following the obviously unnatural deaths of Miss Borden's parents, was held, pursuant to statutory provisions, and such inquest thereafter was merely a normal incident relating to preliminary inquiries. The time consumed in the inquest was not, as I remember such incidents, unusual, nor, because of its length, in any wise notable. It becomes significant, as a part of the legal analysis of the case and the trial only as it involved the admissibility of Miss Borden's testimony there offered.

I remember of talking with Moody long after the trial and after your father's death. Moody, evidently, thought the case should be officially published, under our statute, and surely the case was of sufficient popular interest to have warranted such publication, and since it had no official review by the Full Court, such publication would have afforded to the Bar the only detailed record of the serious questions involved; but the Attorney General, and I think the Governor, were of opinion that since the result of the trial was an acquittal of the defendant, there might be rational objection to the renewed publicity incident to the production of the volumes.

I am very glad you wrote me and I have much happiness in these moments of close thought of your honored father. I should be glad, if it is in any wise possible, to make any useful suggestion to you or your friend with respect to this famous case.

Faithfully yours,

/s/ Herbert Parker

*Biographical Note:* **Herbert Parker** (American lawyer, District Attorney for Middle District of Massachusetts from 1896-1899, Attorney General of the Commonwealth of Massachusetts from 1902-1906), 1856-1939; **Charles F. Choate Jr.** (American lawyer, partner in the firm of Choate, Hall & Stewart, Boston), 1866-1927; **Damon E. Hall** (American lawyer, former Assistant Attorney General, partner in the law firm of Hurlburt, Jones & Hall, Boston), 1875-1953; **Ralph A. Stewart** (American lawyer, former Assistant Attorney General of Massachusetts under Herbert Parker, partner in the firm of Choate, Hall & Stewart, partner in the firm Stewart & Chase), 1870-1926; **Hosea Morrill Knowlton** (American lawyer, District Attorney for the Commonwealth of Massachusetts from 1879-1893, he led the prosecution against Miss Lizzie A. Borden, and later served as the Attorney General of the Commonwealth from 1894-1902), 1847-1902; **William Henry Moody** (American lawyer, assisted Hosea Knowlton in the prosecution of Lizzie A. Borden, Secretary of the Navy and Attorney General under President Theodore Roosevelt, and justice of the Supreme Court), 1853-1917; **Albert Enoch Pillsbury** (American lawyer, Attorney General, Commonwealth of Massachusetts from 1891-1893), 1849-1930; **William E. Russell** (Governor of the Commonwealth of Massachusetts from 1891-1894), 1857-1896.

## Letter Number 40c:
## Enclosed letter from Asa French to Knowlton - March 6, 1924

————·∘○❈○∘·————

LAW OFFICE OF ASA P. FRENCH
45 Milk Street
Rooms 609 -613
Boston

6 March 1924.

Frank W. Knowlton, Esq.,
30 State Street,
Boston, Mass.

Dear Mr. Knowlton,

I have your letter of March 4th. By a singular coincidence there came to me, in the same mail, a letter from Mr. Pearson, a portion of whose forthcoming volume is to be devoted to the <u>Bram</u> case in which I was of counsel for the defendant.

As to your inquiry, the answer you have made to Mr. Pearson's question regarding the inquest in the Borden case is in accordance with my experience and is quite correct. I will, however, look over, tonight, the published account of the trial which I have at home, and if, after having done so, anything different suggests itself to me, I will call you up, or write you, tomorrow.

Sincerely yours,
/s/ Asa P. French

F/D

**Biographical Note: Asa Palmer French** (American lawyer, US Attorney for the District of Massachusetts from 1906-1914), 1860-1935;

**Case Detail, Thomas Bram:** See Letter #1 for information.

## Letter Number 40d:
## Enclosed letter from James M. Swift to Knowlton - March 6, 1924

————○◦○⑧⑧⑧○◦○•————

JAMES M. SWIFT
Counselor at Law
401-3 Shawmut Bank Bldg.,
82 Devonshire St.,

Boston, Mar. 6, 1924.

Frank W. Knowlton, Esq.,
Choate, Hall & Stewart,
30 State Street,
Boston, Mass.

Dear Frank:

Replying to your letter of March 4th concerning the
Lizzie Borden trial, the case is not so fresh in my mind as it might be, and
the book published about it is in my Fall River library. My recollection,
however, is that the unusual part about it was that the person suspected of
the murder, Miss Borden, was allowed to testify at the inquest. It does not
seem to me very material that it took six days. I do not recall any other
murder inquest that took so long a time as that, although I seem to recall
that the Jane Toppan case, in 1901 or 1902, took at least four days, and
the Angles Snell case, in 1903, consumed quite a few days, but the exact
number I cannot recall.

The situation in the Borden case was, of course, that Miss
Borden occupied at that time so high a standing in the community that it
was thought impossible by the general public that she could be involved,
and I presume that attitude was reflected in the feeling of the presiding
judge at the inquest.

I am sorry that I cannot give you something more definite.

Sincerely yours,
/s/ J.M. Swift.

SW

***Biographical Note:*** **James Marcus Swift** (American lawyer, District Attorney for Southern District of Massachusetts, Attorney General of the Commonwealth of Massachusetts from 1911-1914), 1873-1946; **Charles F. Choate Jr.** (American lawyer, partner in the firm of Choate, Hall & Stewart, Boston), 1866-1927; **Damon E. Hall** (American lawyer, former Assistant Attorney General, partner in the law firm of Hurlburt, Jones & Hall, Boston), 1875-1953; **Ralph A. Stewart** (American lawyer, former Assistant Attorney General of Massachusetts under Herbert Parker, partner in the firm of Choate, Hall & Stewart, partner in the firm Stewart & Chase), 1870-1926.

***Case Detail, Jane Toppan:*** Jane Toppan (1857-1938) confessed to thirty-one murders in 1901. Toppan began her murder spree in 1885 as a nurse in training at Cambridge Hospital in Boston. She used her patients as guinea pigs to experiment with dosages of morphine and atropine and their effects on the nervous system. She later claimed that she derived a sexual thrill when her patients were near death and then came back to life, only for them to finally die. She would administer her drug mixture to patients, lie in bed with them, and hold them close as they passed away. She killed additional victims at the Massachusetts General Hospital in 1890. Toppan returned to Cambridge Hospital but was dismissed for over-prescribing opiates. It was then she began her career as a private nurse and when her poisoning spree began in earnest.

Surviving members of one of the families in her care ordered toxicology tests performed. The report found that the family's youngest daughter had been poisoned. Jane Toppan was arrested for murder on October 26, 1901. She soon confessed to the other thirty murders. On June 23, 1902, she was found not guilty by reason of insanity and committed for life to Taunton Hospital for the Insane in Taunton, Massachusetts. She died on August 17, 1938.

***Case Detail, Angles Snell:*** See Letter #40a for information.

# Letter Number 41:
## Knowlton to Herbert Parker - March 7, 1924

————⋅∘⊙⊛⊙∘⋅————

March 7, 1924.

Herbert Parker Esq.,
    910 Barristers Hall,
       Boston, Mass.

Dear Mr. Parker:

I have your very nice letter of March 6 and I am very glad to have not only your recollection in reference to the Borden case but your very kind words about my father.

Mr. Pearson writes me, after I had written to him my first impression, as follows:

> "Is it possible that you are confusing the inquest with the preliminary trial?
>
> According to Porter's book on the Borden case, the inquest was held before Judge Blaisdell, August 10-12, 1892. On the last date Miss Borden was arrested, and arraigned in the District Court, before the same Justice, August 13. Mr. Jennings protested at Judge Blaisdell sitting in what he called this "double capacity"; whereupon the District Attorney pointed out that the inquest, which was in itself an action against no one, was still proceeding, and that it had no bearing on the present hearing. The Court overruled Mr. Jennings' motion and sustained the District Attorney's demurrer. Both lawyers then agreed on August 22 for the preliminary hearing, which does not seem to be referred to as an inquest. It was afterwards adjourned until August 25, when it began and lasted for six days. It seems to have been a trial in everything except the

presence of a jury. Cross examinations by counsel, and arguments by them, in closing, at any rate. This was the proceeding which I thought might have been unusual, at least, in length."

This will probably refresh your recollection and would it change your answer to him?

With kind regards, I am

Yours very truly,

FWK:ED

*Biographical Note:* **Herbert Parker** (American lawyer, District Attorney for Middle District of Massachusetts from 1896-1899, Attorney General of the Commonwealth of Massachusetts from 1902-1906), 1856-1939; **Hosea Morrill Knowlton** (American lawyer, District Attorney for the Commonwealth of Massachusetts from 1879-1893, he led the prosecution against Miss Lizzie A. Borden, and later served as the Attorney General of the Commonwealth from 1894-1902), 1847-1902; **Edwin H. Porter** (reporter for the *Fall River Daily Globe* and author of *The Fall River Tragedy: A History of the Borden Murders*, Fall River, MA: George R. H. Buffinton, Press of J. D. Munroe, 1893), 1864-1904; **Josiah Coleman Blaisdell** (American lawyer, District Court Judge of Bristol County, Massachusetts, from 1874-1893, presiding judge at the inquest and preliminary hearing in the Lizzie Borden case), 1820-1900; **Andrew Jackson Jennings** (American lawyer, partner in firm of Jennings & Brayton in Fall River, and a member of the legal team that represented Lizzie A. Borden at her trial), 1849-1923.

## Letter Number 42:
## Knowlton to James M. Swift - March 7, 1924

————··◦◦❀❀❀◦◦··————

March 7, 1924.

James M. Swift, Esq.
    82 Devonshire Street,
      Boston, Mass.

Dear James,

Thank you for your very kind letter of March 6 about the Lizzie Borden case. I have told Mr. Pearson what you say.

In the meantime in answer to my first impressions about the case, Mr. Pearson writes me as follows:

> "Is it possible that you are confusing the inquest with the preliminary trial?

> According to Porter's book on the Borden case, the inquest was held before Judge Blaisdell, August 10 - 12, 1892. On the last date Miss Borden was arrested, and arraigned in the District Court, before the same Justice, August 13. Mr. Jennings protested at Judge Blaisdell sitting in what he called this "double capacity" whereupon the District Attorney pointed out that the inquest, which was in itself an action against no one, was still proceeding, and that it had no bearing on the present hearing. The Court overruled Mr. Jennings' motion and sustained the District Attorney's demurrer. Both lawyers then agreed on August 22 for the preliminary hearing, which does not seem to be referred to as an inquest. It was afterwards adjourned until August 25, when it began and lasted for six days. It seems to have been a trial in everything except the presence of a jury. Cross examinations by counsel, and arguments by

them, in closing, at any rate. This was the proceeding
which I thought might have been unusual, at least, in
length."

This will probably refresh your recollection and I wonder if it
would change your answer to him?

Yours sincerely,

FWK:ED


*Biographical Note:* **James Marcus Swift** (American lawyer, District Attorney for
Southern District of Massachusetts, Attorney General of the Commonwealth of
Massachusetts from 1911-1914), 1873-1946; **Edwin H. Porter** (reporter for the
*Fall River Daily Globe* and author of *The Fall River Tragedy: A History of the Borden
Murders*, Fall River, MA: George R. H. Buffinton, Press of J. D. Munroe, 1893),
1864-1904; **Josiah Coleman Blaisdell** (American lawyer, District Court Judge of
Bristol County, Massachusetts, from 1874-1893, presiding judge at the inquest and
preliminary hearing in the Lizzie Borden case), 1820-1900; **Andrew Jackson Jennings** (American lawyer, partner in firm of Jennings & Brayton, Fall River, and a
member of the legal team that represented Lizzie A. Borden at her trial), 1849-
1923; **Hosea Morrill Knowlton** (American lawyer, District Attorney for the Commonwealth of Massachusetts from 1879-1893, he led the prosecution against Miss
Lizzie A. Borden, and later served as the Attorney General of the Commonwealth
from 1894-1902), 1847-1902.

## Letter Number 43:
## Knowlton to Asa French - March 7, 1924

————·· ∘∘ ✖️ ∘∘ ··————

March 7, 1924.

Asa P. French, Esq.
45 Milk Street,
Boston, Mass.

Dear Mr. French,

Thank you for your very good letter of March 6.

After I had given Pearson my first impressions about the case, he writes me as follows:

> "Is it possible that you are confusing the inquest with the preliminary trial?
>
> According to Porter's book on the Borden case, the inquest was held before Judge Blaisdell, August 10 - 12, 1892. On the last date Miss Borden was arrested, and arraigned in the District Court, before the same Justice, August 13. Mr. Jennings protested at Judge Blaisdell sitting in what he called this "double capacity" whereupon the District Attorney pointed out that the inquest, which was in itself an action against no one, was still proceeding, and that it had no bearing on the present hearing. The Court overruled Mr. Jennings' motion and sustained the District Attorney's demurrer. Both lawyers then agreed on August 22 for the preliminary hearing, which does not seem to be referred to as an inquest. It was afterwards adjourned until August 25, when it began and lasted for six days. It seems to have been a trial in everything except the presence of a jury. Cross examinations by counsel, and arguments by them, in closing, at any rate. This was the proceeding

which I thought might have been unusual, at least, in
length."

This will perhaps refresh your recollection and I wonder if you
would have any different feeling in view of what he states?

Yours very truly,

FWK:ED

*Biographical Note:* **Asa Palmer French** (American lawyer, US Attorney for the
District of Massachusetts from 1906-1914), 1860-1935; **Edwin H. Porter** (reporter
for the *Fall River Daily Globe* and author of *The Fall River Tragedy: A History of the
Borden Murders*, Fall River, MA: George R. H. Buffinton, Press of J. D. Munroe,
1893), 1864-1904; **Josiah Coleman Blaisdell** (American lawyer, District Court
Judge of Bristol County, Massachusetts, from 1874-1893, presiding judge at the
inquest and preliminary hearing in the Lizzie Borden case), 1820-1900; **Andrew
Jackson Jennings** (American lawyer, partner in firm of Jennings & Brayton, Fall
River, and a member of the legal team that represented Lizzie A. Borden at her
trial), 1849-1923; **Hosea Morrill Knowlton** (American lawyer, District Attorney
for the Commonwealth of Massachusetts from 1879-1893, he led the prosecution
against Miss Lizzie A. Borden, and later served as the Attorney General of the
Commonwealth from 1894-1902), 1847-1902.

## Letter Number 44:
## James M. Swift to Knowlton - March 8, 1924

# JAMES M. SWIFT
## COUNSELOR AT LAW
401-3 SHAWMUT BANK BUILDING
82 DEVONSHIRE STREET

BOSTON, Mar. 8, 1924.

Frank W. Knowlton, Esq.
Choate, Hall & Stewart,
30 State Street,
Boston, Mass.

Dear Frank:-

Replying to yours of March 7th. re the Lizzie Borden case, if your friend has Porter's book on the trial, he has about everything you could get at the present time, except the court records.

Of course, under our statutes inquests and preliminary hearings are entirely separate, and may be independent of each other.

The usual practice is, I believe, to use the inquest to a sufficient extent to get sufficient evidence to swear out a warrant for the arrest of the suspected person, who then would be put on trial at the preliminary hearing to ascertain whether there is sufficient evidence to bind the person over for the grand jury.

While I haven't any definite recollection of cases in mind as to length of time of preliminary hearings, my general impression is that the course as outlined in your letter followed in the Borden case, was not particularly unusual under our practice.

Sincerely yours,
J.M. Swift

SW

***Biographical Note:*** **James Marcus Swift** (American lawyer, District Attorney for Southern District of Massachusetts, Attorney General of the Commonwealth of Massachusetts from 1911-1914), 1873-1946; **Charles F. Choate Jr.** (American lawyer, partner in the firm of Choate, Hall & Stewart, Boston), 1866-1927; **Damon E. Hall** (American lawyer, former Assistant Attorney General, partner in the law firm of Hurlburt, Jones & Hall, Boston), 1875-1953; **Ralph A. Stewart** (American lawyer, former Assistant Attorney General of Massachusetts under Herbert Parker, partner in the firm of Choate, Hall & Stewart, partner in the firm Stewart & Chase), 1870-1926; **Edwin H. Porter** (reporter for the *Fall River Daily Globe* and author of *The Fall River Tragedy: A History of the Borden Murders*, Fall River, MA: George R. H. Buffinton, Press of J. D. Munroe, 1893), 1864-1904.

## Letter Number 45:
## Knowlton to James M. Swift - March 10, 1924

————•○○⊕⊛⊕○•———

March 10, 1924.

James M. Swift, Esq.,
　　82 Devonshire Street
　　　Boston, Mass.

Dear Jim:

Thank you for your letter of March 8. I shall send your opinion on to my New York author friend.

Yours very truly,

FWK:ED

*Biographical Note:* **James Marcus Swift** (American lawyer, District Attorney for Southern District of Massachusetts, Attorney General of the Commonwealth of Massachusetts from 1911-1914), 1873-1946.

## Letter Number 46:
## Knowlton to George A. Sanderson - March 10, 1924

————··∘⊶❦⊶∘·· ————

March 10, 1924.

Hon. George A. Sanderson,
      Hampson Court,
         Brookline, Mass.

Dear Judge Sanderson:

      Thank you very much for your letter of March 8, not only for the suggestions you make as to the proper answer to give to my New York author friend, but also the very interesting incident of the Eastman case.

      The book, I think is likely to be very interesting and I am rather inclined to think that its preparation is in good hands.

Yours very truly,

FWK:ED

*Biographical Note:* **George Augustus Sanderson** (American lawyer, Associate Justice of the Massachusetts Supreme Court from 1924-1932), 1863-1932.

*Case Detail, Charles R. Eastman:* Charles R. Eastman, a geology and paleontology instructor at Harvard University, was charged with the murder of his brother-in-law, Richard H. Grogan, on July 4, 1900, while the two were participating in target practice. Eastman contended that the shooting death was an accident—that the antique revolver he was using had discharged unexpectedly, hitting Grogan just above his heart.

In January of 1901, Grogan's body was exhumed to recover the bullet fragment. Testing proved that the weapon that fatally wounded Grogan was not from an old gun but a modern weapon. The bullet extracted contained tin while an older weapon would have produced lead fragments. Mrs. Mary Milner, a professional nurse, claimed that she saw Grogan on the ground with Eastman nearby. Grogan, she said, looked at Eastman and said "There is the man who shot me."

Eastman replied that he did kill Grogan but that he did not mean to do it. Grogan allegedly responded, "He did mean it." All eyewitness testimony was ruled inadmissible at trial, which was a considerable blow for the prosecution.

The trial lasted three weeks, with forty witnesses, and two days of closing arguments. The jury deliberated five hours and on May 11, 1901 returned a verdict of not guilty. Reportedly, a cheer broke out among the spectators in the courtroom.

Eastman later worked for the American Museum of Natural History in New York and was a naturalist with an international reputation. He was recovering from the influenza of 1918 when he collapsed, fell into the ocean, and drowned.

## Letter Number 47:
## Asa P. French to Knowlton - March 10, 1924

—∘∘❦∘∘—

## LAW OFFICE OF ASA P. FRENCH
## 45 MILK STREET
### ROOMS 609-613
## BOSTON

TELEPHONES   MAIN 16

MAIN 17

ASA P. FRENCH

JAMES S. ALLEN, JR.

JONATHAN W. FRENCH

10 March 1924.

Dear Mr. Knowlton,

Regarding the <u>Borden</u> case and the suggestion of Mr. Pearson quoted in your letter to me of March 7th, it occurs to me to say, further, -

    1. That the public hearing before Judge Blaisdell should not be referred to by Mr. Pearson as a "trial", although it is carelessly so denominated in Mr. Porter's narrative of the case; it was, of course, merely a preliminary hearing to determine whether or not there was probable cause to hold the accused for the grand jury.

    2. It was undoubtedly of unusual length, explicable, of course, by the intricacy of the case, the number of witnesses called, and the laudable determination of Miss Borden's counsel to fight every inch of the ground.

It was unique, I am sure, only in the fact that a person under suspicion was examined at the inquest, and the testimony there given was used against her at the hearing upon probable cause. Why it was admitted without objection (as I believe it was) I cannot understand, unless her counsel did not know what she had said and wished to ascertain, or because a request for its exclusion would have had an unfavorable influence upon public opinion which then seemed to be very strongly in her favor, and upon which the ultimate result may have largely depended. I need not remind you that this testimony was excluded at the trial, for you refer to that fact in your earlier letter.

I should be very glad if, at some time, you would tell me how your father explained the verdict. The evidence seems as nearly a positive demonstration of guilt as one could possibly conceive of.

Sincerely yours,
Asa French

Frank W. Knowlton, Esq.,
  30 State Street, Boston.

F/D

*Biographical Note:* **Asa Palmer French** (American lawyer, US Attorney for the District of Massachusetts from 1906-1914), 1860-1935; **James Sidney Allen Jr.** (American lawyer, Assistant US District Attorney for Massachusetts from 1912-1917, lawyer in the firm of Asa P. French, Clerk of US District Court in Boston from 1917-1950), 1876-1917; **Jonathan Wales French** (American lawyer, son of Asa Palmer French, lawyer in the firm of Asa P. French, Boston, later legal counsel for Mayors Association of Massachusetts), 1891-1964; **Josiah Coleman Blaisdell** (American lawyer, District Court Judge of Bristol County, Massachusetts, from 1874-1893, presiding judge at the inquest and preliminary hearing in the Lizzie Borden case), 1820-1900; **Edwin H. Porter** (reporter for the *Fall River Daily Globe* and author of *The Fall River Tragedy: A History of the Borden Murders*, Fall River, MA: George R. H. Buffinton, Press of J. D. Munroe, 1893), 1864-1904; **Hosea Morrill Knowlton** (American lawyer, District Attorney for the Commonwealth of Massachusetts from 1879-1893, he led the prosecution against Miss Lizzie A. Borden, and later served as the Attorney General of the Commonwealth from 1894-1902), 1847-1902.

## Letter Number 48a:
## Knowlton to Asa P. French - March 11, 1924

———·∘○❀❀❀○∘·———

March 11, 1924.

Asa P. French, Esq.,
    45 Milk Street,
        Boston, Mass.

Dear Mr. French:

Thank you very much for your letter of March 10 which I think will be very helpful to Mr. Pearson.

Unfortunately nobody seems to be able to find the stenographic report of the inquest and for that reason Mr. Pearson has had to rely upon newspaper accounts and a book published by a newspaper man at the time. However, I am going to send your letter on to him for his assistance.

You ask me how my father explains the verdict. He knew the strength of public opinion and knew the way in which it was used by church organizations and others to bring about an atmosphere. The conduct of the judges did not help at all to dissipate that atmosphere and I think that the result was about as he expected. I am sending you a copy of a letter that father wrote to Mr. Pillsbury a little over a month before the trial which shows his frame of mind just before the trial and indicates clearly that he had no delusions about it.

Thank you very much for your kindness.

Yours very truly,

FWK:ED
Enc.

*Biographical Note:* **Asa Palmer French** (American lawyer, US Attorney for the District of Massachusetts from 1906-1914), 1860-1935; **Hosea Morrill Knowlton** (American lawyer, District Attorney for the Commonwealth of Massachusetts from 1879-1893, he led the prosecution against Miss Lizzie A. Borden, and later served as the Attorney General of the Commonwealth from 1894-1902), 1847-1902; **Albert Enoch Pillsbury** (American lawyer, Attorney General, Commonwealth of Massachusetts from 1891-1893), 1849-1930.

## Letter Number 48b:
## Copy of letter from Hosea M. Knowlton to Pillsbury
## dated April 24, 1893

———•∘∘🙣🙡∘∘•———

*HOSEA M. KNOWLTON. ARTHUR E. PERRY.*
*COUNSELLORS AT LAW.*
*OFFICE:*
*38 NORTH WATER STREET.*

{Dictated}.

NEW BEDFORD, MASS. April 24, 1893.

Hon. A. E. Pillsbury, Attorney General:
    My Dear Sir:-
        I have thought more about the Lizzie Borden
case since I talked with you, and think perhaps it may be well to write
you, as I shall not be able to meet you probably until Thursday, possibly
Wednesday afternoon.
        Personally I would like very much to get rid of the trial of the
case, and fear that my own feelings in that direction may have influenced
my better judgment. I feel this all the more upon your not unexpected
announcement that the burden of the trial would come upon me.
        I confess, however, I cannot see my way clear to any disposition
of the case other than a trial. Should it result in disagreement of the jury
there would be no difficulty then in disposing of the case by admitting
the defendent [sic] to bail: but a verdict either way would render such
a course unnecessary. The case has proceeded so far and an indictment
has been found by the grand inquest of the county that it does not seem
to me that we ought to take the responsibility of discharging her without
trial, even though there is every reasonable expectation of a verdict of not
guilty. I am unable to concur fully in your views as to the probable result.
I think it may well be that the jury might disagree upon the case. But even
in my most sanguine moments I have scarcely expected a verdict of guilty.
        The situation is this: nothing has developed which satisfies

either of us that she is innocent, neither of us can escape the conclusion that she must have had some knowledge of the occurrence. She has been presented for trial by a jury which, to say the least, was not influenced by anything said by the government in the favor of the indictment.

Without discussing the matter more fully in this letter I will only say as above indicated that I cannot see how any other course than setting the case down for trial, and trying it will satisfy that portion of the public sentiment whether favorable to her or not, which is worthy of being respected.

June seems to be the most satisfactory month, all things considered. I will write more fully as to the admission of her confession after I have looked the matter up.

Yours Truly,<br>
H M Knowlton

*Biographical Note:* **Arthur Ebenezer Perry** (American lawyer, partner in the firm of Knowlton & Perry and later Knowlton, Perry & Cook), 1857-1909; **Albert Enoch Pillsbury** (American lawyer, Attorney General, Commonwealth of Massachusetts from 1891-1893), 1849-1930; **Hosea Morrill Knowlton** (American lawyer, District Attorney for the Commonwealth of Massachusetts from 1879-1893, he led the prosecution against Miss Lizzie A. Borden, and later served as the Attorney General of the Commonwealth from 1894-1902), 1847-1902.

## Letter Number 49:
## Knowlton to Frederick H. Chase - March 11, 1924

———··◦○❀○○·———

March 11, 1924.

Hon. Frederick H. Chase.
    6 Beacon Street.
        Boston. Mass.

Dear Judge Chase:

    Thank you for your letter of March 10 giving me the result of your experience in the matter I asked you about.

    I think there was more to the Borden inquest than appears on the surface of this correspondence but I am afraid after this lapse of time it will be difficult to determine just what influenced the proceedings.

    However. I am grateful to you for your help in making the situation clear to my New York author friend.

        Yours very truly

FWK:ED

*Biographical Note:* **Frederick Hathaway Chase** (American lawyer, partner in the firm of Stewart & Chase, and Stewart, Chase & Baldwin, Assistant District Attorney for Suffolk County, Massachusetts), 1870-1948.

## Letter Number 50a:
## Knowlton to Pearson - March 11, 1924

❦

March 11, 1924.

Edmund L. Pearson, Esq.
    476 Fifth Avenue
      New York City.

My dear Pearson:

I send you herewith three more letters that I have received from ex-prosecutors about the Borden case.

Robert O. Harris, the present U. S. District Attorney, was for a number of years the District Attorney of the Southeastern District of Massachusetts. The longhand letter is from George A. Sanderson, now a Judge of our Superior Court, who was for a number of years Assistant District Attorney of Middlesex County. Frederick H. Chase was for many years an Assistant District Attorney of Suffolk County and later a Judge of our Superior Court. He is now one of our leading practitioners.

I don't know that these letters give you much help, although you will notice in Judge Sanderson's letter that my father's judgment about the admissibility of testimony at preliminary hearings was vindicated by our Court. The case he refers to is the one of Professor Eastman of Harvard; which you will recall and which you and I have spoken of.

Yours very truly,

FWK:ED

***Biographical Note:*** **Robert Orr Harris** (American lawyer, Representative from Massachusetts from 1911-1913, US Attorney for District of Massachusetts from 1921-1924), 1854-1926; **George Augustus Sanderson** (American lawyer, Justice of the Superior Court of Massachusetts from 1907-1924, Associate Justice of the Massachusetts Supreme Court from 1924-1932), 1863-1932; **Frederic Hathaway Chase** (American lawyer, partner in the firm of Stewart & Chase, and Stewart, Chase & Baldwin, Assistant District Attorney for Suffolk County, Massachusetts), 1870-1948; **Hosea Morrill Knowlton** (American lawyer, District Attorney for the Commonwealth of Massachusetts from 1879-1893, he led the prosecution against Miss Lizzie A. Borden, and later served as the Attorney General of the Commonwealth from 1894-1902), 1847-1902.

***Case Detail, Charles R. Eastman:*** See Letter #46 for information.

## Letter Number 50b:
## Robert O. Harris to Knowlton - March 7, 1924

————— ·∘∘🙵🙷🙷🙵∘∘· —————

Address reply to
85 Devonshire St.,
Rooms 904-906

DEPARTMENT OF JUSTICE
United States Attorney's Office
District of Massachusetts
Federal Building

Boston, March 7, 1924

Frank W. Knowlton, Esq.,
Attorney at Law,
30 State Street, Boston.

Dear Mr. Knowlton:

Yours of the 4th in regard to "Studies in Murder" is at hand.

The Borden case is so far back that I have myself forgotten some of the proceedings. The hearing before Judge Blaisdell at the inquest was not so unusual in length as to be remarkable or extraordinary. The case was a difficult one and the inquest was necessarily one of some length. I should say it was not at all unprecedented, for while I was the State District Attorney in the Southeastern District I had several cases that were at least equal in length to this one.

I think I should answer this question by saying, as I have above, "not unusual to the extent of being remarkable and not unprecedented."

Yours very truly,
/s/ Robert O. Harris.

*Biographical Note:* **Robert Orr Harris** (American lawyer, Representative from Massachusetts from 1911-1913, US Attorney for District of Massachusetts from 1921-1924), 1854-1926; **Josiah Coleman Blaisdell** (American lawyer, District Court Judge of Bristol County, Massachusetts, from 1874-1893, presiding judge at the inquest and preliminary hearing in the Lizzie Borden case), 1820-1900.

## Letter Number 50c:
## George A. Sanderson to Knowlton - March 8, 1924

HAMPTON COURT
Brookline, Mass.

My dear Mr. Knowlton,

In answer to your question I should say that inquests in this Commonwealth are the usual procedure in cases of death under suspicious circumstances. I do not know that I can recall another that lasted as long as six days but it would not surprise me if others could be found that were of that length. I have known hearings of this kind to start and then be continued from time to time for the purpose of discovering and presenting evidence that may not be obtainable at first or for the purpose of enabling the officers to make further investigations and present further evidence, that may aid the court and prosecuting officers in relieving from suspicion those who may have been unjustly suspected or in fixing the guilt upon those who are responsible for the crime.

I remember that your father said after he had argued in the Eastman case for the admission of Eastman's statement before the Grand Jury and quoting from his argument in the Borden case that he was going to keep on offering this kind of evidence until some judge would have the courage to admit it. Such statements made before the Grand Jury have since been held to be admissible.

I believe that it is good practice in a case surrounded with mystery to continue the inquest hearings so long as the inquiry is likely to throw light on the case.

Very truly yours,
/s/ George A. Sanderson

March 8, 1924.

***Biographical Note:*** **George Augustus Sanderson** (American lawyer, Justice of the Superior Court of Massachusetts from 1907-1924, Associate Justice of the Massachusetts Supreme Court from 1924-1932), 1863-1932; **Hosea Morrill Knowlton** (American lawyer, District Attorney for the Commonwealth of Massachusetts from 1879-1893, he led the prosecution against Miss Lizzie A. Borden, and later served as the Attorney General of the Commonwealth from 1894-1902), 1847-1902.

***Case Detail, Charles R. Eastman:*** See Letter #46 for information.

## Letter Number 50d:
## Frederic H. Chase to Knowlton - March 10, 1924

STEWART & CHASE

6 Beacon St.,

Boston

March
tenth
1 9 2 4

Frank W. Knowlton, Esq.,
30 State Street,
Boston, Massachusetts

Dear Mr. Knowlton: -

I am sorry that I have not had a chance to answer your letter of March 4th before this, but am glad now to send you what little information I have upon the subject.

According to my observation and information, inquests are generally of rather brief duration. While the hearings are not exactly perfunctory in character, yet the absence of examining counsel and the ex parte nature of the hearing is rather conducive to brevity. In my own personal experience I can recall but one inquest which was lengthy, or where the District Attorney appeared and took part in the examination. I refer to the so-called "Subway Explosion" case where, as perhaps you will recall, a number of people were killed or injured by an explosion during the construction of the subway at the corner of Tremont and Boylston Streets. An inquest was held by Judge Ely of the Municipal Court and Judge McLaughlin, who was then an Assistant District Attorney, conducted the examination of witnesses. This hearing covered a number of weeks, as I recall it.

The "Lizzie Borden" case was unusual in that the person who was suspected of causing the deaths, and who afterwards was charged by indictment with murder, testified before the examining magistrate. I do not now recall whether she was summoned as a witness or whether she appeared voluntarily. I am informed that oftentimes a person upon whom suspicion rests makes a request or permission to appear and testify at the inquest. I understand that this request is generally denied and that the magistrate holding the inquest endeavors to confine the inquiry to an examination of witnesses who are not suspected of wrong in the matter.

I feel that I would have to answer your friend's question just as you did, to the effect that while a hearing such as was held in the Borden case was unusual, it was not unprecedented.

Very truly yours,
Frederic H. Chase.

*Biographical Note:* **Frederick Hathaway Chase** (American lawyer, partner in the firm of Stewart & Chase, and Stewart, Chase & Baldwin, Assistant District Attorney for Suffolk County, Massachusetts), 1870-1948; **Ralph A. Stewart** (American lawyer, former Assistant Attorney General of Massachusetts under Herbert Parker, partner in the firm of Choate, Hall & Stewart, partner in the firm Stewart & Chase), 1870-1926; **Frederick David Ely** (American lawyer, partner in the firm of Ely & Gates, Boston, member of US House of Representatives from 1885-1887, and Justice of the Municipal Court of Boston from 1888-1914), 1838-1921; **John Dwyer McLaughlin** (American lawyer, Assistant District Attorney of Suffolk County, Massachusetts, from 1894-1904, Justice of the Superior Court of Massachusetts from 1911-1931), 1865-1931.

*Case Detail, "Subway Explosion":* Twelve persons and multiple horses were killed, as well as at least sixty people seriously injured in a gas explosion at the junction of Boylston and Tremont Streets in Boston on March 4, 1897. An old break in the six-inch gas main along the south side of Boylston Street was the culprit. Gas had accumulated under the planking of the construction of the new subway system, with complaints being made for weeks in advance of the disaster. In 1900, an action against the Boston Gas Light Company was heard before the Superior Court. The jury returned a verdict for the plaintiff for personal injury.

## Letter Number 51:
## John C. Hammond to Knowlton - March 13, 1924

---

John C. Hammond                    Thomas J. Hammond

HAMMOND & HAMMOND
Attorneys At Law
NORTHAMPTON, MASS.

March 13,1924.

Frank W. Knowlton, Esq.,
    Attorney at Law,
       30 State St. Boston, Mass.

    Dear Knowlton, - Your letter of March 4th has gone too long unanswered, probably because I did not know of anything that would be of assistance. At any rate it has escaped my mind for a few days.

    I have not had my attention called to any inquest of unusual length. I do not recollect in the many times I met your father hearing him say anything about it. It does not seem that six days was an extreme length for an inquest in a difficult capital case. This does not help you any I am sorry to say.

    With personal regards, I am

Very truly yours,
\s\ J. C. Hammond

*Biographical Note:* **John Chester Hammond** (American lawyer, Northwestern District Attorney of Massachusetts from 1897-1903, partner in firm of Hammond & Hammond), 1842-1926; **Thomas Jasper Hammond** (American lawyer, partner in firm of Hammond & Hammond, Northampton, Massachusetts, District Attorney for Northampton from 1903-1909, Justice with the Superior Court of Massachusetts from 1929-1946), 1876-1946; **Hosea Morrill Knowlton** (American lawyer, District Attorney for the Commonwealth of Massachusetts from 1879-1893, he led the prosecution against Miss Lizzie A. Borden, and later served as the Attorney General of the Commonwealth from 1894-1902), 1847-1902.

## Letter Number 52:
## Pearson to Knowlton - March 13, 1924

476 Fifth Avenue
New York
March 13, 1924

Dear Knowlton, -

It was good of you to make these further inquiries, and
I believe that I am perfectly safe in leaving my cautious statement as I first
wrote it. As I remember (I haven't the manuscript here at my office) it was to
the effect that few preliminary trials in Massachusetts could have been longer.

I have been emboldened to write to Mr. Herbert Parker
to ask him if he has any newspaper clippings about the Tucker case - and
the agitation after the trial - and if he has, and will lend them, I think I
shall add a short essay on that case. I have always been interested in it,
and the record of the trial is of course easily available. In fact, I own the
first volume of it, and can easily get the other.

Miss Lizzie has gone to the ~~printer~~ publisher; she and
one other will make up about half the book, as the Borden case has run
to 30,000 words. My publisher did not seem to object at the length of it;
he may do so, later. They are to begin composition on these, while I finish
the other cases, - four or five shorter ones. So I shall be able to return
your material soon and to send back the record to the patient Mr. Freeze.
Before June 1, I hope to send you a copy of the book.

In the meantime I am sending you a copy of a book of
mine, one which came out last year, has been out of print for a month or two,
and has now appeared in a new edition, in a fearfully meretricious dress, for
which I am partly to blame. I hope you will find some things of interest in it;
one of the chapters, the last, was written as a try-out for the murder book. It is
sent as a souvenir of my gratitude to you for your help in the later one.

Sincerely yours
/s/ E. L. Pearson

*Biographical Note:* **Herbert Parker** (American lawyer, District Attorney for Middle District of Massachusetts from 1896-1899, Attorney General of the Commonwealth of Massachusetts from 1902-1906), 1856-1939; **Louis Freeze** (Chief Clerk at the office of the Attorney General of the Commonwealth of Massachusetts), 1866-1956.

**Editor's Note:** The book given by Mr. Pearson to Mr. Knowlton was *Books in Black or Red*, published by Macmillan in 1923, and the title of the essay on the Lizzie Borden case is titled "The Borden Case," published in *Studies in Murder*, New York: Random House, 1924.

*Case Detail, Charles Lewis Tucker:* See Letter # 6 for information.

## Letter Number 53:
## Knowlton to Pearson - March 14, 1924

————·∘⊸☙☙⊷∘·————

March 14, 1924.

My dear Pearson:

I am quite excited about your letter of March 13. I am looking forward not only to your "Studies in Murder" but to the book of yours which you tell me is in its way to me. I shall be very glad indeed to have it.

In the meantime, although I assume it is now too late, I am sending you for what it is worth a clipping I found in my desk today which has been there for a great many years about the Borden case. It looks as if it appeared in the "Providence Journal". When, I do not know, but it could not have been long after the trial. If it is too late to be of any service or interest, just put it with the others.

Yours very gratefully,

FWK:ED
Enc.


Mr. Edward Pearson,
　　476 Fifth Avenue,
　　　　New York City.

## Letter Number 54:
## Knowlton to John C. Hammond - March 14, 1924

March 14, 1924.

Dear Mr. Hammond:

Thank you very much indeed for your letter of March 13 in answer to my inquiry about the "Lizzie Borden" case.

Yours very truly,

FWK:ED

Hon. John C. Hammond,
        Northampton,
                Mass.

*Biographical Note:* **John Chester Hammond** (American lawyer, Northwestern District Attorney of Massachusetts from 1897-1903, partner in firm of Hammond & Hammond), 1842-1926;.

## Letter Number 55:
## Knowlton to Pearson - March 18, 1924

————··○○⊕⊛⊕○○·· ————

March 18, 1924.

My dear Pearson:

Your kind present arrived yesterday and I had a very pleasant half hour with it last evening, all the time that was permitted to me, and I look forward to several pleasant evenings.

At first the color of the cover was rather disturbing, particularly as it brought to mind the bright yellow book that I have had for several years, "Memoirs of Li Hung Chang", a book which I have enjoyed and which has been loaned perhaps more than any book in my library, but when I read the title of the first essay, I could see at once the happy significance of the color of the cover you have put on your book. The disclosure that that was a literary hoax came too recently to permit you to treat it.

By the way, as an authority on such matters, is Ossendowski's "Beasts, Men and Gods" another such and like the eternal question of which came first, the hen or the egg, did Ossendowski's story suggest Locke's "The Tale of Triona" or did Locke's book suggest the Ossendowski tale?

In your little note to me on the front page you have accurately hit upon the weakness which I have been endeavoring to conceal for years. Of course I ate Conan Doyle alive and still go back time and again to Gaboriau and his wonderful "M. Le Coq", but even one who has to cultivate a severe legal style of correspondence must be entitled to his secret weaknesses.

I have peeked ahead in the book and see much delight in store for me. Like yourself, I was not forbidden dime novels and consequently read few, but the illustrations are delightful. I can see that you refer to books like "Oliver Optic" books which I was supposed to read as a youth but never could get much thrill out of. The principal ideal of the young hero was to have some rich man come and say to his parents, "Put money in his pocket and let him know that his uncle put it there." Really, my greatest thrill came from the wonderful Castleton [*sic*] series of "Frank" books. - "Frank, the Young Naturalist", "Frank at Don Carlos Rancho" and others. I got such wonderful thrills from those that I inquired the other day at our library in Weston to see if boys still read them, and I was told by the hard hearted librarian that their style was considered a little low for proper reading by youths of today. When I see the "Motorcycle Boys In Europe and Elsewhere" series and others such as my boys have. I really wonder if they get as much from their books as I got from the wonderful Castleton Series. Perhaps you discuss all these matters later on. In any event, I know that I am going to have some very pleasant evenings and I am very grateful to you for your kindness in affording me them.

By the way, J.H. Wigmore's book "The Principles of Judicial Proof", paragraphs 369 and 370, at pages 734 and 735, has reference to a part of the argument in the Borden case.

Yours sincerely,

FWK:ED

Mr. Edmund L. Pearson,
476 Fifth Avenue,
New York City.

***Biographical Note:*** *Memoirs of Li Hung Chang,* a fabricated memoir exposed as a forgery in 1923, after the author's death (**William Francis Mannix**, 1858-1920); **Li Hongzhang** (Chinese politician, general, and diplomat in late Qing Dynasty), 1823-1901; *Beasts, Men and Gods* by **Ferdynard Antoni Ossendowski** (Polish writer, explorer, university professor, anti-Communist activist), 1876-1945; *The Tale of Triona* by **William John Locke** (British novelist, dramatist, playwright), 1863-1930; **Sir Arthur Ignatius Conan Doyle** (British writer and physician, author of fifty-six Sherlock Holmes stories), 1859-1930; **Emile Gaboriau** (French writer, novelist, journalist, pioneer in detective fiction, created character of Monsieur Le Coq), 1832-1873; **Oliver Optic**, pseudonym for **William Taylor Adams** (American academic, author, and member of the Massachusetts House of Representatives), 1822-1897; **Harry Castlemon**, pseudonym for **Charles Austin Fosdick** (American prolific writer of juvenile stories and novels for boys), 1842-1915; **Ralph Marlow** (author of "Five Big Motorcycle Boys" series of books published from 1914-1916, probably a pseudonym); **John Henry Wigmore** (American lawyer and legal scholar, known for his expertise in the law of evidence, author of "The Borden Case," *American Law Review* 17, November/December, 1893, 819-45), 1863-1943.

## Letter Number 56:
## Pearson to Knowlton - March 19, 1924

———••○○◦✿❀✿◦○○••———

# The New York Public Library
### Astor, Lenox and Tilden Foundations

476 FIFTH AVENUE

*New York,*  *March 19, 1924*

Mr. Frank W. Knowlton
    30 State Street
        Boston, Mass.

Dear Knowlton:

Have you seen the new edition of "The Memoirs of Li Hung Chang", with the essay by Ralph Paine telling about Mannix and the circumstances under which the book was written? It is well worth reading and if you like, I will lend you my copy. As for "Beasts, Men and Gods", everybody seems to suspect that that and its recent successor are full of fake, but your suggestion that Locke's novel is similar is news to me as I have never read "The Tale of Triona". I believe by the way, that Mr. Macrae, President of the Company which publishes Ossendowski's books, trusts in him as a teller of truth. I am in perfect agreement with you about Oliver Optic. I have never read one of his books to the end, while I shared your admiration for Harry Castlemon. I can still recall my excitement when the ~~stone~~ stolen horses were carried into Don Carlos Rancho over the bridge of clouds. Librarians are unnecessarily ~~smithy~~ sniffy about these books and as you suggest "The Motor Cycle Boys" and "The Submarine Boys" are no better, - nor are they as good.

Thank you for the reference to Wigmore, which I shall look

up immediately. Have you seen Algernon Blackwood's "Episodes before Thirty"? It contains one sentence about the Borden case and scores about five appalling blunders in that one sentence.

Sincerely yours,

Edmund L. Pearson

*Biographical Note:* Memoirs of Li Hung Chang, a fabricated memoir exposed as a forgery in 1923 after the author's death (**William Francis Mannix**, 1858-1920); **Li Hongzhang** (Chinese politician, general, and diplomat in late Qing Dynasty), 1823-1901; **Ralph Delahaye Paine** (American journalist and author of popular fiction in the early 20th century), 1871-1925; *Beasts, Men and Gods* by **Ferdynard Antoni Ossendowski** (Polish writer, explorer, university professor, anti-Communist activist), 1876-1945; *The Tale of Triona* by **William John Locke** (British novelist, dramatist, playwright), 1863-1930; **John Macrae Sr.** (president of E.P. Dutton Company), 1866-1944; **E.P. Dutton, Publishers** (American book publishing company founded as a book retailer in Boston in 1852 by **Edward Payson Dutton**, 1831-1923); **Oliver Optic**, pseudonym for **William Taylor Adams** (American academic, author, and member of the Massachusetts House of Representatives), 1822-1897; **Harry Castlemon**, pseudonym for **Charles Austin Fosdick** (American prolific writer of juvenile stories and novels for boys), 1842-1915; **Ralph Marlow** (author of "Five Big Motorcycle Boys" series of books published from 1914-1916); "Submarine Boys" series (American adventure books for boys, published in 1909-1920, by **Victor G. Durham**, pseudonym of **H. Irving Hancock**, American chemist and author of children's literature and juveniles, 1868-1922); **John Henry Wigmore** (American lawyer and legal scholar, known for his expertise in the law of evidence, author of "The Borden Case," *American Law Review* 17, November/December, 1893, 819-45), 1863-1943; **Algernon Henry Blackwood** (British broadcasting narrator, journalist, novelist, short story writer, and prolific ghost story author), 1869-1951.

## Letter Number 57:
## Knowlton to Pearson - April 5, 1924

April 5, 1924.

My dear Pearson:

I have been so busy that I have not had a chance to write you since I finished reading "Books in Black and Red" [*sic*]. I cannot tell you how much pleasure I had with it. It is a delightfully interesting, chatty little book and you have succeeded in whetting my appetite for the book you are to publish by the last essay, which, I think, I enjoyed as much as any of them.

Strangely enough, it was only about a month ago in reading of the life of Caleb Cushing that I ran across references to the eccentric Lord Timothy Dexter so that I was quite anxious to read the tale about him.

Thank you for offering to loan me your copy of the new edition of the "Memoirs of Li Hung Chang". At the time it was issued, the Boston Globe gave one Sunday the whole of Ralph Paine's essay which appears in the new edition, and I cut it out and pasted it into the front of my edition.

Yours sincerely,

Edmund L. Pearson,
476 Fifth Avenue,
New York City.

*Biographical Note:* **Caleb Cushing** (American Democratic politician and diplomat, Congressman from Massachusetts from 1835-1843, Minister to China under President Zachary Taylor in 1844, 23rd Attorney General of the United States under President Franklin Pierce from 1853-1857, and Minister to Spain under President Ulysses S. Grant from 1874-1877), 1800-1879; **Lord Timothy Dexter** (American businessman and author, noted for his eccentricities), 1747-1806; *Memoirs of Li Hung Chang*, a fabricated memoir exposed as a forgery in 1923 after the author's death (**William Francis Mannix**, 1858-1920); **Li Hongzhang** (Chinese politician, general, and diplomat in late Qing Dynasty), 1823-1901; **Ralph Delahaye Paine** (American journalist and author of popular fiction in the early 20th century), 1871-1925.

**Editor's Note: Editor's Note:** The book given by Mr. Pearson to Mr. Knowlton was *Books in Black or Red*, published by Macmillan in 1923. It would appear there is a break in the correspondence at this point. Letters are missing between April 5 and May 9, 1924.

## Letter Number 58:
## Pearson to Knowlton - May 8, 1924

## The New York Public Library
### Astor, Lenox and Tilden Foundations

476 FIFTH AVENUE

*New York,* May 8, 1924

Mr. Frank W. Knowlton
c/o Choate Hall & Stewart
30 State Street
Boston, Massachusetts

My dear Knowlton:

As soon as I hear from you whether you wish them sent to your office or to your home, and in the latter instance, as soon as you give me your home address, I will return to you the letters, memoranda, pictures, and other things which you so kindly lent me for use in work on the Borden case.

They were very useful to me and not only of interest to me personally and valuable in giving me some idea of the public state of mind at the time, but also I made direct use, as you know, of the letter from your father to Mr. Pillsbury, and I got information from the photographs from the curious letters to your father, and quoted from the newspaper clippings, and from one or two police reports and memoranda in typewriting.

I hope the book will be out before long, say about the middle or last of June.

Sincerely yours,
Edmund L. Pearson

ELP:AP

**Editor's Note**: Handwritten at the bottom of this letter was the following:

*I still have <u>one</u> photograph of the Borden house, which is being copied for an illustration. That is all not returned, I think. Will send that as soon as the publishers return it to me.*

*Biographical Note:* **Charles F. Choate Jr.** (American lawyer, partner in the firm of Choate, Hall & Stewart, Boston), 1866-1927; **Damon E. Hall** (American lawyer, former Assistant Attorney General, partner in the law firm of Hurlburt, Jones & Hall, Boston), 1875-1953; **Ralph A. Stewart** (American lawyer, former Assistant Attorney General of Massachusetts under Herbert Parker, partner in the firm of Choate, Hall & Stewart, partner in the firm Stewart & Chase), 1870-1926; **Hosea Morrill Knowlton** (American lawyer, District Attorney for the Commonwealth of Massachusetts from 1879-1893, he led the prosecution against Miss Lizzie A. Borden, and later served as the Attorney General of the Commonwealth from 1894-1902), 1847-1902; **Albert Enoch Pillsbury** (American lawyer, Attorney General, Commonwealth of Massachusetts from 1891-1893), 1849-1930.

## Letter Number 59:
## Knowlton to Pearson - May 9, 1924

————⋅∘○🙦🙤○∘⋅————

May 9, 1924.

My dear Pearson:

I have your letter of May 8 and I think it would perhaps be better for you to send the Borden data to me at my home address which is just Weston, Mass., and that being a simple country town nobody bothers about names of streets and there are no numbers. I am very glad that you found them useful and of interest, and I am looking forward eagerly to the book. Our librarian at Weston told me the other night that she was quite disappointed to hear from the publishers from whom she had ordered it that it was not yet out. So, you see that it is being anxiously awaited.

With best regards, I am

Yours sincerely,

Mr. Edmund L. Pearson,
New York Public Library,
476 Fifth Avenue
New York City

## Letter Number 60:
## Pearson to Knowlton - May 12, 1924

---•○◦❀❁❀◦○•---

# The New York Public Library
### Astor, Lenox and Tilden Foundations

476 FIFTH AVENUE

*New York,* May 12, 1924

Mr. Frank W. Knowlton
c/o Choate Hall & Stewart
30 State Street
Boston, Massachusetts

Dear Knowlton:

      I am sending you the Borden material by parcel post, insured. I hope you have a rural free delivery and that you will not have to call for it, as it is a rather large box. But this seemed the better way, rather than to ship it by express, as then, so far as I can find out, you would have had to call at Waltham for it.

                Gratefully yours,
                  E.L.P.

ELP:AP

*Biographical Note:* **Charles F. Choate Jr.** (American lawyer, partner in the firm of Choate, Hall & Stewart, Boston), 1866-1927; **Damon E. Hall** (American lawyer, former Assistant Attorney General, partner in the law firm of Hurlburt, Jones & Hall, Boston), 1875-1953; **Ralph A. Stewart** (American lawyer, former Assistant Attorney General of Massachusetts under Herbert Parker, partner in the firm of Choate, Hall & Stewart, partner in the firm Stewart & Chase), 1870-1926.

## Letter Number 61:
## Knowlton to Pearson - May 20, 1924

May 20, 1924.

Mr. Edmund L. Pearson,
  The New York Public Library,
   476 Fifth Avenue,
    New York City.

Dear Pearson:

  This is to acknowledge the safe arrival in Weston of the package of Borden papers which you sent so carefully packed.

  I am still looking forward with eager interest to the book when it comes out next month.

      Yours very truly,

FWK:ED

## Letter Number 62:
## Handwritten Letter from Pearson to Knowlton - July 8, 1924

---

# The New York Public Library
### Astor, Lenox and Tilden Foundations

476 FIFTH AVENUE

*New York,* July 8 '24

Dear Knowlton:

Even books about murder will out – at last - and mine goes to you today or tomorrow, by mail.

Sincerely yours,
E.L. Pearson

## Letter Number 63:
## Knowlton to Pearson - July 19, 1924

———◦◦○❈○◦◦———

July 19, 1924.

Edmund Lester Pearson,
    New York Public Library,
        476 Fifth Avenue,
            New York City.

My dear Pearson:

I have been in Greenfield in Franklin County, trying jury cases in the quiet hills at the foot of the Mohawk Trail and when your book arrived it was forwarded to me up there. Twenty-seven years ago my father tried the famous case of Commonwealth v. John H. O'Neil for the murder of Harriet McLeod upon the lonely hillside of the Town of Buckland. Everywhere I went I found that, the most famous case in Greenfield County for a century, was being still talked of. Consequently your book came to me when I was in an atmosphere of murder. I have had a delightful time with it and while there I loaned it two or three times just to whet the appetites of friends who immediately rushed and bought it. I think you have done an admirable piece of work, the Borden case particularly. I speak of that case because that is the one I am most familiar with. So far I have killed with you seven of the people, five of whom I have chopped to death with axes, the sixth I have beaten to death with an iron bar, and the seventh I have stabbed. I still have to dream with Uncle Amos but before I dream I want to thank you for sending me the book and tell you how much I am enjoying it.

Of course I am naturally proud of what my father did in the Borden case and I am very glad to have it resurrected thirty years later for everyone to know about and appreciate so I owe you my thanks for that as well as for the book. I am today sending copies to different members of my family and I know that they will be equally pleased.

Yours gratefully,

FWK*PS

**Biographical Note: Hosea Morrill Knowlton** (American lawyer, District Attorney for the Commonwealth of Massachusetts from 1879-1893, he led the prosecution against Miss Lizzie A. Borden, and later served as the Attorney General of the Commonwealth from 1894-1902), 1847-1902.

**Case Detail, Hattie McCloud murder (O'Neil case):** John "Yank" O'Neil (1873-1908), an unemployed machinist with a drinking problem, was accused of strangling Mrs. Harriet "Hattie" Evelyn McCloud (1859-1897), then raping her corpse on a country lane near Shelburne Falls, Massachusetts, on January 8, 1897. Convicted later that year, O'Neil was executed on January 7, 1898. A few months after O'Neil's hanging, a dying soldier who was fighting the Spaniards in Cuba confessed to the crime to ace newspaper reporter, Eddie Collins. The soldier originated from the area of the murder and died before his oral confession could be backed up by a written one.

**Case Detail, Jesse and Stephen Boorn (Uncle Amos reference):** See Letter #6 for information.

## Letter Number 64:
## Pearson to Knowlton - July 22, 1924

476 Fifth Avenue
July 22

Dear Knowlton,

I remember the O'Neil case, although imperfectly, as I read the report years ago. I had forgotten that your Father prosecuted it. The murderer had, as I recollect, a narrow space of time for the killing, but he could not account for that time. I seem to recall that he confessed afterwards.

Thank you for what you say about the book. I am interested in lawyers' comments, although so far they have been open to suspicion because of courtesy and friendliness toward the author. One lawyer, a very charming woman, asked me, after reading the Borden essay, asked me if I believed Lizzie was guilty!

There was a long article in the New Bedford Standard last Sunday. I think you will surely see it. I was interested when the editor wrote me that all Lizzie's inquest testimony was printed in the Standard in June '93.

Sincerely yours
Edmund Pearson

*Biographical Note:* **Hosea Morrill Knowlton** (American lawyer, District Attorney for the Commonwealth of Massachusetts from 1879-1893, he led the prosecution against Miss Lizzie A. Borden, and later served as the Attorney General of the Commonwealth from 1894-1902), 1847-1902.

*Case Detail, Hattie McCloud murder (O'Neil case):* See Letter #63 for information.

**Editor's Note:** Cooper Gaw, "The Borden Case Has No Parallel in Country," *The Sunday Standard*, New Bedford, Massachusetts, July 20, 1924; transcribed in Appendix B.

## Letter Number 65:
## Knowlton to the New Bedford Standard

————◦∘◦❊❊❊◦∘◦————

July 25, 1924.

New Bedford Standard,
Pleasant Street,
New Bedford, Mass.

Gentlemen:

I would like to have you send me if you will the New Bedford Standard for Sunday, July 20th. What I am anxious for is the copy that has the long article on Edmund Lester Pearson's book "Studies In Murder".

I enclose ten cents herewith, which I hope will be sufficient for the purpose.

Yours very truly,

FWK/Y

**Editor's Note:** Cooper Gaw, "The Borden Case Has No Parallel in Country," *The Sunday Standard*, New Bedford, Massachusetts, July 20, 1924; transcribed in Appendix B.

**Letter Number 66:**
**Pearson to Knowlton - August 28, 1924**

---

# The New York Public Library
### Astor, Lenox and Tilden Foundations

**476 Fifth Avenue**

*New York,* August 28 1924

Dear Knowlton:

My egregious publishers have already let the "Studies" get temporarily out of stock, and it maybe that there will, some day, be another edition. I may be allowed to correct, emend, ~~an~~ and alter it.

If possible, will you note and some day let me know of any corrections, additions, or changes which you think ought to be made, especially, of course, in the Borden case?

These occur to me: (1) a better resume of Lizzie's inquest testimony, which I now know can be found in the New Bedford Standard of June 13, 1893, where the whole thing was printed; (2) a clearer statement about the handle-less hatchet, - as it stands it seems to intimate, to some readers, that the killing was done with a hatchet which had no handle at the time; (3) possibly a little more about the dresses, although this is a long and wearying topic.

In addition, I may decide to put in a few more strokes of pure "litrachoor", here and there although it is possible that I got most of the effects I tried for, as well as I could expect to get them, not being a De Quincey, a Lafcadio Hearn, or a Poe.

Oh, and I guess I will not be so tender with the Judge. I think more of a description of the charge should be given, and perhaps some of Judge Davis's admirable analysis.

I have had an autograph letter of Miss Lizzie given me by

a man in Forest Hills, and a poem about her sent me by an army chaplain in California, written by an Iowa poet. Also, I am besought to aid a prisoner of the law in Tennessee, most unjustly charged with homicide, - so says his attorney, who has sent me ten pounds of briefs to read.

I have had what the English would call "a simply ripping press" on the subject of the book, of which an article by a neurologist in the September Bookman, and Asa P. French's article in "Book-Notes" have been especially pleasant and intelligent, as ~~they are~~ both writers are learned in the literature of crime. Brander Matthews tells me that he has done a long article, with pictures, for the September International Book Review. I shall take a look, some day two or three months hence, to see if any legal periodicals have stooped to notice my popularization of the law, and how they think I ought to be admonished about it.

Please do not let my request weigh heavily upon you, but if you think of anything I ought to do, or have undone, in the event of another edition, please give me the straight dope.

Sincerely yours
E.L. Pearson

*Biographical Note:* Thomas De Quincey (English essayist, best known for *Confessions of an English Opium-Eater* in 1821), 1785-1859; **Patrick Lafadio Hearn**, later **Koizumi Yakumo** (American author of books on Japanese culture, legends, and ghost stories), 1850-1904; **Edgar Allan Poe** (American poet and short story writer, known for his tales of mystery and macabre), 1809-1849; **Charles Gideon Davis** (American lawyer, District Court Judge, Massachusetts, author of "The conduct of the law in the Borden case, with suggestions of changes in criminal law and practice," in *A Collection of Articles Concerning the Borden Case*, Boston Daily Advertiser, 1894), 1820-1903; **Asa Palmer French** (American lawyer, US Attorney for the District of Massachusetts from 1906-1914), 1860-1935; **Brander Matthews** (American writer and educator, professor of dramatic literature at Columbia University), 1852-1929.

## Letter Number 67:
## Knowlton to Pearson - September 4, 1924

—··◦·◦❈❈◦·◦··—

September 4, 1924.

My dear Pearson:

I am just back from a rather extended vacation and find your letter of the 28th.

I am very glad to know that the "Studies" has had such a fine sale. I have noticed in the Saturday night list in the Boston papers for some weeks that it has appeared in the list of best sellers for this neighborhood, and all the reviews that I have seen have been very favorable. I am gratified to find my own opinion so well corroborated by all the distinguished reviewers.

I am interested to know that you already contemplate another edition and I am going to wait a while before I make any suggestions, if any occur to me, because I want to re-read the Borden essay before replying. Unfortunately my copy has been almost constantly borrowed for the last three or four weeks by different neighbors and I have not had a chance to sit down and re-read it in a more critical frame of mind. I read it before with the idea simply of enjoying it.

Now that we have found what is undoubtedly a verbatim report of the inquest testimony, I wonder if you would not want back that summary by Moody of the points upon which they had counted for proof by the inquest testimony. You may remember that there was in Moody's handwriting a list in rather cryptic form of certain points which seemed important which would be wholly lost if the inquest testimony were excluded with some suggestions as to how a few of the matters might otherwise be covered. If so, I should be glad to dig it out and send it to you.

I think perhaps a few words about the tendency of the judge's charge and its possible influence upon the verdict might be in order. As I read it I thought you showed good judgment and perhaps good taste in not commenting at length upon it, but two or three of my friends have spoken of some curiosity which they had after reading the book as to what part the charge really played. They had always understood that it played a rather large part and perhaps Judge Davis' analysis of the charge might take off the curse of any assumption that a layman should comment upon a charge of the judge.

After I had read your book and while I was trying in Greenfield. I ran across in the Franklin County law library an edition of English trials called "Notable English Trials Series" published during the last few years by some publisher in Edinburgh and I skimmed through several of these while I was there. They are not particularly interesting reading as they are almost entirely a report of the evidence and arguments, but to one brought up in this country where the functions of a judge have been more or less curtailed until he is becoming a little better than a moderator at the trial it comes with rather a shock to see the vehemence and virulence of some of the English judges in their efforts to get convictions. After reading the remarks of some of the English judges in those trial series, Dewey's performance would perhaps seem tame on the other side. By the way, in those trial series I can commend to you as very interesting reading the introductions by a chap named Filson Young in the volume containing the trial of Dr. H. H. Crippin and in the last volume the trial of Edith Thompson and her paramour Bywaters. They stand out as gems in a rather otherwise dull edition, and Filson Young's analysis of characters and motives of the defendants and of the skill with which their defense was handled is very interesting reading and I commend it to you.

I am rather interested to see that you are being bombarded by the same sort of people who bombard the prosecution in these notable cases. What are you going to do for the poor fellow in Tennessee?

Thank you again for the compliment in asking my humble suggestions and I will write you further after I have thought the matter over somewhat.

With congratulations upon the success that you have made of this book, I am

Yours sincerely,


FWK:ED

Mr. Edmund L. Pearson,
476 Fifth Avenue,
New York City.

*Biographical Note:* **William Henry Moody** (American lawyer, assisted Hosea Knowlton in the prosecution of Lizzie A. Borden, Secretary of the Navy and Attorney General under President Theodore Roosevelt, and justice of the Supreme Court), 1853-1917; **Charles Gideon Davis** (American lawyer, District Court Judge, Massachusetts, author of "The conduct of the law in the Borden case, with suggestions of changes in criminal law and practice," in *A Collection of Articles Concerning the Borden Case, Boston Daily Advertiser,* 1894), 1820-1903; **Justin Dewey** (American lawyer, Justice of the Massachusetts Superior Court, one of the three presiding justices who served at the superior court trial of Lizzie Andrew Borden), 1836 - 1900; **Alexander Bell Filson Young** (Irish journalist, essayist, war correspondent, novelist, organist, and conductor), 1878-1938.

*Case Detail, Dr. Hawley Harvey Crippen:* Born in the United States in 1862, Dr. Hawley Harvey Crippen, a homeopath, ear and eye specialist, and medical dispenser, moved with his second wife, Corrine "Cora" Turner, to England in 1894. Corrine performed under her stage name Belle Elmore, and the doctor was unable to practice as a doctor in the United Kingdom. While a manager of Drouet's Institution for the Deaf, Crippen hired Ethel Le Neve, a young typist. By 1900, the two were having an affair. In 1905, the Crippins moved to 39 Hilldrop Crescent, Camden Road, Holloway, London, and took in boarders to offset the doctor's meager income. Apparently, Cora also openly had affairs, including one of the lodgers, so Crippen took Le Neve as his mistress in 1908. In 1910, Cora disappeared. Her husband claimed that she had returned to America to visit family, then changed the story to say that she had died and had been cremated in California. Le Neve moved in with Crippen and was seen wearing Cora's clothes and jewelry.

A friend of Cora's, Kate Williams, known as Vulcana the Strongwoman, reported her disappearance to her friend at Scotland Yard and an investigation was begun. Crippen admitted fabricating the story but claimed she had left him and he was too embarrassed to tell the truth. Crippen panicked following the questioning and he and Le Neve fled to Canada aboard the *SS Montrose*.

Crippen's disappearance inspired the police to do a more thorough search of his house. During the fourth such search, the police found a human torso buried under the brick floor of the basement. The body was found to contain the calming drug scopolamine. Cora was identified by a piece of skin on her abdomen, a scar that she was known to have.

With Crippen and Le Neve, masquerading as a boy, aboard the *SS Montrose*, Chief Inspector Walter Dew was on the faster White Star liner *SS Laurentic*, which arrived in Quebec one day before Crippen. The couple were arrested before they could depart the ship.

Crippen was tried and found guilty of murder after a four-day trial and twenty-seven minutes of jury deliberation. Crippen was hanged at Pentonville Prison on November 23, 1910.

***Case Detail, Edith Thompson and Frederick Bywaters:*** Edith Thompson was born Edith Jessie Graydon in 1893 in London. In 1909, she met Percy Thompson, three years her senior. They were married after a six-year engagement. By that time, Edith was a successful chief buyer for Carlton & Prior, wholesale milliners, making regular trips to Paris as part of her job. The married couple lived in a fashionable London suburb and enjoyed a comfortable life.

In 1920, the Thompsons met eighteen-year-old Frederick Bywaters, although Edith had known him as a childhood friend of her younger brother. Edith was attracted to the young and virile Bywaters and Percy gradually realized that his wife was having an affair with the young man.

On October 3, 1922, Edith and Percy attended a performance at the Criterion Theatre in Piccadilly Circus. After the show, as they were walking along Belgrave Road, a man jumped out and attacked Percy with a knife and knocked Edith to the ground. Bywaters was suspected and brought to the police station. When Edith arrived to be questioned, they informed her that he had confessed (he had not). She admitted she knew the attacker and that they had had an affair. The police discovered some sixty love letters from Edith to Bywaters, proving their emotional connection. Both were charged with murder.

At the trial, Edith made the fatal mistake of testifying on her behalf (in order, she said to save Bywaters) and bungled things badly, contradicting herself and presenting herself as an unappealing witness. Both Edith and Bywaters were convicted and sentenced to death by hanging. Edith faced the gallows on January 9, 1923, and Bywaters was hung at exactly the same time in a prison a half-mile away.

## Letter Number 68:
## Pearson to Knowlton - September 8, 1924

# The New York Public Library
### Astor, Lenox and Tilden Foundations

**476 FIFTH AVENUE**

*New York,* September 8, 1924

Dear Knowlton:

Thanks for your letter. Yes, I think Moody's notes would be useful, although I may have to ask your advice about them; they were rather cryptic to me. Maybe with the full inquest testimony they will be clearer. There is no rush; the book has been reprinted already, but it is another matter to be allowed to make extensive alterations of the plates, and when the publishers will allow that, I do not know.

Indeed, I do know the Notable British Trials, and own about ten of them. I agree with you about Filson Young on the Crippen case; the Byewaters and Thompson was to me somewhat of a disappointment. But did you miss the very brilliant introduction by Eric Watson to the extraordinary trial of George Joseph Smith - the most peculiar of all murderers - if so, do look it up, as well as William Roughead's introduction to the trial of Burke and Hare, and to that of Mrs. M'Lachlan. Mary Blandy-- I am a great fan for Roughead, and an admirer of his work in this series, as well as his independent volumes of old crimes:

The Riddle of the Ruthvens
Twelve Scots Trials
Glengarry's Way
The Fatal Countess (published this summer)

and you have a winter's delight awaiting you if you have not read them. The first three should be easily available through libraries, as they have been put on sale in America by Dutton.

I have had most amusing letters from him on my book, and have convinced him of the attractions of Miss Lizbeth Borden. In his latest he writes, imploring me to get him Porter's book, and adding: "If I were a bachelor, instead of the bald headed father of four, I should come to Fall River to pay my addresses to the ~~attaches~~ attaching Miss Lizzie, in the hope of getting something out of her in the intimacy of domestic life."

And earlier, "I am sending you The Fatal Countess (Countess of Somerset, the Poisoner) but ~~als~~ alas, she pales before the stupendous Lizzie."

His comments - he is a Scotch lawyer, a "Writer to the Signet", upon our Judicial procedure is also interesting.

Be sure to look up these books, and you will bless me.

Sincerely yours,

E.L. Pearson

*Biographical Note:* **William Henry Moody** (American lawyer, assisted Hosea Knowlton in the prosecution of Lizzie A. Borden, Secretary of the Navy and Attorney General under President Theodore Roosevelt, and justice of the Supreme Court), 1853-1917; **Alexander Bell Filson Young** (Irish journalist, essayist, war correspondent, novelist, organist, and conductor), 1878-1938; **Eric Russell Watson** (British author of legal works), 1879-1927; **William Roughead** (Scottish lawyer, amateur criminologist, editor, true crime essayist), 1870-1952; *The Riddle of the Ruthvens and Other Studies* by William Roughead (Edinburgh: W. Green & Son, 1919); *Twelve Scots Trials* by William Roughead (Notable English Trials series, 1913); *Glengarry's Way and Other Studies* by William Roughead (Edinburgh: W. Green & Sons, 1922); *The Fatal Countess and Other Studies* by William Roughead (Edinburgh: W. Green & Sons, 1924); **Edwin H. Porter** (reporter for the *Fall River Daily Globe* and author of *The Fall River Tragedy: A History of the Borden Murders*, Fall River, MA: George R. H. Buffinton, Press of J. D. Munroe, 1893), 1864-1904

*Case Detail, Dr. Hawley Harvey Crippen:* See Letter #67 for information.

*Case Detail, Edith Thompson and Frederick Bywaters:* See Letter #67 for information.

*Case Detail, George Joseph Smith:* See Letter #6 for information.

*Case Detail, Burke & Hare:* See Letter #6 for information.

*Case Detail, Jessie McLachlan (Sandyford Place Murder):* In June of 1862, Jessie McPherson, as servant, was murdered in Glasgow, Scotland. A month later, Jessie McLachlan, her friend, was arrested for the crime. The Sandyford case was the first Scottish crime in which forensic photography played a role. The trial was held in September 1862. McLachlan declared her innocence and accused the father of McPherson's employer, James Fleming, age 87, of killing her after McPherson refused his sexual advances. After only nineteen minutes deliberation, the jury returned a verdict of guilty. She was sentenced to death by hanging. There was a public outcry and the case was re-investigated by a Court Commission, which reduced her sentence to life in prison. McLachlan served fifteen years and was told she would be released if she left the country. She moved to the United States, married, and died in 1899.

*Case Detail, Mary Blandy ("The Fatal Countess"):* Mary Blandy (1720-1752) was convicted of poisoning her father, Francis Blandy, with arsenic in 1751. She claimed it was all a mistake because she believed that she was giving her father a love potion that would make him approve of her relationship with William Henry Cranstoun, a man he did not approve of. The trial was held in 1752 and Mary Blandy was found guilty and hanged outside Oxford Castle prison in 1852.

**Editor's Note:** It would appear there is a break in the correspondence at this point. Letters are missing between September 8, 1924 and February 6, 1925.

## Letter Number 69:
## Knowlton to Pearson - February 6, 1925

———— ·∘-◦❀◦-∘· ————

February 6, 1925.

Mr. Edmund Pearson,
        276 Fifth Avenue,
                New York City.

My dear Pearson:

I have your letter of February 4. I shall be very glad to get hold of the "Juridical Review" and read the discussions.

You have no idea from how many different sources people come to me to talk about your book. In the most unexpected places people bob up to discuss phases of it with me.

I have just been laid up with and recovering from an appendicitis operation and one of the books which was sent to me to help pass the time was "Murder and its Motive" [*sic*] by Miss F. Tennyson Jesse. Probably you have seen it too. If not, I should be glad to send it on to you. It is rather interesting, although I have not much sympathy with her attempt to fit a ready made cloak of one of six styles onto every case. It seems me that motives are often mixed in so many cases that it can hardly be classified as a definite type. However, her accounts of the cases were rather interesting and she has added a little something to the literature of murder.

My good friend Loring Young, who was for a number of years a Selectman of Weston and was Selectmen at the time of the Page murder, tells me that he has had correspondence with you in reference to the Page case. This summer just before he was going away he asked me to get from the Town Hall archives an envelope that had to do with the distribution of the reward offered in the Page case and which contains some contemporaneous affidavits and other documents bearing upon the solution of the mystery. He wanted me to send it on to you so that if a second edition of your book was published you could have the material if it interested you.

I have the file now and I should be glad to send it on to you if you desire it. I don't want to wish it on you, however, if you haven't any particular desire for it at this time.

One of my neighbors, a lady, tells me that shortly after reading your book, and being very much interested in it, she had a rather thrilling experience. She went into a rather expensive but small tailor shop run by a humble Hebrew and while waiting for her fitting was attracted by a terrible dressing down which some wooman [sic] was giving to the tailor. The language was scathing and caustic and aroused the admiration of my friend, who asked the tailor when the lady left who the customer was. He told her it was Miss Lizzie Borden of Fall River.

With best regards, I am

Sincerely yours,

FWK:ED

*Biographical Note:* The Juridical Review: Law Journal of Scottish Universities, Edinburgh, London, W. Green & Sons, 1889; **Fryniwyd Tennyson Jesse** (Mrs. Harold Marsh Harwood), author of *Murder and its Motives*, London: W. Heinemann, 1924 (English criminologist, journalist, author), 1888-1958; **Benjamin Loring Young** (American lawyer, politician, Speaker of the Massachusetts House of Representatives from 1921-1924), 1885-1964.

*Case Detail, Charles Lewis Tucker (referred to here as the Mabel Page murder):* See Letter # 6 for information.

## Letter Number 70:
## Handwritten Letter from Pearson to Knowlton
## February 7, 1925

———◦○❊○◦———

# The New York Public Library
### Astor, Lenox and Tilden Foundations

**476 FIFTH AVENUE**

New York,  Feb. 7. 1925

Dear Knowlton:

Thank you for your letter and all it contains. Sorry about the appendix; hope all is well again. Yes, I have read Tennyson Jesse's book, and agree with you about it. It has good points, but the Constance Kent story was better told in Atlay's book on celebrated trials. Try Sir John Hall's "Bravo Case & other mysteries" [*sic*] just published here (I believe) and Roughead's "The Fatal Countess."

I would like to see the Loring Young material about Tucker.

That story of Lizzie is odd; time does not wither nor custom stale her infinite vivacity.

Sincerely yours,
E.L. Pearson

*Biographical Note:* **Fryniwyd Tennyson Jesse** (Mrs. Harold Marsh Harwood), author of *Murder and its Motives*, London: W. Heinemann, 1924 (English criminologist, journalist, author), 1888-1958; **James Beresford Atlay** (British historian, and author of legal and biographical works), 1860-1912; *The Bravo Mystery and Other Cases* (London: John Lane the Bodley Head, Ltd, 1923) by **Sir John Richard Hall**, 9th Baronet of Dunglass, UK (British author of war and mystery works),

1865-1928; *The Fatal Countess and Other Studies* (Edinburgh: W. Green & Sons, 1924) by **William Roughead** (Scottish lawyer, amateur criminologist, editor, true crime essayist), 1870-1952; **Benjamin Loring Young** (American lawyer, politician, Speaker of the Massachusetts House of Representatives from 1921-1924), 1885-1964.

*Case Detail, Constance Kent:* In 1860, three-year-old Francis Saville Kent disappeared from his father's home in Wiltshire, England. His body was found in a privy on the property wrapped in a blanket. He had stab wounds to his chest and hands and was almost decapitated. Initially, the boy's nursemaid, Elizabeth Gough, was accused and arrested. She was released when Detective Inspector Jack Whicher of Scotland Yard had his suspicions about the boy's half-sister, Constance, who was sixteen-years old. She was arrested but released when there were public accusations that the working-class detective was biased against the well-bred aristocratic young lady.

The Kent family moved to Wales and Constance was sent to a finishing school in France. Five years later, she confessed to Rev. Arthur Wagner that she had killed the boy in an act of revenge against her father for his attentions to his new family. She said she took the boy and her father's razor to the privy, where she had secreted away matches to light the act of murder. This premeditated killing suggested to the authorities that Constance was possibly mentally unbalanced.

Speculation that she had given a false confession surrounded her arrest. Her father, Samuel Saville Kent was a known adulterer with the nursemaid and that, in a fit of rage, had murdered his son.

Constance Kent plead guilty and was sentenced to death, but her punishment was commuted to life in prison because she had only been sixteen at the time of the killing. She served twenty years, moved to Australia, changed her name to Ruth Emilie Kay, trained as a nurse, working at the Parramatta Industrial School for Girls and then as matron of the Pierce Memorial Nurses' Home in New South Wales from 1911-1932. She died at the age of 100 in 1944.

Kate Summerscale in her book *The Suspicions of Mr. Whicher or The Murder at Road Hill House* (2008) concluded that Constance Kent's confession was false and she was protecting her brother, William Saville-Kent, with whom she was extremely close. Kent never recanted her confession, even after the deaths of both her father and brother.

*Case Detail, Charles Lewis Tucker (Mabel Page murder):* See Letter # 6 for information.

## Letter Number 71:
## Knowlton to Pearson - February 17, 1925

————————·∘○❧❦☙○∘·————————

February 17, 1925.

My dear Pearson:

In accordance, with the suggestion in your letter of February 7, I am sending you the file that Loring Young referred to and which I found in the vault at the Weston Town Hall. I don't know that any of this will add anything to what you already know. The pictures in the "Green Bag" of the knife and of the cards I had not seen before. It is, however, interesting to show that when the curtain falls upon the last act and the villain receives his rich reward and the audience has all left the theatre, somebody has to come and clean up and set the stage for a new performance. As Loring Young was one of the principal cleaners, this file ought to be interesting on that account.

Yours sincerely,

Mr. Edmund L. Pearson,
476 Fifth Avenue,
New York City.

*Biographical Note:* **Benjamin Loring Young** (American lawyer, politician, Speaker of the Massachusetts House of Representatives from 1921-1924), 1885-1964; "The Tucker Trial," by **Hugh Bancroft**, in *The Green Bag: A Monthly Illustrated Magazine Covering the Higher and Lighter Literature of the Law*, edited by Sidney R. Wrightington, Boston Book Co., Boston, 1905; **Hugh Bancroft** (American lawyer, Assistant District Attorney for Middlesex County, Massachusetts, partner in the law firm of Stone, Dailinger & Bancroft, Boston), 1879-1933.

*Case Detail, Charles Lewis Tucker (Mabel Page murder) referred to here in the 1905 edition of "The Green Bag":* See Letter # 6 for information.

## Letter Number 72:
## Pearson to Knowlton - February 25, 1925

———·∘○❀❀○∘·———

### THE NEW YORK PUBLIC LIBRARY
#### 5TH AVENUE & 42ND STREET
#### NEW YORK CITY

February 25. 1925

Dear Knowlton:

It was kind of you - and of Mr. Speaker Young - to send me that file and the article. I am reading it all, with interest. There was some trepidation in my bosom as I read Hugh Bancroft's article, but it subsided, as I discovered that I had made no serious errors, even of omission, in my story of the crime. I would have liked to have had the picture of the knife and of the notes, though, and I may yet – when that hypothetical second edition comes along - try to get the originals, or the plates, from Mr. Faxon of the Boston Book company, which used to publish The Green Bag. As long as the present edition of the Studies sells fairly well, however, I suppose they will simply reprint from time to time, and there may not be a revised edition for years.

I enclose two clippings, comprising the Broun - Pearson correspondence in re the Bram case. Will you kindly return them at your convenience? I showed these to Mr. Asa French and I think that my first impression may have been right: that it was Herbert Parker, in the Tucker case, who timed a minute for the jury. I own only the first volume of that trial, so I could not verify it. When I was working on the Tucker I had the second volume from the Newburyport Public Library, as well as one which Mr. Parker very obligingly lent me. The point is not important but I think that you may be amused to read these clippings.

I am sending a copy of your latest Lizzie anecdote to William Roughead in Edinburgh. He is a lover of hers, and I have furnished him with a copy of a fine picture (from Leslie's Weekly) which I found this winter. It shows Miss Borden in Court, and Governor Robinson standing beside her, examining a witness. An excellent sketch from life by Clinedinst.

The retiring U.S. Attorney General, Mr. Stone, has not only been instrumental lately in the President's re-nomination of my sister-in-law as Judge of the Juvenile Court of the District of Columbia, but he further attracted my favorable notice, 30 years ago, when he gave me a high mark in a chemistry examination in the Newburyport High School. I therefore departed from my invariable ~~custom~~ rule, which is never to send ~~copies of~~ my books to strangers, especially to eminent persons (who think that you are seeking letters of praise to use as advertisements) and sent him a copy of the Studies, thinking that he might recall the Massachusetts cases. It struck me that after a suitable interval - allowing for the fact that he has been rather busy - he might write me something to this effect: "It may interest you to know that I was at the White House the other evening, and Mr. Coolidge begged to be excused early. He said that he had had practically no sleep the night before, as he and the Chief Justice had sat up all night, taking turns in reading out loud to each other from 'Studies in Murder'".

Of course, I could make no use of such a note, but it might please my nephews and nieces, and go well in my Life and Letters, when these are published, post-mortem.

Nothing of the sort has come yet, however, Mr. Stone acknowledged my letter, and later, the book, in two very courteous and conventionally crafty notes, - the "I-shall-lose-no-time-in-reading-your-valuable -book", sort of thing which is said to have originated with Disraeli. I have used the formula myself. And if the President's rest has been broken into, I haven't heard about it.

Yours faithfully
E.L. Pearson

**Biographical Note: Benjamin Loring Young** (American lawyer, politician, Speaker of the Massachusetts House of Representatives from 1921-1924), 1885-1964; "The Tucker Trial," by **Hugh Bancroft**, in *The Green Bag: A Monthly Illus-*

*trated Magazine Covering the Higher and Lighter Literature of the Law*, edited by Sidney R. Wrightington, Boston Book Co., Boston, 1905; **Hugh Bancroft** (American lawyer, Assistant District Attorney for Middlesex County, Massachusetts, partner in the law firm of Stone, Dailinger & Bancroft, Boston), 1879-1933; **Frederick Winthrop Faxon** (American writer, editor, bibliographer, photographer, lifelong champion of libraries, President and Treasurer of the Boston Book Company, a law book publisher, later the F. W. Faxon Company, Boston), 1866-1936; *The Green Bag: A Monthly Illustrated Magazine Covering the Higher and Lighter Literature of the Law*, edited by Sidney R. Wrightington, Boston Book Co., Boston, 1899-1914; **Heywood Broun** (American journalist, sportswriter, newspaper columnist, editor), 1888-1939; **Asa Palmer French** (American lawyer, US Attorney for the District of Massachusetts from 1906-1914), 1860-1935; **Herbert Parker** (American lawyer, District Attorney for Middle District of Massachusetts from 1896-1899, Attorney General of the Commonwealth of Massachusetts from 1902-1906), 1856-1939; **William Roughead** (Scottish lawyer, amateur criminologist, editor, true crime essayist), 1870-1952; **George Dexter Robinson** (American lawyer, Governor of Massachusetts from 1883-1886 and principal attorney for the defense in the Commonwealth of Massachusetts vs. Lizzie A. Borden), 1834-1896; **Benjamin West Clinedinst** (American illustrator and portrait painter), 1859-1931; **Harlan Fiske Stone** (American lawyer, Associate Justice US Supreme Court from 1925-1941, Chief Justice of the United States from 1941-1946), 1872-1946; **John Calvin Coolidge Jr.** (American lawyer, 30th President of the United States), 1872-1933; **Kathryn Sellers** (American lawyer, Judge of the Juvenile Court in Washington D.C. from 1918-1934, distinction of being first woman appointed judge of the court in the United States), 1870-1939; **Charles Evans Hughes** (American lawyer, 11th Chief Justice of the Supreme Court from 1930-1941), 1862-1948; **Benjamin Disraeli** (British politician, twice Prime Minister of the United Kingdom, novelist), 1804-1881.

*Case Detail, Thomas Bram:* See Letter #1 for information.

*Case Detail, Charles Lewis Tucker (Mabel Page murder) referred to here in the 1905 edition of "The Green Bag":* See Letter # 6 for information.

## Letter Number 73:
## Pearson to Knowlton - April 14, 1925

————— ∘∘⊙⚬⊙∘∘ —————

THE NEW YORK PUBLIC LIBRARY
5TH AVENUE & 42ND STREET
NEW YORK CITY

April 14, 1925

Dear Knowlton:

I spent some hours Sunday looking again at the Tucker papers, and I am very grateful to you and to Mr. Loring Young for the privilege. I found the deposition of Carberry, the Globe reporter, particularly interesting, and made a number of notes from that and others. I am again relieved in my feelings to discover that my ignorance of Hugh Bancroft's article in The Green Bag did not betray men into any serious blunders. I do wish I had had the picture of "the fatal knife" for my book.

They are all packed and ready to be expressed. To what address will it be most convenient to have me send them?

Sincerely yours,
E.L. Pearson

*Biographical Note:* **Benjamin Loring Young** (American lawyer, politician, Speaker of the Massachusetts House of Representatives from 1921-1924), 1885-1964; **John W. Carberry** (American journalist, reporter for the *Boston Globe* for more than twenty years, covered the Borden murders, first as Henry G. Trickey's assistant, and then by himself upon Trickey's death), 1869-1914; "The Tucker Trial," by **Hugh Bancroft**, in *The Green Bag: A Monthly Illustrated Magazine Covering the Higher and Lighter Literature of the Law*, edited by Sidney R. Wrightington, Boston Book Co., Boston, 1905; **Hugh Bancroft** (American lawyer, Assistant District Attorney for Middlesex County, Massachusetts, partner in the law firm of Stone, Dailinger & Bancroft, Boston), 1879-1933.

*Case Detail, Charles Lewis Tucker (Mabel Page murder):* See Letter # 6 for information.

## Letter Number 74:
## Knowlton to Pearson - April 15, 1925

————·∘○◦❀◦○∘·————

April 15, 1925.

My dear Pearson:

I am sorry I did not see you when I was in New York a little while ago. I stopped at your office to have a chat with you but you were out and I left for home before you were expected to return.

Simply send the papers to me at my Boston office.

The picture of "the fatal knife" was to me very impressive. It had in it tangible evidence of guilt beyond any conception that I had formed from reading the accounts of it and of the circumstances under which it was found. To read that a hunting knife, broken in three pieces, was found in Tucker's pocket carried of course the suggestion of guilt. To see a picture of the knife and realize what a wicked looking instrument it was and to realize also how much force and strength it must have taken to break the knife up as it was broken brought home to me more than any description of it could have done the guilty conscience of Tucker and the realization by him of sure conviction if the knife were ever found in its original form. I of course hope some day that you will have a second edition and I hope you will have that picture of the knife in your book.

I don't thank you for your suggestion about the "Juridical Review". I went up to the Social Law Library one day, full of important work, and got out the volume of that Review and read the two references to your book in full. Then I discovered that Roughead had been a frequent contributor, and I began reading back volumes of it until I found my whole day spoiled and no work accomplished. You really should not put such temptation in my path.

I hope to be over in New York again shortly and I will drop in and see you.

Yours sincerely,

FWK:ED

Mr. Edmund L. Pearson,
476 Fifth Avenue,
New York City.

*Biographical Note:* "The Tucker Trial," with the photo of "the fatal knife," by **Hugh Bancroft**, in *The Green Bag: A Monthly Illustrated Magazine Covering the Higher and Lighter Literature of the Law*, edited by Sidney R. Wrightington, Boston Book Co., Boston, 1905; **Hugh Bancroft** (American lawyer, Assistant District Attorney for Middlesex County, Massachusetts, partner in the law firm of Stone, Dailinger & Bancroft, Boston), 1879-1933; *The Juridical Review: Law Journal of Scottish Universities*, Edinburgh, London, W. Green & Sons, 1889; **William Roughead** (Scottish lawyer, amateur criminologist, editor, true crime essayist), 1870-1952.

*Case Detail, Charles Lewis Tucker (Mabel Page murder):* See Letter # 6 for information.

# Letter Number 75:
## Handwritten Letter from Pearson to Knowlton - April 16, 1925

HARVARD CLUB
27 WEST 44TH STREET

<u>April 16</u> /25

Dear Knowlton:

The papers will be expressed to your office in a day or two.
You should get your Library in Weston to buy Roughead's <u>books</u>.
Dutton publishes some of them.

What you say about the knife is true. Still have to have that picture.

I don't want to miss you next time you come over; try to arrange to
take lunch with me here, and to do that let me know by letter or 'phone,
or Indian, in advance. I am out of my office a good deal, and on some
days - Fridays especially - I am at my other office, - at <u>The Outlook</u>. But
I will always be glad to see you, and if I know in advance, will come up
town, or wherever you are. This is a good place to eat and talk.

Sincerely,

E.L. Pearson

*Biographical Note:* **William Roughead** (Scottish lawyer, amateur criminologist,
editor, true crime essayist), 1870-1952; "The Tucker Trial," with the photo of "the
fatal knife," by **Hugh Bancroft**, in *The Green Bag: A Monthly Illustrated Magazine Covering the Higher and Lighter Literature of the Law*, edited by Sidney R.
Wrightington, Boston Book Co., Boston, 1905; **Hugh Bancroft** (American lawyer,
Assistant District Attorney for Middlesex County, Massachusetts, partner in the
law firm of Stone, Dailinger & Bancroft, Boston), 1879-1933; *The Outlook* (weekly
magazine published in New York City from 1879-1935).

*Case Detail, Charles Lewis Tucker (Mabel Page murder):* See Letter # 6 for information.

## Letter Number 76:
## Albert E. Pillsbury to Knowlton - November 10, 1925

————•◦○❀❀❀○◦•————

6 Beacon Street, Boston.
10 Nov. 1925

Dear Frank: - -

I am very much obliged to you for your prompt execution of your proposal to send me a copy of the "Studies in Murder". I have not yet had time to read it, but on opening it I can see at a glance that the Borden part, at least, is done with a skillful hand and is vastly superior to the other "History" of the Borden case published many years ago, which is so inconsequential that I have even forgotten the name of the author. I may have something more to say about this book when I have finished the reading of it. In the meantime, with renewed thanks, I remain as ever,

Yours truly,
A.E. Pillsbury

Frank W. Knowlton, Esq.

*Biographical Note:* **Albert Enoch Pillsbury** (American lawyer, Attorney General, Commonwealth of Massachusetts from 1891-1893), 1849-1930.

## Letter Number 77:
## Knowlton to Pearson - December 18, 1925

————·∘∘❀❀❀∘∘·————

December 18, 1925.

Edmund L. Pearson, Esq.,
New York Public Library,
Fifth Avenue,
New York City.

My dear Pearson:

I am sending you, under separate cover two books, one a bound copy of the trial of Ephraim K. Avery charged with the murder of Sarah M. Cornell in May 1833. The interesting part of this to me is that this pamphlet and the cartoon which is pasted in the front of it belonged to my great aunt, Nancy Almy, who at the time of the murder and the trial lived in Portsmouth, N.H., which was, as you will see by the map which appears in the pamphlet, just over the river from the place of the murder, and according to the report on page 10, it appears that my grandfather, Benjamin Almy, was excused from service as a juror because he had formed an opinion.

I am also sending you another bound volume containing the trial of Henry Joseph and Amos Otis for the murder of James Crosby, Captain of the Brig Juniper, on the-high seas, in 1834; the report of the trial of Dr. Samuel Thomson, the founder of the Thomsonian practice, for an alleged libel in warning the public against the impositions of Paine D. Badger, as a Thomsonian physician sailing under false colors in 1839; the report of the trial of Albert John Tirrell for the murder of Mary Ann Bickford, together with the lives of Albert J. Tirrell and Mary Ann Bickford, in 1846, and which contains a report of Rufus Choate's famous argument in the case; the trial of Dr. Valorous P. Coolidge for the murder of Edward Mathews of Waterville, Maine, in 1848; two reports of the trial of Professor John W. Webster for the murder of Dr. George Parkman, in 1850, together with the extraordinary confession of Dr. Webster and his petition for pardon on the ground of innocence and the proceedings before the Governor and council; what is alleged to be the only full report of the trial of Reverend I. S. Kalloch on the charge of adultery, with what are said to be accurate portraits of Kalloch and the beautiful lady in black in the lecture room of the Lechemere; and a luridly illustrated edition of the trial of the Honorable Daniel E. Sickles for shooting Philip Barton Key, Esq., in 1859.

You may find some of these of interest, although I presume you have seen most of them. Don't hurry about returning these because as long as I get them back, time is not of the essence. If you want to take any photostats, don't hesitate to do so.

I was glad to have a chat with you the other day and wish I could have seen more of you.

With best wishes for a very happy Christmas, I am

Yours very truly,

FWK:ED

*Biographical Note:* **Nancy Almy**, 1802-1896; **Benjamin Almy**, 1810-1892; **Rufus Choate** (American lawyer, orator, and Congressman, US Senator from Massachusetts from 1841-1845, Massachusetts Attorney General from 1853-1854), 1799-1859.

*Case Detail, Sarah Cornell murder:* On December 21, 1832, the body of twenty-nine year old Sarah Maria Cornell, a pregnant mill worker, was found hanging from a stack pole in the south end of Fall River, Massachusetts (then Tiverton, Rhode Island), on the John Durfee farm. Cornell had been counseled by Rev. Ephraim Kingsbury Avery (1799-1869), a Methodist minister from Bristol, Rhode Island, who had met her in Lowell, Massachusetts, and later at a Methodist Camp in Connecticut. Among Cornell's effects was found a note she had written and dated the day of her death: "If I should be missing, enquire of Rev. Mr. Avery of Bristol, he will know where I am."

Cornell had spoken to a doctor and told him that the married Reverend Avery was the father of her unborn child. Avery was then suspected. A coroner's jury determined that she had "committed suicide by hanging herself upon a stake ... and was influenced to commit said crime by the wicked conduct of a married man."

A second coroner's jury accused Avery as the probable accessory in her death.

Avery was arrested but released on his own recognizance while awaiting trial.

Avery was absolved of culpability after two Justices of the Peace found at the inquest that there was insufficient evidence to try him for the crime of murder. There was a large public outcry at this decision, which influenced Harvey Harnden (1795-1863), the deputy sheriff of Fall River to obtain an arrest warrant for Avery from a Rhode Island Superior Court judge. However, Avery had fled and the warrant could not be served.

Harnden tracked Avery to New Hampshire and took him to the Newport, Rhode Island, jail to await his trial. On May 8, 1833, Avery was indicted for murder by a Newport County grand jury. At his arraignment, he plead not guilty.

In an unusual turn of events, there were actually two trials where Reverend Avery was accused of murder. The first was convened on May 6, 1833, and lasted twenty-seven days. According to Rhode Island law in the early 19th century, Avery was not allowed to testify in his own defense.

On June 2, 1833, the jury found him not guilty. After this acquittal, Avery returned to his position as a minister in the Methodist Church. However, public outrage was again high. Rallies were held that hanged and burned effigies of Avery, and he was almost lynched in Boston. In response to this public outcry, the Methodist Church's New England Conference convened a trial of their own. Avery was acquitted once again.

The murder remains unsolved. In 1836, Avery left the ministry and moved first to Connecticut, then upstate New York, finally settling with his family in Ohio, where he became a farmer. He died in 1869 in Ohio, where he is buried in South Pittsfield Cemetery, Lorain County, Ohio. Sarah Cornell was buried on the farm near where her body was discovered. Many years later when the farm was annexed to Massachusetts and became part of Fall River and the farm became South Park, her body was exhumed and moved to Oak Grove Cemetery where it remains in Plot 2733 on Whitethorn Path to this date.

***Case Detail, James Crosby murder:*** In the early morning hours of August 14, 1834, Captain James Crosby of the brig *Juniper* was stabbed to death on his ship. On September 2, Henry Joseph, a black cook, and Amos Otis were apprehended on board the ship in the port of Boston. A grand jury on October 20 indicted them for the murder. Both men plead not guilty.

The trial was held on October 28, 1834, with Judge Joseph Story, Associate Justice of the Supreme Court, presiding, and Andrew Dunlap, US Attorney for the District of Massachusetts, prosecuting. The defendants had two able court-appointed defense attornies to plead their cases.

Witnesses testified as to the events of the night of murder, each presenting a similar tale. James H. Peterson, the second mate, had heard a scream late in the night from the captain's cabin. He went to assist and helped the captain to the deck. Captain James Crosby had been stabbed twice, once in the chest and once in the abdomen. He died soon after. He helped the captain to the deck, with Eldrid, his mate, following, Henry Joseph slashed at his Edlrid's legs (Eldrid had been stabbed multiple times during the attack on the captain).

Peterson grabbed an oar and struck Joseph, but Joseph grabbed it away from him. He then ran to get the cook axe and found that it was not where it was supposed to be. He kept calling for Amos Otis to aid him, asking him to bring him a handspike or axe, but Otis did not come or reply. He noticed Otis climbing the fore-rigging quickly. Peterson grabbed a spar and struck Joseph twice but didn't strike him a third time for fear he would hit Eldrid. He grabbed a rope and attempted to strangle Joseph, and called for assistance once again. Another mate assisted in tying Joseph, who called to Otis to bring him his knife. Otis replied that he didn't have it.

Eldrid was badly injured but survived the attack. Since there was no money on the ship—the cargo consisted of fish, beef, pork, flour, and lumber, and the cook and mate Otis could not navigate a ship—there was speculation that this seemed to be a motiveless crime.

The defense argued that it could have been a conspiracy amongst the other crew members as their stories were "too similar" to not be the product of comparing notes and statements. Since there was no "moral certainty" that the two had participated in the death of Captain Crosby they must be found not guilty.

The jury deliberated for ninety minutes and found both men guilty—Henry Joseph of first degree murder and Amos Otis for second degree murder. Both were scheduled to hang on December 2.

While awaiting his execution, many individuals came forward, some recanting their testimony against Amos Otis. An especially telling statement was given by Mary Wildermuth, the keeper of a boarding house. She said that Peterson had told her that he had made up the parts about Otis and that there had been talk of William Sutherford, another mate on the ship, talking about taking over the ship and sailing her to Cuba.

A minister who met with Joseph in jail made a sworn statement that the black man (Sutherford) had confessed to the crime and exonerated Amos Otis of his involvement. He said he acted completely alone in the murder, but stopped short of providing a motive for the attacks.

Henry Joseph was executed on the scheduled date. Amos Otis was granted a ten-day reprieve and then a full pardon by President Andrew Jackson on December 12, 1834.

**Case Detail, Dr. Samuel Thomson libel trial:** Samuel Thomson (1769-1843) was a self-taught American botanist, herbalist, healer, and founder of the alternative system of medicine named after him—Thomsonian Medicine. It was widely practiced and popular in the US in the 19th century.

Thomson believed that the main cause of illness and disease was one's exposure to cold temperatures, which only could be treated by restoring the body's natural heat. To that end, he recommended steam baths, the use of cayenne pepper, laxatives, and emetic Lobelia inlata ("puke weed"). He published *New Guide to Health; or Botanic Family Physician* in 1822, where he suggested many home-made preparations for their curative properties while expressing a contempt for conventional and expensive traditional medicine.

In 1839, Thomson was taken to court for warning the public against the practices of Paine D. Badger's use of Thomsonianism. On April 14, 1839, the jury returned with a verdict of guilty in the case of the Commonwealth v. Dr. Samuel Thomson for libel. He was sentenced to pay a fine of $50. He then published his account of the trial in *Report of the trial of Dr. Samuel Thomson, the founder of the Thomsonian practice, for an alleged libel in warning the public against the impositions of Paine D. Badger, as a Thomsonian physician sailing under false colors, before Judge Thacher* (1839).

This experience taught Thomson to take care to guard his patented cures and he used those patents to prevent anyone from manufacturing his "medicines" under his name. He sold rights to use his system of medicine to any family for $20. Right-holders were able to purchase Thomson's herbs and formulas, which he distributed from a central warehouse, and a copy of Thomson's book. He had sold over 100,000 patents by 1840.

***Case Detail, Albert John Tirrell trial:*** Albert Tirrell (1824-1880) lived in Weymouth, Massachusetts with his wife and two children. In 1945, he left his family in order to be with Maria Bickford, a married prostitute who lived in a Boston brothel. Soon they were living together as husband and wife, even though she never stopped conducting her line of work. On October 27, 1845, she was found brutally murdered and Tirrell was charged with slitting her throat, nearly severing her head from her body. He then allegedly set fire to the brothel, which awakened the owner, who then discovered the body of Maria.

The case was a sensation, not only for the circumstances of Tirrell leaving his wife to live with Bickford (under a charge of adultery), but the gruesome manner in which she was killed. Tirrell's family hired the famous Boston attorney Rufus Choate, who was known for his innovative and successful defense strategies.

While there were many people who could testify as to Tirrell and Bickford's unusual relationship, there were no eyewitnesses to the murder. Choate argued that Tirrell had no motive to commit the attack and set forth two possible explanations: that Bickford had committed suicide or that Tirrell, who was an habitual sleepwalker, murdered her under the influence of a nightmare or night trance. Choate related to the jury many descriptions of violence that had occurred while people had been sleepwalking. He emphasized that the punishment for this crime was death and if there was even the remotest chance that he was innocent, they needed to acquit him.

The jury deliberated less than two hours and on March 30, 1846, returned a verdict of not guilty. The trial became famous for Choate's successful use of the sleepwalking defense.

***Case Detail, Edward Mathews murder:*** On September 30th, 1847, the body of bookstore owner Edward Mathews was found in the cellar of David Shorely's store in Waterford, Maine. It first appeared that Mathews had been killed by a blow to the top of his head. The body was moved to the Williams House to facilitate the autopsy, conducted by Dr. Plaistead, Dr. Thayer, and Dr. Valorous P. Coolidge, with Thomas Flint assisting. Coolidge made the incisions and removed the stomach, which smelled of brandy. The scent was so strong that Coolidge suggested it be removed from the room. Williams, the owner of the inn, put the bowl with the stomach in it into a locked icehouse in the rear of the building.

The next day, Dr. Loomis tested the contents of the stomach and found it contained prussic acid and was likely the cause of death. Apparently, the poison had been administered in a glass of brandy.

Dr. Valorous P. Coolidge was a man of great debt. He had borrowed money from many individuals with each person unaware that there were other lenders because of Coolidge's requests for discretion. On the evening of the murder, Coolidge was to receive a loan of $1,500 from Edward Mathews. Witnesses had seen Mathews withdraw the funds from his bank earlier in the day.

Thomas Flint, a young medical student, was Dr. Coolidge's assistant. He was walking home about 9:00 p.m. when he was stopped by the doctor who led him to his office and said he had a secret to share. Coolidge told him that Ed Mathews wanted to borrow $200 from him and had poured himself a brandy, took a sip, and instantly died. Panicking, the doctor had taken a stick and "thumped" him on the head to make it appear like he was murdered and dragged the body into the next room. He asked Flint to help him move the body to the cellar, beneath the store below. In his confusion over the events, Flint agreed.

The body was discovered, the autopsy performed, and Dr. Coolidge pronounced the death to be of natural causes. Flint reported what had happened to the authorities and, on October 7, 1847, Dr. Coolidge was indicted on a charge of first degree murder. The trial ran from March 14 to March 22. A parade of witnesses testified to the doctor's indebtedness and his actions during the autopsy. The prosecution asserted that Mathews was killed because Coolidge didn't want to have to repay him the $1,500 he was to borrow. The defense asserted that Coolidge was the one who was loaning Mathews money, some $200, and expected payment the following day, thus eliminating this motive for the crime.

Evidence was presented showing that Coolidge had purchased a large quantity of prussic acid, an unusual amount in fact, and more than he would need as a physician. This and the fact that there was no need for Mathews to borrow money from Coolidge since he had so much in his pockets that day made a strong case for conviction.

The jury found Dr. Valorous P. Coolidge guilty of murder and he was sentenced to die by hanging. Maine law allowed for one year before the carrying out of a sentence of death. During that time, Coolidge's sentence was reduced to life in prison at hard labor and solitary confinement. He was eventually allowed some liberties, including the use of the prison yard for recreation and lighter duties instead of hard labor. It was during this time that he plotted his revenge against Thomas Flint. He hatched a plan to have Flint killed and a confession letter discovered following his "suicide" that stated that he alone had killed Mathews.

The plot was discovered before it could be carried out and a further charge was forthcoming for the doctor. Before any action could be taken, Dr. Coolidge was found dead in his cell with his head in a bucket. His brother was sent to collect the body but claimed that the dead man was not his brother as his sibling had part of his right thumb missing from a childhood accident and this man had two complete thumbs, fueling decades of public speculation about what happened to him.

*Case Detail, Dr. Parkman Murder:* See Letter # 1 for information.

*Case Detail, Reverend Isaac Smith Kalloch adultery case:* Isaac Smith Kalloch (1832-1887) was a Baptist minister who had moved to California from his native Maine to spread the word of God. In 1879, he made the decision to run for mayor of San Francisco. Another candidate in the race was backed by the *San Francisco Chronicle*'s editor in chief, Charles de Young. Hoping to take Kalloch out of the race, de Young accused the minister of having an affair. In retaliation, Kalloch accused de Young's mother of running a brothel. Perhaps this was too much for de Young because he ambushed Kalloch on the street and shot him twice. Surviving his wounds, Kalloch gained the sympathy of the voters and was elected the 18th Mayor of San Francisco, serving from 1879 to 1881. On April 23, 1880, Isaac Milton Kalloch, the son of the minster, shot and killed Charles de Young in his office at the *Chronicle*. After his term of office, Kalloch moved to the Washington Territory and died at the age of fifty-five of diabetes.

*Case Detail, Philip Barton Key Jr. murder:* Philip Barton Key Jr. (1818-1859) was the son of Francis Scott Key, was an American lawyer, and US Attorney for the District of Columbia from 1853 until his death. He was allegedly the most handsome man in Washington and, by 1859, was a widower with four children. Sometime in 1858, Key began an affair with a married woman, Teresa Sickles. Her husband was a serial adulterer himself, but was incensed when he received a poison pen letter informing him of his wife's affair. He forced her to write out a confession of her actions and then confronted Key in Lafayette Square and shot him. Key died soon after.

Sickles was put on trial for the murder but acquitted based on temporary insanity, the first successful use of this defense in the United States.

## Letter Number 78:
## Pearson to Knowlton - January 1, 1926

———◦∘❈❈❈❈❈∘◦◦——

# The New York Public Library
### Astor, Lenox and Tilden Foundations

**476 FIFTH AVENUE**

New York,____January 1 1926

Dear Knowlton:

Thank you heartily for the books, which came in good order, and for permission to keep them for a while. They are great, and the picture of the Rev'd Avery is priceless.

Happy New Year.

Faithfully yours
Edmund Pearson

*Case Detail, Sarah Cornell murder (referred to here as the picture of Reverend Avery):* See letter #77 for information.

## Letter Number 79:
## Pearson to Knowlton - July 7, 1926

THE NEW YORK PUBLIC LIBRARY
5TH AVENUE & 42ND STREET
NEW YORK CITY

July 7, 1926

Dear Frank: I send you today by parcels post, insured, the two books you kindly lent me last December. I used the report of the trial of Mr. Avery in a chapter I have written on him; also I had the caricature of him reproduced for probable use in the new book, which is completed, and should appear next October.

In the other book, the Webster material was of service; while I got much amusement from some of the other pamphlets, especially the trial of Mr. Kalloch for ~~crim~~ crim. con. at the felicitously named hotel, - Lechmere; and the illustrations in the Sickles-Key pamphlet, especially the one of the Companion of Mr. Sickles in his Confinement. Look it up.

Thank you for both of these. By the way, I had always thought that the Rev. Avery was probably guilty, merely, I suppose, because I thought Methodist ministers always were. But, before I got through, I came to think that there are grave doubts about it. The case against him, when it came to any legal sifting, was full of holes.

I think rather better of Atty. Gen. Pillsbury than I did, after his crustiness about that letter from your Father. A man from the Transcript told me the other day that the old gentleman recommended to him "Studies in Murder", as "a very ingenious book".

With kind regards,

Sincerely yours
Edmund Pearson

*Biographical Note:* **Albert Enoch Pillsbury** (American lawyer, Attorney General, Commonwealth of Massachusetts from 1891-1893), 1849-1930.

*Case Detail, Sarah Cornell murder (referred to here as the trial of Mr. Avery):* See letter #77 for information.

*Case Detail, Dr. Parkman Murder (referred to here as the Webster material):* See Letter # 1 for information.

*Case Detail, Reverend Isaac Smith Kalloch adultery case:* See letter #77 for information.

*Case Detail, Philip Barton Key Jr. murder (referred to here as the Sickles case):* See letter #77 for information.

## Letter Number 80:
## Knowlton to Pearson - July 14, 1926

------ ·∙○◦❊◦○∙· ------

July 14, 1926.

Mr. Edmund L. Pearson,
  New York Public Library,
   Fifth Avenue,
    New York City.


My dear Pearson:

   Your letter of July 7 came while I was away on a short vacation, and I find that the books have arrived safely.

   I am very glad to know that another book is coming out, and I am eagerly looking forward to it.

   Aren't these pamphlets very interesting human documents? I enjoy the Avery trial particularly and the naive descriptions of the witnesses made by the reporter are often very amusing and very helpful. It helps a good deal to know that Mary Hicks was an elderly friend, and that Miss Jane A. Sprague was a maiden lady, and that Abbie Hathaway was beyond middle age, a cautious statement. I felt after reading the trial that the verdict was proper. It is pretty hard to tell just what the real truth was. There seems back in the 30's to be the same common rallying of associations to overbear the court so that I look with a good deal of suspicion upon the evidence for the defense, but the whole thing left an impression of doubt in my mind so that I think the Scotch verdict "not proven" would have been proper.

   By the way, do you remember the testimony of Ezra Parker "(a queer tall old man)"? He said that Maria Cornell came to his house the last of March, or the first of April.

   " . . . . She said she belonged to the Methodist Church, and appeared to be very much engaged in the work of God; very much indeed. At seven o'clock in the evening, Charles and William Taylor called for entertain-

~ 164 ~

ment Maria Cornell sot by the fire, with my family. The
devil, says William Taylor, Maria, be you here? Yes, says
she, and you can't help yourself, William Taylor!"

I am glad to know what you tell me about Pillsbury. I
met the old crab on the street a year or so ago and walked along with him
and I found out that he had not seen your book and was curious about it,
so I got a copy and sent it to him. He immediately acknowledged receipt
of the book and said he looked forward to reading it with a good deal of
pleasure, and I have never seen nor heard from him since. I am glad to get
in this indirect way his appreciation of the book.

With best wishes, I am

Yours very truly,

PWK:ED

*Biographical Note:* **Albert Enoch Pillsbury** (American lawyer, Attorney General,
Commonwealth of Massachusetts from 1891-1893), 1849-1930.

*Case Detail, Sarah Cornell murder (referred to here as the trial of Mr. Avery):*
See letter #77 for information.

**Editor's Note:** Mary Hicks, Jane A. Sprague, Abbie Hathaway, Ezra Parker, Charles
and William Taylor are all real people in the case of Sara Maria Cornell, but as
minor characters in this story, their biographical particulars are, unfortunately,
difficult to determine.

## Letter Number 81:
## Pearson to Knowlton - October 25, 1926

——————•∘○𝕰𝖃𝕰○∘•——————

### THE NEW YORK PUBLIC LIBRARY
#### 5TH AVENUE & 42ND STREET
#### NEW YORK CITY

October 25, 1926

Dear Knowlton:

In about two weeks I hope to have advance copies of "Murder at Smutty Nose", when I shall send you one. The Parson Avery case is in it, and that odd picture, - thanks be to you. I was so taken with the quotation from the inn-keeper's testimony about Maria Cornell and William Taylor, which you mentioned in your letter, and so impressed by the fact that it struck you as amusing, that I added that passage to the chapter after the whole thing was in proof. I had always supposed that Mr. Avery was probably guilty, but my sympathies were aroused for him when they intimated that a man who went on a long walk alone on a winter's day must necessarily be about the devil's business. I am fond of long and purposeless walks, and in consequence have often known what it is to be suspected of being goofy.

Usually, as you know, I incline to the side of the State, but in the present ecclesiastical case of the late Rev. Dr. Hall in New Jersey, I am in a ~~decided~~ minority in my belief that Prosecutor Simpson is a good deal of a wind-mill, and that the prisoners are probably telling ~~ght~~ the truth. I have done the incautious thing of writing about it – in the November Vanity Fair - an act which, professionally, you are bound to disapprove.

If there is ever a revised edition of "Studies in Murder" - which I fear is not very likely; it has twice been reprinted, but the publishers may never care to go to the expense of altering the plates - but if there is such an edition, the enlarged comments on the judge's charge, and the references to Moody's memorandum, which we have discussed, may go into the chapter on the Borden case. In my new book, I have a few pages of comment on the case, - all that it seemed wise to print there and now. Neither of the points mentioned above would be ~~intelligible~~ valuable - or so it seemed to me - unless they were added to the <u>original</u> chapter.

I was twice told last spring that Sir Edmund Gosse, who with some of his club-mates had been reading the Studies, had sighed that he "did wish he could hear something more about Miss Lizzie Borden". This fall, getting an opportunity at last, I sent him ten or fifteen typed pages of unpublishable material about it. He replied, with his thanks, saying that he could see no escape from the conclusion of her guilt. (I have heard, by the way, that Booth Tarkington does argue for her innocence.) Gosse added that he was visiting his old friend, Lord Haldane, as he wrote, and that he (Haldane) also was much interested in Miss Lizzie. So we have added an ex-Lord-Chancellor to the devotees! Are you keeping up with the Notable British Trials Series? I hope so; some good ones are appearing: Abraham Thornton, Henry Fauntleroy (forger) and Katharine Nairn, who was convicted, with her brother in law of murder <u>and</u> incest. They didn't do things by halves in the 1700's. There are some good ones coming: Charles Peace and H.R. Armstrong. Take a look at the Nairn trial, and especially the dedication. When you consider the heavy guns of English law and letters to whom the other volumes in the series have been dedicated, and see this one inscribed to the chronicler of the Borden case and the biographer of Mate Bram, you will know why the elevator man has got all my old hats, and why I had to buy new ones.

Always sincerely yours,

Edmund Pearson

**Editor's Note:** Pearson included the following letter with the above.

THE MURDER ON THE BARGE GLENDOWER.

How's that for a title? Do you remember the case, - about a dozen years ago, I guess; maybe more. Coal barge from Philadelphia to Newburyport; captain found murdered; cook, a hump-back, tried in a U. S. court, in Boston, I think, and acquitted. After the acquittal, he confessed! And disappeared. Did it for revenge; Captain had abused him, and caused his deformity, by knocking him out of the rigging something like 20 years earlier.

Doesn't that sound like a looloo? I was about to ask you if you could use your good graces to get me a view of the report of the trial, when I hear from a friend that Dr. George MacGrath [sic] - if that's the way he's spelled - the med. examiner in Boston is writing it himself. He was in on it, officially. My friend thinks I must layoff. I don't agree, but shall probably do nothing about it for the present. The doctor will probably write for a professional journal, - and I for a most unprofessional one. But quite ethically; and I can quote him with all due credit. So I may, some time or another, ask you what chance there is of getting hold of the record.

*Biographical Note: Murder at Smutty Nose: and Other Murders,* by Edmund Pearson, Doubleday, Page & Company, 1927; **Reverend Edward Wheeler Hall** (Episcopal priest, murder victim), 1881-1922; **Alexander Simpson** (American lawyer, journalist, and Democratic politician, served in both houses of the New Jersey Legislature, Assistant Attorney General of New Jersey), 1872-1953; **William Henry Moody** (American lawyer, assisted Hosea Knowlton in the prosecution of Lizzie A. Borden, Secretary of the Navy and Attorney General under President Theodore Roosevelt, and justice of the Supreme Court), 1853-1917; **Sir Edmund William Gosse** (English poet, author, critic), 1849-1928; **Newton Booth Tarkington** (American novelist and dramatist, Pulitzer Prize winner, author of *The Magnificent Ambersons* in 1918), 1869-1946; **Richard Burden Haldane** (British lawyer, influential politician, and philosopher, British Secretary for War from 1905-1912), 1856-1928; **Dr. George Burgess Magrath** (American doctor, professor of legal medicine at Harvard University, Medical Examiner for Suffolk County from 1907-1935), 1870-1938.

*Case Detail, Sarah Cornell murder (referred to here as Parson Avery case):* See letter #77 for information.

*Case Detail, Hall-Mills murder:* On September 16, 1922, the bodies of Eleanor Mills and the Reverend Edward Wheeler Hall were discovered in a field near a farm in Somerset, New Jersey. The couple, both of whom were married, had been having an affair. They were both shot in the head, the man once and the woman three times. Eleanor Mills also had her throat severed. Because there were maggots in the wounds, it was believed that their deaths had occurred at least twenty-four hours earlier.

There was a jurisdictional issue over the initial investigation because while the crime scene was in Somerset County, the Middlesex County police arrived first. While the authorities were attempting to negotiate this crisis, spectators and the curious trampled the scene and took souvenirs.

The suspects were Halls' wife, Frances Noel Stevens, her two brothers, Henry Hewgill Stevens and William "Willie" Carpender Stevens, and a cousin, Henry de la Bruyere Carpender. Unfortunately, the investigation, led by Joseph E. Stricker (1870-1926) produced no indictments. A second investigation was ordered when newspaper-fueled speculation was published. The group was arrested, with Henry Capender set to be tried separately (ultimately, this trial never occurred).

The trial began on November 3, 1926 and lasted thirty days, garnering huge national attention. Alexander Simpson was the prosecutor and Robert H. McCarter and Timothy N. Pfeiffer were the defence attornies. The key witness for the prosecution was a pig farmer by the name of Jane Gibson, on whose property the bodies were discovered. She claimed to have heard a dog barking and went outside and saw a man standing near the tree where the bodies were later discovered. She rode her mule to the location and saw four people there and heard the gunshots. She then turned her mule home, hearing additional gunshots as she went in the opposite direction. Her account, however, had varied depending on whom she spoke to—the newspapers, the police, and the court. She was portrayed by the defense as crazy as they tried to ruin her credibility.

All of the defendants were found not guilty.

***Case Detail, Abraham Thornton:*** In 1817, Abraham Thornton, the twenty-four-year-old son of a builder from Castle Bromwich, a village in the English county of the West Midlands, met Mary Ashford, twenty, at a party at The Three Tuns, a public house known as the Tyburn House. Apparently, the couple enjoyed each others company. Ashford left the event about 11 p.m. with her friend Hannah Cox, with Thornton walking behind them. After a while, Cox went home, breaking off from the group, with Ashford and Thornton walking off together. A laborer saw Thornton at 2:45 a.m. leaving a friend's house with a woman who had her head down. Before 4 a.m., Ashford woke up Cox to get her working clothes, changed, and hurried off, saying she had to get home before her uncle left for the market. A passerby saw her walking quickly.

Around 6 a.m., a laborer saw some woman's items near a water-filled pit, including a woman's shoe with blood upon it. He alerted others and they raked the pit, finding Mary Ashford's dead body. There were footprints nearby, of a man and a woman, as if walking to the edge of the pit, with the men's footprints retreating alone.

Thornton was soon arrested and searched. His underclothing was stained with blood and he admitted they had sex the previous night. Thornton's shoes fit the footprints at the scene. The post-mortem revealed that Ashford had drowned and that there were two lacerations in the genital area. It was decided that she was a virgin prior to the intercourse, which caused the bleeding. In addition, Ashford was menstruating at the time of her death.

The prosecution alleged that Thornton had lain in wait for her to pass by on her way home from her friend's house and raped Ashford near the pit. She had nothing in her stomach and had fainted from the experience. He panicked and threw her unconscious body in the pit, where she drowned.

The defense brought forth eleven witnesses who established an alibi for Thornton. They contended that in order for the prosecution's case to work, Thornton would have had to chase down Ashford, rape her, kill her, and then travel three miles in only eleven minutes.

The judge, in his charge, told the jury that it was not possible for Thornton to have committed the acts and make it back to where he was witnessed to be in the time frame. Additionally, he stressed that Thornton didn't act like a guilty man, had admitted to the sex with Ashford, and that it was better to let a murderer go free than convict an innocent man. The jury didn't even deliberate. They conferred together in the court and found Thornton not guilty in six minutes time.

Mary's brother, William Ashford, filed an appeal and Thornton was arrested again. He then claimed the English law right to a trial by battle, which was a medieval legal doctrine that had never been repealed. Ashford declined the offer and Thornton was freed. In 1819, statutes were passed to abolish this law. After the final legal proceeding, Thornton immigrated to the United States.

***Case Detail, Henry Fauntleroy forgery:*** Henry Fauntleroy (1784-1824) was managing the London bank of Marsh, Sibbald & Co., where his father had been one of the founders. In 1824, he was arrested on the charge of forging trustees' signatures and appropriating trust funds. It was estimated that the amount he absconded with was close to £250,000, which, it was said, was "squandered in debauchery."

He admitted his guilt at his trial but said he used the funds to pay the debts of his firm. He was found guilty and sentenced to be hanged, as forgery was still a capital crime. Influential businessmen and politicians appealed to the court on his behalf, but to no avail. Henry Fauntleroy was hanged in November of 1824. Forgery ceased to be a capital crime in 1836.

***Case Detail, Katharine Nairn and Patrick Ogilvie:*** In 1765 in Eastmiln, Glenisla, Scotland, Thomas Ogilvie was murdered by poison and his wife, Katharine Nairn, and his brother, Patrick, were arrested and tried for murder and incest (both capital crimes), it being illegal for a woman to be in a sexual relationship with the brother of a husband. The most important witness at their trial was the youngest Ogilvie brother Alexander's mistress, Anne Clark, a former prostitute. Some doubt her testimony, which was lengthy, because Alexander was in line to inherit the estate if both brothers died childless. Clark testified that Nairn told her she was going to poison Thomas and had overheard (spied on) Patrick and Katharine having sex. Both Patrick and Katharine were found guilty and sentenced to death. Katharine's execution was delayed because she was pregnant and then successfully escaped execution, prison, and even her own country, after stealing away from her cell in the uniform of an old family servant and making her way to France. She was never seen again.

***Case Detail, Charles Peace:*** Charles Peace (1832-1879) was born in Sheffield, England, the son of a shoemaker and a naval surgeon's daughter. When he was fourteen, he was permanently crippled in an accident at a steel-rolling mill. He was a serial burglar who had served at least three sentences in prison for his actions. In 1876, about midnight, he was seen in Manchester by two policeman entering the grounds of a house. In the ensuing encounter with the authorities, Peace shot PC Nicholas Cook, who died the next day. It was dark and he was not clearly seen by the other policeman, so two brothers, who lived nearby, were arrested and charged with killing Constable Cook. One brother was acquitted, but the other, William Habron, was sentenced to death, later commuted to penal servitude for life. Peace had even attended the trial to make sure his name was not mentioned in connection with the crime.

Later that year, Peace became obsessed with Mrs. Dyson, even threatening to kill her husband if she did not acquiesce to his advances. The couple moved at one point to escape his advances. He found out their new home and, on November 29, observed her leaving the house by the back door and entering the outhouse. He confronted her on her exit shouting, "Speak, or I'll fire!" She jumped back into the outhouse and her husband came out to see what the commotion was about. Peace fired twice at Dyson, killing him with the second shot in the temple.

He changed his appearance and name and started a relationship with Mrs. Sue Thompson, but he ended up betraying his whereabouts to the authorities when he moved to London with Thompson and committed further burglaries. He was caught on October 10, 1878, in a shoot out with police, injuring Constable Robinson in the arm. He refused to give his name and it took a bit of time for the police to determine who they had arrested. Under the name of John Ward, he was tried for burglary and the attempted murder of PC Robinson and sentenced to penal servitude for life.

He was then taken to Sheffield and charged with the murder of Mr. Dyson. His lawyer tried to convince the magistrate that Mrs. Dyson was a willing participant in their relationship and Peace was merely acting in self-defense in the shooting. He was committed to take his trial at Leeds Assizes, to begin on February 4, 1879.

The jury returned with a verdict of guilty and a sentence of death was imposed. Apparently having nothing more to lose, Peace made a full confession to the murder of Constable Cook to help exonerate William Habron, who was given a free pardon and £800 in compensation. Peace still asserted that Mrs. Dyson was his mistress and he was the slighted lover who had been treated with ingratitude. He was executed on February 25, 1879, at the age of forty-six.

*Case Detail, Herbert Rowse Armstrong:* Herbert Rowse Armstrong (1869-1922) was born in Plymouth, Devon, England. He studied the law at St. Catharine's College, Cambridge, and became a solicitor in February of 1895. The next year he married Katharine Mary Friend; the couple had three children: two girls and a boy.

He was a hard working lawyer and had his own law firm—Cheese & Armstrong. Armstrong was a Major in the Royal Engineers Territorial Force in the World War I, serving in France. Thereafter, he was referred to as Major Armstrong.

In 1919, his wife began to get sick, but the local physician could not determine the exact nature of her illness. She would get better, then her health would deteriorate once again. Her mental state was suffering and she was admitted to Barnwood, a private mental asylum near Gloucester. When she was admitted, she was suffering from pyrexia, vomiting, heart murmurs, and albumen in the urine. She also exhibited partial paralysis in her hands and feet and was delusional.

Her condition improved at Barnwood and she was discharged on January 22, 1921. Her symptoms returned and she died one month later. Her death certificate stated that the cause of death was gastritis, aggravated by heart disease and nephritis.

In Hay, the town where Armstrong practiced law, there was only one rival solicitor—Oswald Martin. Armstrong invited Martin to his home for a meeting on a property sale on which they were on opposing sides. He was served tea, cakes, and buttered scones. When Martin returned home, he became violently ill. Martin's father-in-law was the chemist in town and he had made several sales of arsenic to Armstrong in the past. He became suspicious of Martin's sudden illness. The doctor treating Martin had also treated Mrs. Armstrong and he noticed similarities between the symptoms. He advised the Martins to avoid all gifts or invitations with Armstrong again.

Armstrong was arrested on December 31, 1921, and charged with the attempted murder of Oswald Martin. While he claimed he was innocent, police found a packet of arsenic in his pocket and many more at his home. The authorities exhumed the body of Mrs. Armstrong and the eminent Home Office pathologist Dr. Bernard Spilsbury examined her remains. She was riddled with arsenic ten months after her death. On January 19, 1922, Armstrong was additionally charged with the willful murder of his wife.

Even though he maintained his innocence in both cases, he was found guilty on April 13, 1922, and sentenced to death. He was hanged at Gloucester Prison on May 31, 1922.

*Case Detail, Thomas Bram:* See Letter #1 for information.

*Case Detail, Glendower Murder:* The story of the mystery of the coal barge *Glendower* begins on June 9, 1911. On that date, she was part of a three-ship flotilla and her captain was fifty-five year old Charles Wyman, an experienced seaman.

His crew consisted of three men, William De Graff, the cook, William Nilsen, and Antonio Priskich. When the ships were approaching their destination of Newburyport, Massachusetts, the barge sent out a whistling signal, indicating it wanted the tug *Monocacy* to come alongside. The *Monocacy's* pilot, Captain Camp, steered the tug to approach the barge. As he got close, the ship's cook shouted to him that the captain was dead. The cook said that Wyman had died about noon and that there was blood in his bunk. He invited Camp to come aboard and inspect the situation. Sensing something untoward, Camp declined and the ships made their way to Boston, where they went ashore. The police and local coroner, Dr. George Burgess Magrath, were called to the scene.

De Graff, who was a hunchback, was mild-mannered and matter of fact about the discovery of the captain's body. He had been a sailor for nearly forty years but had just joined the crew of the *Glendower* a month before. It was determined that Captain Wyman had been attacked with a hammer or axe, as his head was battered and there was a very large amount of blood soaking the sheets around him. No murder weapon was located.

The trio faced a Boston grand jury, and evidence was presented that seemed to implicate De Graff in the attack, mostly because he was the only one of the three who had not been seen for a period of time during the day, while Nilsen and Priskich worked together on many of the daily tasks. De Graff was accused of the murder and the trial began on February 19, 1912.

While testimony showed that De Graff had opportunity to commit the crime, there was no known motive for the seemingly senseless killing. Because there was no witness to murder, even though it seemed obvious that it was De Graff (because who else could it have been?), the jury determined he was not guilty. Following the verdict, De Graff disappeared into history.

**Editor's Note:** William Taylor is a real person in the case of Sara Maria Cornell, but as a minor character in this story, his biographical particulars are, unfortunately, difficult to determine.

## Letter Number 82:
## Knowlton to Pearson - October 28, 1926

———o○○❦○○o———

October 16, 1926.

My dear Pearson:

Thank you very much for your chatty and very interesting letter of October 25. I am delighted at the prospect of receiving soon a copy of "Murder at Smutty Nose". I shall peruse it with great interest.

I am also interested in what you say about the Hall case. Are you in a minority in your opinion? I haven't heard much talk about it here, but I have heard a good deal of doubt expressed, largely on account of the conduct of the case by this man Simpson rather than on the merits of the testimony. He seems to be quite a loud-mouth and whoever is guilty, there is aroused in me a distinct desire to see him get licked. Your opinion, coming from you who are an expert on murder, gives me great courage to believe that he may be in danger of coming into his own.

I haven't kept up with my reading lately, largely because I have been a little too hard driven by my work, and I am glad to get the list of the five cases that I am to buy and read. I certainly must own the trial of Katharine Nairn, for having accomplished two crimes for which she is charged, in the order you name, it is novel to be guilty of murder and incest if you do it in that order.

I am afraid that age is affecting my memory. I don't remember the "Barge Glendower" case, although several of the boys here in the office seem to have a very fresh recollection of it.

Dr. McGrath, the medical examiner here, is quite a character although, confidentially, he is not nearly so much as he is willing to admit that he is or that some people think he is. I do not believe Dr. George McGrath will write for anything other than a medical journal, but if you want me to do anything about hunting up the evidence at any time, just let me know.

By the way, I hope some day not too far off I shall be released from my professional obligations and be free to tell you some things that come within my knowledge which makes me wonder a good deal about what really happened on the "Herbert Fuller." You know I am not now nearly so convinced as I was that the jury and the conventional opinion about the case were right.

Do you think it strange that Booth Tarkington argues for Lizzie Borden's innocence? You see Tarkington has lived in the realm of fiction for a generation and that quite poorly prepares a man for the strange things that happen in life. Only possibilities happen in fiction; improbabilities happen in real life. That is why Sir Edmund Gosse from his contact with the real woman is ready to believe that Lizzie Borden <u>could</u> chop in the heads of her stepmother and father (~~notice the order~~) while Booth Tarkington would never dare to put such a thing into a story.

I expect to be in New York shortly, or at least in the course of the next four or six weeks, and I am going to make it a point to get hold of you and take you out to lunch with me.

With best regards, I am

Sincerely yours,

FWK:ED

Mr. Edmund Lester Pearson,
    The New York Public Library,
        5th Avenue,
            New York City.

**Biographical Note:** *Murder at Smutty Nose: and Other Murders*, by Edmund Pearson, Doubleday, Page & Company, 1927; **Alexander Simpson** (American lawyer, journalist, and Democratic politician, served in both houses of the New Jersey Legislature, Assistant Attorney General of New Jersey), 1872-1953; **Dr. George Burgess Magrath** (American doctor, professor of legal medicine at Harvard University, Medical Examiner for Suffolk County from 1907-1935), 1870-1938; **Newton Booth Tarkington** (American novelist and dramatist, Pulitzer Prize winner, author of *The Magnificent Ambersons* in 1918), 1869-1946. **Sir Edmund William Gosse** (English poet, author, critic), 1849-1928.

*Case Detail, Hall-Mills murder:* See Letter #81 for information.

*Case Detail, Katharine Nairn and Patrick Ogilvie:* See Letter #81 for information.

*Case Detail, Glendower Murder:* See Letter #81 for information.

*Case Detail, Thomas Bram (referred to here as the "Herbert Fuller"):* See Letter #1 for information.

## Letter Number 83:
## Pearson to Knowlton - November 9, 1926

---

### THE NEW YORK PUBLIC LIBRARY
#### 5TH AVENUE & 42ND STREET
#### NEW YORK CITY

November 9, 1926

Dear Knowlton:

Much excited over Bram rumor.

Please let me know in advance when you are coming; desire to take you to luncheon at either Harvard or Coffee House Club.

Sincerely yours
E.L.P.

**Biographical Note:** The Harvard Club, located in New York City, was founded in 1865 by alumni of Harvard University. The Coffee House Club, also in NYC, was formed in 1914 by two members of the Knickerbocker Club. It was located in the Hotel Seymour at 54 West 45th Street. Both social clubs still exist.

**Case Detail, Thomas Bram:** See Letter #1 for information.

## Letter Number 84:
## Knowlton to Pearson - November 11, 1926

—∘∘❈∘∘—

November 11, 1926.

Mr. Edmund L. Pearson,
New York Public Library,
Fifth Avenue,
New York City.

Dear Pearson:

Thank you very much for your invitation to lunch with you. I am very happy to accept. The time, however, is a little indefinite still. I will let you know as soon as I find I can get away.

Yours sincerely,

FWK:ED

## Letter Number 85:
## Knowlton to Pearson - November 23, 1926

———••○❈○•○——

November 23, 1926.

My dear Pearson:

I am very grateful to you for sending me the advanced copy of the "Murder at Smutty Nose". I am afire with anticipation of the pleasure that I am going to get from the book.

Let me congratulate you upon the startling yellow cover. How anybody can pass a book store window without going in and buying the book, I cannot imagine.

I am going to write you later after I have had a chance to read it. In the meantime, I have to guard it very carefully against its being lugged off before I have had my chance at it.

Gratefully yours,

Mr. Edmund L. Pearson,
New York Public Library,
Fifth Avenue,
New York City.

**Biographical Note:** *Murder at Smutty Nose: and Other Murders*, by Edmund Pearson, Doubleday, Page & Company, 1927.

## Letter Number 86:
## Knowlton to Pearson - November 24, 1926

November 24, 1926.

My dear Pearson:

My partner, Frederick Nash, looked through your book as it lay on my desk and he wants me to ask you if you know where he can get a copy of the second edition of Lewis and Bombaugh's book, published in 1896, entitled "Stratagems and Conspiracies to Defraud Life Insurance Companies", or even the earlier one published in 1878.

He also wants me to call to your attention two books appearing in the Catalogue No. 144 of Dulau & Company, Ltd., 34 Margaret Street, Cavendish Square, London, W.I. They are as follows:

440 on p. 40. "Crime. The life of David Haggart, alias John Wilson, alias John Morison, alias Barney M'Coul, alias John M'Colgan, alias Daniel O'Brien, alias The Switcher. Written by Himself, while under sentence of death. Bound in between pp. VIII and I is a blank leaf, of the same paper as the frontispiece, on which is written, signed and dated by David Haggart from the Iron Room, Edinburgh Jail the 14th July, 1821, 'This is a true account of my Life partly written by myself and partly Taken down, from my own lips while under Sentence of Death.' And: Phrenological Observations on the Cerebral Development of David Haggart. By George Combe, Esq. Inscribed presentation copy from the author. 2 Vols. in 1, post 8vo., half calf. A Nice Copy. Edinburgh, 1821. £ 5s."

1114 on p. 91. "Portraits, Memoirs and Characters of Remarkable Persons from the Revolution in 1688 to the end of the Reign of George II, collected by James Caulfield. About 150 portraits of Convicts, Highwaymen, Rebels, Giants, Beggars, etc. 4 vols., large 8vo., half roan. 1819. £3 3s."

These apparently rare publications he thought you might possibly want to acquire, either for yourself, or for your library.

Sincerely yours,

Mr. Edmund Lester Pearson,
  The New York Public Library,
    5th Avenue,
      New York City.

*Biographical Note:* **Frederick Hapgood Nash** (American lawyer, member of law firm of Choate, Hall & Stewart, Boston), 1873-1949; **Dr. John Benjamin Lewis** (American physician, Civil War surgeon, Medical Director and Adjuster at Travelers Insurance Co. from 1868-1914), 1832-1914; **Dr. Charles Carroll Bombaugh** (American physician, Civil War veteran, writer, lecturer, editor, Medical Examiner for Life Insurance and Editor for Baltimore Underwriter), 1828-1906; *Stratagems and Conspiracies to Defraud Life Insurance Companies: An Authentic Record of Remarkable Cases*, by John B. Lewis, MD, and Charles C. Bombaugh, AM MD, Baltimore: James H. McClellan Publisher, 1896; **David Haggart**, 1801-1821; **George Combe** (Scottish lawyer, founded Edinburgh Phrenological Society), 1788-1858; **James Caulfield**, 1764-1826.

# Letter Number 87:
## Pearson to Knowlton - November 28, 1926

―――――・∘◦⊷§⊷◦∘・―――――

### THE NEW YORK PUBLIC LIBRARY
5TH AVENUE & 42ND STREET
NEW YORK CITY

November 28, 1926

Dear Knowlton:

Thank you for those two titles; I shall look to see if we have them here. I know a little about Haggart, as Roughead has written about him in one of his books. For the most part, these rare English books are, so far as my own library goes, outside my scheme of life.

I have never seen but one copy of each of the editions of Lewis and Bombaugh's book. I am not sure that we even have it here. I would advise your partner to ask Smith & McNance, or Lauriat, or some other good Boston book-dealer, to advertise for the second edition of it, in the Publisher's Weekly. This ought to get it, if anything will. It will cost say, about 50 cents for the advertisement.

Sincerely yours
E.L.P

*Biographical Note:* **David Haggart**, 1801-1821; **William Roughead** (Scottish lawyer, amateur criminologist, editor, true crime essayist), 1870-1952; **Dr. John Benjamin Lewis** (American physician, Civil War surgeon, Medical Director and Adjuster at Travelers Insurance Co. from 1868-1914), 1832-1914; **Dr. Charles Carroll Bombaugh** (American physician, Civil War veteran, writer, lecturer, editor, Medical Examiner for Life Insurance and Editor for Baltimore Underwriter), 1828-1906; *Stratagems and Conspiracies to Defraud Life Insurance Companies: An Authentic Record of Remarkable Cases*, by John B. Lewis, MD, and Charles C. Bombaugh, AM MD, Baltimore: James H. McClellan Publisher, 1896.

## Letter Number 88a:
## Knowlton to Pearson - December 16, 1926

—◦◦◦ ⊛❦⊛ ◦◦•—

December 16, 1926.

Dear Pearson:

Although somewhat delayed, I have concluded my reading
of "Murder at Smutty Nose" and I had a very enjoyable time reading
it. Some of them were crimes wholly new to me. Some of the others, of
course, are old favorites. I found my interest so revivified that I went
back to your older book and read your first treatise on murder as a fine
art. I think perhaps the most tragic picture in the whole book is poor old
Dr. Crippen and his inamorata looking hopefully for the promised land,
standing side by side at the ship's rail, and the suddenness of the destruc-
tion of all their plans and hopes. I think I shall have to re-read Crippen's
trial in the British Trials Series.

Thank you very much for writing the book, and also, for
sending it to me. You have solved the question of what I shall give a good
many of my friends for Christmas.

I am also deeply indebted to you for sending the "Outlook"
for December 15. My partners, John Hall, who has always enjoyed your
books, came to me this morning and told me you had his unbounded
admiration because you put into words all of his inarticulate feelings
about the trial in New Jersey. The result of reading the article is a letter to
the editor of the Herald, a copy of which I an enclosing herewith. I am in
hope that this will bring forth a snappy editorial.

My grievance against Senator Simpson is the same grievance I
felt against Senator Walsh and Senator Wheeler at the time of the Daugherty investigation in Washington, that the methods adopted by this class
of prosecutor and the kind of evidence they fathered and produced,
together with their obvious newspaper propaganda, make it so difficult
for a fair minded person to have any idea where the truth really lies. I
never felt at all sure whether Daugherty was guilty until he was tried in a

reasonably sane and restrained atmosphere in the Federal Court in New York, and while I have always felt the probable innocence of the Hall side of the family in the Hall-Mills case, I am indignant that the attitude of the New York Mirror and Simpson makes it impossible for a great many other people to reach in their own minds a sound conviction of the innocence of these people.

Gratefully yours,

FWK:ED

*Biographical Note: Murder at Smutty Nose: and Other Murders*, by Edmund Pearson, Doubleday, Page & Company, 1927; *The Outlook* (weekly magazine published in New York City from 1879-1935); **John Loomer Hall** (American lawyer, senior partner in law firm of Choate, Hall & Stewart), 1872-1960; **Alexander Simpson** (American lawyer, journalist, and Democratic politician, served in both houses of the New Jersey Legislature, Assistant Attorney General of New Jersey), 1872-1953; **Thomas James Walsh** (American lawyer and Democratic politician, Senator from Montana from 1913-1933), 1859-1933; **Burton Kendall Wheeler** (American lawyer and Democratic politician, Senator from Montana from 1923-1947), 1882-1975; **Harry Micajah Daugherty** (American politician, Attorney General of United States under Presidents Warren G. Harding and Calvin Coolidge, involved in Teapot Dome scandal during Harding's presidency), 1860-1941; **Teapot Dome scandal**, a bribery scandal involving the administration of United States President Warren G. Harding from 1921 to 1923 when Secretary of the Interior Albert Bacon Fall leased Navy petroleum reserves at Teapot Dome in Wyoming, as well as two locations in California, to private oil companies at low rates without competitive bidding (subject of an investigation by Senator Thomas J. Walsh).

*Case Detail, Dr. Hawley Harvey Crippen:* See Letter #67 for information.

*Case Detail, Hall-Mills murder (referred to here for Senator Simpson):* See Letter #81 for information.

## Letter Number 88b:
## Knowlton to R. L. O'Brien, Boston Herald - December 16, 1926

————·∘○❀○∘·————

December 16, 1926.

Robert Lincoln O'Brien, Esq.,
    The Boston Herald,
        Boston, Mass.

Dear Mr. O'Brien:

The undersigned wish to call to your careful and thoughtful consideration an article in "The Outlook" for December 15, 1926, entitled "Five Hours in Court at the Hall-Mills Trial" by Edmund Pearson.

We suggest that whatever need there may be for reform in the medical or legal professions the need that cries to Heaven is for reform in the quality of the men who report the news.

Sincerely yours,

*Biographical Note:* **Robert Lincoln O'Brien** (American journalist and editor of the *Boston Herald* from 1910-1928), 1865-1955; *The Outlook* (weekly magazine published in New York City from 1879-1935).

*Case Detail, Hall-Mills murder:* See Letter #81 for information.

## Letter Number 89:
## Pearson to Knowlton - May 13, 1927

———·∘○❦○∘·———

### THE NEW YORK PUBLIC LIBRARY
#### 5TH AVENUE & 42ND STREET
#### NEW YORK CITY

May 13, 1927

Dear Knowlton:

I am disappointed because you never came over here, to
tell me about the Bram news.

In June and July I shall be in Boston and Cambridge, and
shall try to salute you briefly. I have no less than three books on my hands
during the next two years, and one of them - on murder - has to be done
this year. I am resigning from the Library, on July 1, to enable me to do
this, and other work, so - to get in practise - you might teach your secre-
taries and scriveners my home address: 44 West Tenth St., New York City.
I keep my connection with The Outlook, and shall also be available at the
Harvard Club, for people from Boston who may be in this vicinity, and
will lunch with me. Lawyers, especially.

I plan none of the articles now appearing in Vanity Fair
for the next book, but five or six select and curious cases. One is the
strange Hart-Meservey case in Tennant's Harbor, Maine, about 1878; 1
have one book on it. Another is Mr. Small of Ossippee, N.H. about 1916,
but the nearest to a Massachusetts case is the one tried in the Federal
Court in Boston, and known as the murder on the Barge Glendower. If
you look at your letter to me of October 28, 1926, you will see that I have
mentioned it to you before. I am to see Dr. McGrath about this in order
to get - if I can - some pictures from him. But, - here is the nigger in the
woodpile: -

I do not now know the name of the defendant, nor the
date of the trial. You say some of your bright young men remember the
case well. Will you of your unfailing kindness do this for me? Ask them

the names and the dates, and of yourself tell me what lines of inquiry I should pursue to get hold of the stenographic minutes of the trial. He was acquitted (alas!) so there is no record on appeal. He was also guilty, for he confessed! I suppose that it will mean finding who were some of the counsel, and then to discover which eminent Boston barrister whom I have the honor of knowing - Knowlton or Rob Dodge or F M Ives – can be imposed on to pull the wires for me.

Hopefully yours
Edmund the Cadger

**Biographical Note:** *The Outlook* (weekly magazine published in New York City from 1879-1935); **Dr. George Burgess Magrath** (American doctor, professor of legal medicine at Harvard University, Medical Examiner for Suffolk County from 1907-1935), 1870-1938; **Robert Gray Dodge** (American lawyer, partner at Storey, Thorndike, Palmer & Dodge, Boston, later senior partner in Palmer, Dodge, Gardner & Bradford, Boston), 1872-1964; **Frederick Manley Ives** (American lawyer, partner at Johnson, Clapp, Ives & Knight, Boston), 1880-1960.

**Case Detail, *Thomas Bram*:** See Letter #1 for information.

**Case Detail, *Hart-Meservey murder*:** Thirty-seven-year-old Sarah Meservey was married to Captain Luther Meservey, a mariner who spent a lot of time at sea. The couple lived in Tenants Harbor, Maine. She was used to his time away and by all accounts lived a quiet and uneventful life. Her husband had gone out to sea in October of 1877 and Sarah was left to spend the winter alone. On December 22, she was paid a visit by a neighbor and then, late in the day, she walked to the village post office to collect her mail. She then disappeared from sight. No one saw her for weeks and no one inquired about her whereabouts in the small community.

Questions were finally raised on January 29, 1878, when her husband's cousin, Albion Meservey, went to the mayor, Whitney Long, and suggested that an investigation be made. The two men and a neighbor, Frederick Hart, went to Sarah's house to try to find her. They pried open a window and, in the spare bedroom, found a lot of blood, furniture in disarray, and the body of Sarah wrapped in a blanket, wearing the clothes she had on three days before Christmas.

She had been beaten badly and was covered in bruises. She had been strangled with her own scarf and her hands tied behind her with fishing line. The killer left blood marks in the kitchen as he had washed his hands in the sink.

Some matches were also found at the scene, but for what reason, no one could determine.

A note was found near her body that read, "i cam as A Womn She was out and i [waited] till she Come back, not for Mony but i kiled her."

Three weeks later, her husband returned from the sea to learn the gruesome news. He was devastated and could think of no one who would have done this to her. On February 19, Mrs. Levi Hart, one of the Meservey's neighbors, received a curious note that advised Sarah's husband to take care and that the killer will never be caught. It was signed "D.M."

On March 8, Nathan F. Hart, Sarah's nearest neighbor and a sea captain, was arrested on the flimsiest of evidence: the handwriting on the letter and his use of the same matches as those found on the scene. Hart stood trial in October 1878. The prosecution claimed the killer was skilled in tying knots, that Hart had proximity living next door, and would know her whereabouts. He alleged that Hart had come to rob Sarah but she had come home and surprised him and he had no choice but to kill her. The defense asserted that the so-called handwriting experts were wrong, and that his client did not write the letters. In addition, Nathan had an alibi as his wife and stepdaughter testified that he had been home all day on December 22.

The jury returned a verdict of guilty in the first degree and Hart was sentenced to life in prison. Five years later he died of "malignant jaundice."

Fifty years later, Hart's attorney, J.H. Montgomery said that Nathan Hart had killed Sarah Meservey but had not intended to murder her, merely choke her into submission.

***Case Detail: Frederick L. Small:*** On September 28, 1916, the burned body of thirty-seven-year-old Florence Aileen Curry Small was found in the ruins of a burned two-story cottage near Ossipee Lake in New Hampshire. In addition to being burned, her skull was crushed, a cord was wrapped around her neck, she had been shot, and there was evidence she had been chloroformed. Frederick L. Small, forty-nine, was away in Boston at the time of the fire and seemed to have a good alibi, until it was discovered that the fire had been started with a timed device. Small had taken out an insurance policy for $20,000 on March 16, 1916. He was arrested, tried for her murder, convicted, and executed by hanging on January 15, 1918.

***Case Detail, Glendower Murder:*** See Letter #81 for information.

## Letter Number 90:
## Knowlton to Pearson - May 16, 1927

———·○○⊗⊛⊗○○·———

May 16, 1927.

Dear Pearson:

Your very welcome letter of May 13, with its interesting news, makes me also sorry that I haven't had a chance to see you in New York. I hope to be there some this summer, but I haven't been there for several months.

I am glad you are going to be able to put out more work and I shall look forward to your efforts when you are unhampered by your duties at the Library.

I shall surely remember your address – 44 West 10th Street.

The Tennant's Harbor case I do not remember. The Mr. Small case I remember quite distinctly. The Barge Glendower case, however, I think I can help you on. Your friend Asa French tried that case for the Government. I called him up as soon as I got your letter and he thinks there is no doubt that he can get the stenographic minutes. If he hasn't them himself he is sure he can get them from the office of the Federal Attorney in Boston. He told me that John Feeney, who is today our leading lawyer in Massachusetts specializing on criminal work and by far the most successful, defended him. Judge Putnam, a strong and forceful judge of the old school, presided. French tells me that the man did not confess, so far as he knows, but that he was a sympathetic figure; that Judge Putnam charged violently against the Government and that when the man was acquitted and sought to shake the hands of the jurors who had acquitted him, two or three of them either refused to do so or did so with admonitions that he should not do it again. French promises to let me hear from him in two or three days, and let me know about getting the record.

A friend of mine dropped at my house the other day a large size calf bound report of the Webster case. It is by far the most complete record I have seen and I suppose it was available to you when you wrote your book. The thing that particularly interested me in it was Webster's speech to the jury just before the charge of the court, - the famous speech in which he accuses lawyers of having suppressed evidence that would have acquitted him.

By the way, a friend of my partner, Mr. Choate, turned over to him the other day an old family possession, a manuscript in Chief Justice Shaw's handwriting of his remarks to the jury at the time of the sentence of Webster, and Mr. Choate presented it to Harvard Law School to put in their archives.

Looking forward to your promised visit in June or July, I am

Yours very truly,

FWK:ED

*Biographical Note:* **Asa Palmer French** (American lawyer, US Attorney for the District of Massachusetts from 1906-1914), 1860-1935; **John Patrick Feeney** (American lawyer, offices in Boston), 1872-1937; **William Lowell Putnam** (American lawyer, United States Circuit Court Judge), 1861-1924; **Daniel Webster** (American lawyer and statesman, US. Secretary of State under Presidents William Henry Harrison, John Tyler, and Millard Fillmore), 1782-1852; **Charles F. Choate Jr.** (American lawyer, partner in the firm of Choate, Hall & Stewart, Boston), 1866-1927; **Lemuel Shaw** (American lawyer, Chief Justice of the Massachusetts Supreme Court), 1781-1861.

*Case Detail, Hart-Meservey murder (referred to here as Tennant's Harbor case):* See Letter #89 for information.

*Case Detail: Frederick L. Small:* See Letter #89 for information.

*Case Detail, Glendower Murder:* See Letter #81 for information.

*Case Detail, Commonwealth vs Knapp (referred to here as the Webster case):* See Letter # 2 for information.

## Letter Number 91:
## Knowlton to Pearson - June 7, 1927

———•∘○❋○∘•———

June 7, 1927.

Mr. Edmund L. Pearson,
    44 West 10th Street
      New York City

Dear Pearson:

Of course you did not fail to notice that our old and dear friend Lizzie Borden died last week. The number of people who have commented on it show I think not so much a reflection of the everlasting interest in the case as much as the influence of your book. Many people have said that her secret died with her. Personally, I have my doubts. I think the truth was no secret to her sister Emma who apparently is still alive although in some unidentified sanitarium.

Thinking that they might interest you, I have collected the comments that appeared in the New Bedford papers last week. These clippings you may keep or do with as you may see fit. Eventually, however, I should like to have them back as the closing chapter of my book of clippings with reference to the trial.

Mr. Choate's secretary, who is a devoted admirer of yours, told me of her reaction on reading of the death of this distinguished lady. She said she would have liked to have been a fly on the wall when Lizzie met her father and step-mother in that house of many mansions. Apparently her grave has been dug beside the graves of her victims. I wonder if she will rest in peace.

I can't give you any definite information yet about the transcript of the record in the case of the United States v. deGraf [*sic*]. Asa French tells me that he has made careful search among his papers and is convinced that he hasn't the Government's copy. He feels sure that he can locate it in the United States Attorney's office and that they will let him have it perhaps permanently.

I ran across John Feeney who defended deGraf [*sic*]. He tells me that Dr. Boos, (I think that is the doctor he spoke of) who is the leading expert on poisons in this neck of the woods, has his transcript of the testimony, apparently having desire himself to write about it. He also denied with much heat that deGraf [*sic*] ever confessed and poohpoohed the story that the man's deformity was due to the cruelty of the captain who he is supposed to have murdered. However, John is picturesque in his language always, and impulsive rather than accurate.

I am looking forward to seeing you when you come and I hope it will be soon. I shall probably be away about a week or ten days in July starting in about the 27th of this month so I hope it will not be at that time.

Sincerely yours,

FWK:MED

*Biographical Note:* **Charles F. Choate Jr.** (American lawyer, partner in the firm of Choate, Hall & Stewart, Boston), 1866-1927; **Asa Palmer French** (American lawyer, US Attorney for the District of Massachusetts from 1906-1914), 1860-1935; **John Patrick Feeney** (American lawyer, offices in Boston), 1872-1937; **Dr. William Frederick Boos** (American chemist and expert in toxicology, Clinical Chemist at Massachusetts General Hospital from 1906-1912, author of *The Poison Trail*, 1939), 1865-1949.

*Case Detail, Glendower murder (referred to here as case of United States v. De Graff):* See Letter #81 for information.

## Letter Number 92:
## Knowlton to Pearson - June 9, 1927

———∘∘♨♨♨∘∘∘———

June 9, 1927.

My dear Pearson:

Asa P. French called me up last night to tell me that he had just been presented with the Government's copy of the transcript of the record in the case of United States v. de Graf, and that the volume will be at your disposal. I told him that I thought you were going to be around in Boston sometime this month or next, and it would undoubtedly give you a good deal of pleasure to drop in to see him. However, if you are to be delayed and want the book before then, I think French would be very glad to have you write him and ask him for it.

With best wishes, I am

Sincerely,

Mr. Edmund L. Pearson,
44 West 10th Street
New York City.

*Biographical Note:* **Asa Palmer French** (American lawyer, US Attorney for the District of Massachusetts from 1906-1914), 1860-1935.

*Case Detail, Glendower murder (referred to here as case of United States v. De Graff):* See Letter #81 for information.

# Letter Number 93:
# Pearson to Knowlton - June 11, 1927

—·∘○❄○∘·—

## The New York Public Library
### 5th Avenue & 42nd Street
### New York City

Saturday

Dear Knowlton:

The clippings are amazing, and so is today's news of Emma's death. Thank you heartily, and thanks again for good offices re deGraf [*sic*]. I am writing to Mr. French. I will carefully return the clippings in a day or more. See you later.

Sincerely yours

E.L.P.

*Biographical Note:* **Asa Palmer French** (American lawyer, US Attorney for the District of Massachusetts from 1906-1914), 1860-1935.

*Case Detail, Glendower murder (referred to here as case of United States v. De Graff):* See Letter #81 for information.

## Letter Number 94:
## Pearson to Knowlton – July 12, 1927

—·∘°❀°∘·—

# The Outlook
### 120 East 16th Street-New York

EDITORIAL ROOMS

July 12, 1927

Dear Frank:

There was a decisive note in the tones of your telephone girl, the day I called at your office. She said you were away for a week. As I had the Class reunion, a trip to Rockland, one to Ossipee, and a few days of much needed tennis, golf, and swimming at Newbury, I could not manage to get in again. And I regret it. I found Mr. Asa French, after two attempts that day; and later, and not without difficulty (as C. Julius Caesar would say) I had speech with. Dr Magrath. Mr. French has kindly sent me the minutes of the case against De Graff. I am indebted to you, and to him, for this.

Dr Magrath says that the source of the story about De Graff's confession, was a deputy U.S. Marshal, who conducted the prisoner from the jail to the Court each day. After the acquittal, De Graff claimed a previous acquaintance with him, as he said they had both been on a British troop ship, probably in the South African War.* This deputy's name was Cameron, Duncan? or Donald? Of course, I might write to the U.S. Marshal and find if there is such a man, now in office. I hesitate to go at it in that way at first, and will take the risk of imposing on you again, - thus far: could you make an inquiry or two and let me know if Cameron is now in that office? And have I his name right?

*De Graff then told Cameron how he did it, and why.

Sincerely yours
Edmund Pearson

**Biographical Note:** *The Outlook* (weekly magazine published in New York City from 1879-1935); **Asa Palmer French** (American lawyer, US Attorney for the District of Massachusetts from 1906-1914), 1860-1935; **Dr. George Burgess Magrath** (American doctor, professor of legal medicine at Harvard University, Medical Examiner for Suffolk County from 1907-1935), 1870-1938.

**Case Detail, Glendower murder (referred to here as case against De Graff):** See Letter #81 for information.

# Letter Number 95:
## Knowlton to Pearson - April 11, 1928

———◦•◦❦◦•◦———

April 11, 1928.

My dear Pearson:

Great excitement was caused at the office yesterday by the arrival in my absence of your new book "Five Murders" and I find it on my desk this morning. I am looking forward to the pleasure I shall have in reading it and I shall write you further about it after I have read it.

Rather curiously enough, about the time it arrived at my office I was with my mother, who is very ill. In her weakness she has very little interest in anything outside the house, but one matter she did speak of was to ask me whether I felt that you would publish something more about the Borden case, now that both of the sisters had died, and she assured me that she wanted me to send her a copy of anything that you published as soon as it came out. I shall immediately go to the Old Corner Book Store and send her a copy so that it can be read to her when she is stronger.

I have hoped to have the time to see you in New York. Unfortunately, since fall, when my senior partner died rather suddenly, I have been very little the master of my time. When I am somewhat readjusted and next in New York, I certainly will look you up.

I am very grateful to you for sending me the autographed volume.

Gratefully yours,

Mr. Edmund Pearson,
    44 West 10th Street ,
       New York City.

**Biographical Note:** *Five Murders, with a final note on the Borden case*, by Edmund Lester Pearson, New York: Crime Club / Doubleday, 1928; **Sylvia Basset (Almy) Knowlton**, wife of Hosea Morrill Knowlton and mother of Frank Warren Knowlton, 1852-1937; **Charles F. Choate Jr.** (American lawyer, partner in the firm of Choate, Hall & Stewart, Boston), 1866-1927.

## Letter Number 96:
## Pearson to Knowlton - October 24, 1930

————————·-∘-∘🙑🙑🙑∘-∘·————————

44 West Tenth Street
New York City
October 24, 1930

Dear Frank Knowlton:

You have never told me of the new discoveries
you made about the Bram case.

My mail brings me some letters nowadays, saying that it
is high time to quit talking about Lizzie Borden. It also brings me letters,
and portraits, which show that other people are still interested in her. I
have recently had a queer bit of news, incorporated in a long letter from
a newspaper man in Pittsfield. I should like to hear if you have ever heard
anything about the story he tells. Shall I send it to you?

Sincerely yours
Edmund Pearson

*Case Detail, Thomas Bram:* See Letter #1 for information.

## Letter Number 97a:
## Knowlton to Pearson - October 28, 1930

————·-○-◦❁❀❁◦-○-·————

October 28, 1930.

Mr. Edmund Pearson,
    44 West 10th Street,
       New York City

My dear Pearson:

    I am very glad to have your letter of the 24th. I am afraid I
excited your curiosity too much in making some suggestions about the
Bram case. What I discovered had really nothing to do with that case itself,
but gave me a sidelight on the character of Monks and the view which his
family took about him. This I shall have to ask you to keep pretty confidential, owing to the way I got it and the sources from which it came. You
will remember that he died a year or two ago, but before his death and for
several years he led the life of a pretty complete rotter. Rum and women
were his undoing. His family felt that he was insane and wasting what little
property he had without any regard for his wife or child. In that way I came
to know the attitude of his family and of his wife. They were really fearful
that he would resort to extreme violence, even to killing, if they opposed his
will and tried to have him committed. It was to them a real menace and it
affected them so deeply that they finally decided to bear the ills he brought
to them rather than risk an uncertain future and the extreme violence that
they felt he was capable of. That is all there is to that, but in reading the
story of the crime it puts a little different color on things to know what
those who knew him best thought of him.

    I hear occasionally, but not often, of Lizzie Borden. Thirty-five
or more years have not been sufficient to obliterate the memory of that
fascinating crime. I ran across a day or two ago an editorial by Zephaniah
W. Pease, a very able newspaper man of New Bedford, written on the
occasion of her death. I am sending it to you because it is to me rather

interesting. I would like to hear the queer bit of news you got from the newspaper man in Pittsfield.

The really interesting book about the Borden case has not yet been written. Most of what has been written starts with the crime and traces through the circumstances surrounding it and tries to reason back to cause. The real book should work the other way, and work from cause to final result. It should be a psychological study of Lizzie Borden and her family; trace partly in fact and imagination the life she led in the narrow circle in which she moved; the meanness of her father; the entrance of the step-mother into the home; the growing and consuming jealousy that took hold of her, the limited sex-starved life she led with the only outlet the social affairs of her narrow, hardshelled religion and her church; the final overpowering of her caution and reason by the constant contact with the woman she hated; the discovery which undoubtedly she learned from overhearing her father's talk with the cousin; the necessity for action and the subsequent killing of her step-mother and the necessary killing of her father to avoid the certain disclosure of the murder by him. I thought at one time that Julian Green would be the man to do it, after I read his book "The Closed Garden", but I felt my doubts after reading his later book, the name of which escapes me now. It is much too morbid and too thoroughly French in its point of view and I don't believe that Green could appreciate the terribly narrow life such a family led in a small city in the '90's. Who would be the one to do it? Galsworthy might but he doesn't know the New England life and its limitations. There is a real field for somebody there. It could be written, of course, without calling the central figure Lizzie Borden, but with the naive announcement which was made in the preface to "The Elizabethans" which was as I remember it in substance that "no character in this book is wholly fictitious".

I am still dwelling in the hope that some day I shall have enough leisure in New York to look you up.

Yours very sincerely,

FWK:ED

Enc.

## Letter Number 97b:
## Article by Zephaniah W. Pease in the *Morning Mercury*
## New Bedford, Massachusetts
## June 1, 1927

--------·∘∘◉⚜◉∘∘·--------

Lizzie A. Borden, whose name was as conspicuously on the front pages of the newspapers of the world some decades ago as that of Lindbergh just now, died in Fall River Wednesday night. In a certain newspaper office yesterday an editor looked over a proof of a headline, "Lizzie Borden is dead of heart disease," and raised the question whether the headline should further identify her to this generation. His decision was that it could not be possible that anybody could not know, but he took a chance. It is thirty-five years since the hideous crime of which she was accused, and so soon do we forget, as old Rip Van Winkle observed.

It was on a quiet morning in early August in 1982 that Lizzie Borden called to the maid in the attic of the house and told her to call a physician while she notified near-by neighbors that her father had been killed. On a couch where he was taking a nap after an errand down town, Andrew J. Borden was found to have been murdered from more than a dozen blows with an axe, and in a bedroom on the second floor Mrs. Borden was killed by blow after blow on the head and shoulders, also inflicted with an axe, or similar weapon.

Eventually the Fall River police were notified. It was the day of the police picnic at Rocky Point and Chief Hilliard, not appreciating the importance of the case from the manner in which it was reported to him, sent a committing officer who happened to be around to investigate. The officer was sickened at the sight of the human slaughter and didn't stay long in the house. It was late in the day before serious investigation commenced. It is reasonable to believe if there had been efficiency on the part of the police from the start, something might have been discovered—the weapon, the dress that was burned, something that would have afforded a clue. Because of this neglect the murder of the Bordens ranks as the greatest mystery in the United States ever attained.

Lizzie A. Borden was arrested for the crime, tried and adjudged probably guilty in the district court in Fall River, indicted by the grand jury, tried and acquitted in the Superior Court in New Bedford. For months the investigation and speculation and trial filled the columns of the newspapers of the country. The controversy grew so bitter that it divided families and spoiled good neighborhoods. Andrew J. Borden was a God-fearing man, prominent in his church, president of a bank, director in corporations, a man of thrift and fortune and high character, a typical New Englander by birth, breeding and temperament. Lizzie Borden had been brought up amidst such surroundings. She had been active in the Congregational church, taught a Sunday school class, sang in the choir, belonged to the Christian Endeavor society, helped in the fruit and flower mission and worked with the W.C.T.U. Her pastor came to her support and sat by her side or near throughout the days of the trial. That a girl with such upbringing could slaughter her father and stepmother in so barbarous and frenzied an attack seemed an imputation against any cherished views of the value of religious training and a Christian home. All over the country loyal supporters of the church declared it impossible that a woman with such a heritage could do so unnatural an atrocity in such a fiendish blood thirsty way, which was a credit to their loyalty. There was a good deal of talk about the potency of something called "Church politics."

Never before, it is believed was a murder so widely discussed. At the time of the trial in New Bedford there had never been such elaborate plans for reporting a trial. It was among the first, if not the first murder trial where telegraphic reports were sent directly from the court house. From time to time during the trial churchmen, sociologists and authors attended. The late Edward Everett Hale was present. The great newspapers sent their most brilliant men, among them Julian Ralph of the New York Sun who was then regarded as the best reporter in the world. The sun was among those who thought Lizzie Borden innocent. Julian Ralph wrote a fascinating story and likened Lizzie Borden to Hester Prynne of "The Scarlet Letter." We always thought he formed his impression before he left New York. There was nothing about Lizzie Borden to inspire such a comparison. She was heavy, stolid, immobile, unemotional and sodden, if one might judge by appearances. If she ever suffered during the trial or after from the imputation of being a murderess, it was never revealed. One might have looked for some expression of indignation or revolt if the accusation was false or unjust, but no one every heard a protest from her.

Other newspaper men of prominence at the period who reported the case were Joseph Howard, Jr. and Lemuel Eli Quigg. The latter became later a political boss in New York. Hosea M. Knowlton of New Bedford, district attorney at the time, was the prosecutor. It was the practice then for the attorney general to try important murder cases. Attorney General Pillsbury, it was said, was not anxious to act as the prosecuting attorney and was less convinced than Mr. Knowlton, who had no doubts whatever about her guilt. Associated with Mr. Knowlton was William H. Moody who later was made a justice of the United States Supreme Court. Andrew J. Jennings of Fall River, who was the Borden family attorney, represented Lizzie Borden, and associated with him was George D. Robinson, ex-governor of the state. Mr. Robinson made the final plea. As governor, Mr. Robinson had appointed Judge Dewey to the bench. Judge Dewey's charge was regarded as very favorable to Lizzie Borden.

We do not propose to review the case here. The verdict did not end the discussion then any more than that in the Sacco-Vanzetti case which appears not to be held sacred. The chief difficulty which the prosecution suffered was something that might impress the jury as a motive. During the long trial which was reported by this writer, there were nightly conferences at Mr. Knowlton's home with Mr. Moody, and the writer was generally asked around, as Mr. Knowlton like to know what impressions the newspaper men were forming, and what their comments might be. Over and over Mr. Knowlton would say "If John Morse could testify what he and Andrew Borden talked about that night, the jury would know the motive." Morse was a relative of the Bordens and had been visiting at the house. It was Mr. Knowlton's belief that Andrew Borden disclosed to Morse the terms of the will he was contemplating and that the conversation was overheard by Lizzie Borden. As it stood, the only motive Mr. Knowlton could suggest was of a young woman, with a very wealthy father, desirous of travel and a wider outlook, who was cramped and fettered in a home life which lacked the luxury of people of the wealth of her father. That was rather inadequate as a motive. But what motive could have been adequate?

The jury acquitted Lizzie Borden and there was cheering in the court room and the defenders of Lizzie Borden, some of whom were very rabid, exulted over those of opposite view. After the tumult died, the world started forgetting. But before the first notoriety died came a story that Lizzie Borden had committed a theft at the store of Tilden & Thurber in

Providence. There was no denial of this but the case was settled outside the courts. One Fall River newspaper that was dissatisfied with the verdict used to print annually, on the anniversary of the murder, the story of a monster who had done this frightful deed and was somewhere at large. Lizzie Borden and her sister Emma went to live in a larger house on a fashionable street, kept two servants, a car and chauffeur and enlarged their style of living. Then Emma left the establishment and went to live with the little minister who had been their friend. Lizzie Borden was ostracized. Even those who had been loyal to her while she was in the shadow of the jail and the law were haunted and tortured with doubts that persisted in spite of the fact that the jury had declared her guiltless. They held aloof thereafter. There was a story of brief intimacy with an actress of tragedies and the neighborhood was [*illegible*] that the Borden house was alight and entertainment was going on. But that flash was soon over. One of the incomprehensible things is why Lizzie Borden persisted in living on in the city where she was known and gaped at and pointed out whenever she went on the streets. The city held fascination for her that is past understanding. One would have supposed she would have desired to get far away from the terrible suggestiveness of that home that stood in the business center on the street where even to this day pilgrims come to view and shudder, although the house was demolished awhile ago. May it not be possible that it was the sentence she imposed upon herself for an act which set heavy upon her soul?

> "Foul whisperings are abroad; unnatural deeds
> Do breed unnatural troubles; infected minds
> To their deaf pillows will discharge their secrets;
> More needs she the divine than the physician
> God, God forgive us all!"

*Biographical Note:* **Lester Hawthorne Monks** (American businessman, Vice President Shawmut Steamship Company, Director Eastern Steamship Lines, Inc.), 1876-1927; **Zephaniah W. Pease** (American writer, historian, editor, editor of *New Bedford Morning Mercury*, and friend of Franklin Delano Roosevelt), 1861-1933; **Julian Green** (American writer and novelist, first American to be elected to the Académie Française in 1971), 1900-1998; *The Closed Garden*, by Julian Green, New York: Harper & Brothers, 1928; **John Galsworthy** (English novelist and playwright, Nobel Prize for Literature winner in 1932), 1867-1933; *The Elizabethans*, by A.N. Wilson, New York: Farrar, Straus & Giroux, 1912.

*Case Detail, Thomas Bram (also referred to here as Monks character):* See Letter #1 for information.

## Letter Number 98:
## Pearson to Knowlton - October 29, 1930

————————·∘-∘🙙🙑🙚∘-∘·————————

44 West Tenth Street
October 29

Dear Knowlton:

My answer to your good letter is coming, along with the letter from the newspaper man, via William Emery. I am giving him a look at the letter, and asking him to forward it to you. ~~Im~~ I thought that my letter, which comments on the other communication, would be rather meaningless, if it came to you by itself.

Since writing it, I have come across this paragraph, from Cooper Gaw's very interesting column in the New Bedford Standard. I think it will amuse you, as it did me. Will you kindly return it in the enclosed envelope? I think I shall send it to Francis L Wellman, as a specimen of cross-examination carried too far.

Long ago, you mentioned the Angles Snell case to me. His delightful name; the place - Horseneck - and this anecdote make me long to write about it some time. I don't know that I shall ever get to it - it would probably mean coming to Massachusetts to read the papers - or else to the State House for the minutes.

Moreover, I should hesitate to include any joke on Mr. Parker. He was most kind to me, when I wrote about the Tucker case, and my brief allusion to his Chesterfieldian manner (derived from a description given me of ~~this~~ one particular hour in court, by Rob Dodge) caused him to send me an extremely courteous word of explanation - it would be exaggerating to call it a correction. But he noticed it, and politely took exception. (He lent me documents.)

Sincerely yours
Edmund Pearson

*Biographical Note:* **William Morrell Emery** (American journalist, *New Bedford Evening Journal*, covered the Lizzie A. Borden trial), 1866-1951; **Cooper Gaw** (American journalist and editor, editor of *New Bedford Standard*), 1877-1956; **Herbert Parker** (American lawyer, District Attorney for Middle District of Massachusetts from 1896-1899, Attorney General of the Commonwealth of Massachusetts from 1902-1906), 1856-1939; **Robert Gray Dodge** (American lawyer, partner at Storey, Thorndike, Palmer & Dodge, Boston, later senior partner in Palmer, Dodge, Gardner & Bradford, Boston), 1872-1964.

*Case Detail, Angles Snell:* See Letter #40a for information.

*Case Detail, Charles Lewis Tucker:* See Letter #6 for information.

## Letter Number 99:
## Pearson to Knowlton - October 29, 1930

————○•○❦❧❦○•○———

44 West Tenth Street
New York City
October 29, 1930

Dear Knowlton:

Thank you for your good letter. You know Monks was a neighbor of mine, although I saw him but once, when I interviewed him upon the Bram case. ~~Raher~~ Rather a big stuffed shirt, I thought. I heard something of his later difficulties. Someone, a lady, ~~I believe,~~ created a scene at the Harvard Club, one night, demanding to get in and see him. I think you told me that he wrote "The Letters of Down-and-Outer" which I believe were published (anonymously) in the Atlantic.

Aside from some photographs of Miss Lizzie (one of them a sinister looking thing, at the age of sixteen) which I have had presented me by two of her friends, the most interesting information came in a long conversation with Miss Helen Leighton, her residuary legatee, - I think. This had some amusing bits in it, including an account of a house party for Miss Nance O'Neil and her whole company - a party lasting a <u>week</u>, financed by Miss Lizzie! It was at Tyngsboro.

I think to put her into fiction you must resurrect either Aeschylus or Shakespeare. Nobody else can make readers believe in the <u>two</u> murders.

I am sending to William Emery, who will forward it to you, the letter I mentioned. I am asking you both to keep it to yourselves, and you to return it as promptly as convenient. There is only one other man I want to show it to, and he will be in New York in a week.

Perhaps this photographer in this letter is the imaginary artist to write the psychological novel you desire about Miss Lizbeth. His most startling piece of information (among a lot of rather well known stuff) sounds a little fishy to me, - rather like high-school boys' gossip. I have heard all sorts of hints of similar nature about her, but I should like to know at what point in the investigation they had a chance for this photography. Certainly, this discovery would have been a rare addition to the "Black Museum" of the Fall River police headquarters, - if they have one. Chief Feeney didn't mention it to me. But then, there's lots I don't know; I was outside Scotland Yard last month, and never even tried to get in.

Thank you for the interesting article by Mr. Pease, which I will return if you wish it. Otherwise I shall be glad to add it to my notes which fill one or two scrap-books.

Did I tell you that Miss Lizbeth sent a collection of photographs of the scene, bodies, &c., as souvenirs, to Mr. Moody? I have this on the authority of the daughter of Senator Lodge, formerly Mrs. Augustus Gardner, who had it from Mr. Moody himself.

Sincerely yours
Edmund Pearson

*Biographical Note:* **Lester Hawthorne Monks** (American businessman, Vice President Shawmut Steamship Company, Director Eastern Steamship Lines, Inc.), 1876-1927; **Helen Leighton** (friend and one of the executors of the will of Lizzie A. Borden), 1867-1950; **Nance O'Neil** (American stage and film actress, one time friend of Lizzie A. Borden), 1874-1965; **William Morrell Emery** (American journalist, *New Bedford Evening Journal*, covered the Lizzie A. Borden trial), 1866-1951; **Martin Feeney** (Chief of Police of Fall River from 1917-1931), 1862-1937; **Zephaniah W. Pease** (American writer, historian, editor, editor of *New Bedford Morning Mercury*, and friend of Franklin Delano Roosevelt), 1861-1933; **William Henry Moody** (American lawyer, assisted Hosea Knowlton in the prosecution of Lizzie A. Borden, Secretary of the Navy and Attorney General under President Theodore Roosevelt, and justice of the Supreme Court), 1853-1917; **Constance Lodge** (later Mrs. Augustus Peabody Gardner, daughter of Senator Henry Cabot Lodge, Sr., 1850-1924), 1872-1948.

*Case Detail, Thomas Bram (also referred to here as Monks):* See Letter #1 for information.

# Letter Number 100:
## Knowlton to Pearson - October 31, 1930

October 31, 1930.

Dear Pearson:

Thank you very much indeed for your letter of the 29th and for sending me the letter from Mr. Hollister. It is very interesting. The little report from the photographer is interesting and important if true. Of course in those Victorian days Freud had not appeared on the scene, nor had the great significance that should be attached to such things been brought to the attention of the public. We shied off from them as if it wasn't to be spoken of. "The Well of Loneliness" had not appeared nor had "Captive" been played on the stage. However, it seems to be rather fanciful, - a bit of gossip which probably came from some fanciful suggestion. Such tales bob up. There is always some such device being found by a porter on the train to Northampton every so often. Of course I was a fresh and, I hope, clean-minded youth of the early Nineties and I don't remember all the gossip about the Borden case which went the rounds at that time, but I am quite clear that if I had ever heard anything of the sort I would have recalled it.

By all means keep the articles by Pease. You are the authority and collector of all Bordeniana.

I hope you will pardon me if I am a little skeptical about the alleged souvenirs sent to Mr. Moody. We get some pretty fanciful things from the descendants of Mr. Lodge, particularly in the female line, so that I don't take much stock in what I hear. Mr. Moody was a very good friend of my father's and used to visit us almost every summer. There again I am surprised, if it is true, that I never heard of it. Frankly, it is quite improbable.

Yours sincerely,

Mr. Edmund L. Pearson,
44 West Tenth Street,
New York City.

P.S. I am returning with this letter the very interesting newspaper clipping about Attorney General Parker.

F.W.K.

*Biographical Note:* **Sigmund Freud** (Austrian neurologist and founder of psychoanalysis), 1856-1939; *The Well of Loneliness* (lesbian novel), by Radclyffe Hall, London: Jonathan Cape, 1928; *The Captive*, or *La Prisonnière* (French lesbian play), by Édouard Bourdet, 1926; **Zephaniah W. Pease** (American writer, historian, editor, Editor of *New Bedford Morning Mercury*, and friend of Franklin Delano Roosevelt), 1861-1933; **William Henry Moody** (American lawyer, assisted Hosea Knowlton in the prosecution of Lizzie A. Borden, Secretary of the Navy and Attorney General under President Theodore Roosevelt, and justice of the Supreme Court), 1853-1917; **Henry Cabot Lodge Sr.** (American Republican politician and historian, United States Senator from Massachusetts from 1893-1924), 1850-1924; **Hosea Morrill Knowlton** (American lawyer, District Attorney for the Commonwealth of Massachusetts from 1879-1893, he led the prosecution against Miss Lizzie A. Borden, and later served as the Attorney General of the Commonwealth from 1894-1902), 1847-1902; **Herbert Parker** (American lawyer, District Attorney for Middle District of Massachusetts from 1896-1899, Attorney General of the Commonwealth of Massachusetts from 1902-1906), 1856-1939.

# APPENDICES

# APPENDIX A

Lizzie Borden's inquest testimony is reproduced here as an exact transcription of *The Evening Standard*, New Bedford, Massachusetts, June 12, 1893, Monday Evening Edition, p. 8 plus 2 unnumbered supplement pages. It was created by Terence Duniho and Stefani Koorey while writing their article "Will the Real Inquest Testimony of Lizzie Borden Please Stand Up" (*Lizzie Borden Quarterly*: October 2001).

## LIZZIE BORDEN

Q. (Mr. Knowlton.) Give me your full name.
A. Lizzie Andrew Borden.

Q. Is it Lizzie or Elizabeth?
A. Lizzie.

Q. You were so christened?
A. I was so christened.

Q. What is your age, please?
A. Thirty-two.

Q. Your mother is not living?
A. No sir.

Q. When did she die?
A. She died when I was two and a half years old.

Q. You do not remember her, then?
A. No sir.

Q. What was your father's age?
A. He was seventy next month.

Q. What was his whole name?
A. Andrew Jackson Borden.

Q. And your stepmother, what is her whole name?
A. Abby Durfee Borden.

Q. How long had your father been married to your stepmother?
A. I think about twenty-seven years.

Q. How much of that time have they lived in that house on Second street?
A. I think, I am not sure, but I think about twenty years last May.

Q. Always occupied the whole house?
A. Yes sir.

Q. Somebody told me it was once fitted up for two tenements.
A. When we bought it it was for two tenements, and the man we bought it of stayed there a few months until he finished his own house. After he finished his own house and moved into it there was no one else ever moved in; we always had the whole.

Q. Have you any idea how much your father was worth?
A. No sir.

Q. Have you ever heard him say?
A. No sir.

Q. Have you ever formed any opinion[?]
A. No sir.

Q. Do you know something about his real estate?
A. About what?

Q. His real estate?
A. I know what real estate he owned, part of it; I don't know whether I know it all or not.

Q. Tell me what you know of.
A. He owns two farms in Swanzey, the place on Second street and the A. J. Borden building and corner, and the land on South Main street where Mc Mannus is, and then a short time ago he bought some real estate up further south that formerly, he said, belonged to a Mr. Birch.

Q. Did you ever deed him any property?
A. He gave us some years ago, Grandfather Borden's house on Ferry street, and he bought that back from us some weeks ago, I don't know just how many.

Q. As near as you can tell.
A. Well, I should say in June, but I am not sure.

Q. What do you mean by bought it back?
A. He bought it of us, and gave us the money for it.

Q. How much was it?
A. How much money? He gave us $5,000 for it.

Q. Did you pay him anything when you took a deed from him?
A. Pay him anything? No sir.

Q. How long ago was it you took a deed from him?
A. When he gave it to us?

Q. Yes.
A. I can't tell you; I should think five years.

Q. Did you have any other business transactions with him besides that?
A. No sir.

Q. In real estate?
A. No sir.

Q. Or in personal property?
A. No sir.

Q. Never?
A. Never.

Q. No transfer of property one way or the other?
A. No sir.

Q. At no time?
A. No sir.

Q. And I understand he paid you the cash for this property?
A. Yes sir.

Q. You and Emma equally?
A. Yes sir.

Q. How many children has your father?
A. Only two.

Q. Only you two?
A. Yes sir.

Q. Any others ever?
A. One that died.

Q. Did you ever know of your father making a will?
A. No sir, except I heard somebody say once that there was one several years ago; that is all I ever heard.

Q. Who did you hear say so?
A. I think it was Mr. Morse.

Q. What Morse?
A. Uncle John V. Morse.

Q. How long ago?
A. How long ago I heard him say it? I have not any idea.

Q. What did he say about it?
A. Nothing, except just that.

Q. What?
A. That Mr. Borden had a will.

Q. Did you ask your father?
A. I did not.

Q. Did he ever mention the subject of will to you?
A. He did not.

Q. He never told you that he had made a will, or had not?
A. No sir.

Q. Did he have a marriage settlement with your stepmother that you knew of?
A. I never knew of any.

Q. Had you heard anything of his proposing to make a will?
A. No sir.

Q. Do you know of anybody that your father was on bad terms with?
A. There was a man that came there that he had trouble with, I don't know who the man was.

Q. When?
A. I cannot locate the time exactly. It was within two weeks. That is I don't know the date or day of the month.

Q. Tell all you saw and heard.
A. I did not see anything. I heard the bell ring, and father went to the door and let him in. I did not hear anything for some time, except just the voices; then I heard the man say, "I would like to have that place, I would like to have that store. Father says, "I am not willing to let your business go in there." And the man said, "I thought with your reputation for liking money, you would let your store for anything." Father said, "You are mistaken." Then they talked a while, and then their voices were louder, and I heard father order him out, and went to the front door with him.

Q. What did he say?
A. He said that he had stayed long enough, and he would thank him to go.

Q. Did he say anything about coming again?
A. No sir.

Q. Did your father say anything about coming again, or did he?
A. No sir.

Q. Have you any idea who that was?
A. No sir. I think it was a man from out of town, because he said he was going home to see his partner.

Q. Have you had any efforts made to find him?
A. We have had a detective; that is all I know.

Q. You have not found him?
A. Not that I know of.

Q. You can't give us any other idea about it?
A. Nothing but what I have told you.

Q. Beside that do you know of anybody that your father had bad feelings toward, or who had bad feelings toward your father?
A. I know of one man that has not been friendly with him; they have not been friendly for years.

Q. Who?
A. Mr. Hiram C. Harrington.

Q. What relation is he to him?
A. He is my father's brother-in-law.

Q. Your mother's brother?
A. My father's only sister married Mr. Harrington.

Q. Anybody else that was on bad terms with your father, or that your father was on bad terms with?
A. Not that I know of.

Q. You have no reason to suppose that man you speak of a week or two ago, had ever seen your father before, or has since?
A. No sir.

Q. Do you know of anybody that was on bad terms with your step-mother?
A. No sir.

Q. Or that your stepmother was on bad terms with?
A. No sir.

Q. Had your stepmother any property?
A. I don't know, only that she had half the house that belonged to her father.

Q. Where was that?
A. On Fourth Street.

Q. Who lives in it?
A. Her half-sister.

Q. Any other property beside that that you know of?
A. I don't know.

Q. Did you ever know of any?
A. No sir.

Q. Did you understand that she was worth anything more than that?
A. I never knew.

Q. Did you ever have any trouble with your stepmother?
A. No sir.

Q. Have you, within six months, had any words with her?
A. No sir.

Q. Within a year?
A. No sir.

Q. Within two years?
A. I think not.

Q. When last that you know of?
A. About five years ago.

Q. What about?
A. Her stepsister, half-sister.

Q. What name?
A. Her name now is Mrs. George W. Whitehead.

Q. Nothing more than hard words?
A. No sir, they were not hard words; it was simply a difference of opinion.

Q. You have been on pleasant terms with your stepmother since then?
A. Yes sir.

Q. Cordial?
A. It depends upon one's idea of cordiality, perhaps.

Q. According to your idea of cordiality?
A. We were friendly, very friendly.

Q. Cordial, according to your idea of cordiality?
A. Quite so.

Q. What do you mean by "quite so"?
A. Quite cordial. I do not mean the dearest of friends in the world, but very kindly feelings, and pleasant. I do not know how to answer you any better than that.

Q. You did not regard her as your mother?
A. Not exactly, no; although she came there when I was very young.

Q. Were your relations towards her that of daughter and mother?
A. In some ways it was, and in some it was not.

Q. In what ways was it?
A. I decline to answer.

Q. Why?
A. Because I don't know how to answer it.

Q. In what ways was it not?
A. I did not call her mother.

Q. What name did she go by?
A. Mrs. Borden.

Q. When did you begin to call her Mrs. Borden?
A. I should think five or six years ago.

Q. Before that time you had called her mother?
A. Yes sir.

Q. What led to the change?
A. The affair with her stepsister.

Q. So that the affair was serious enough to have you change from calling her mother, do you mean?
A. I did not choose to call her mother.

Q. Have you ever called her mother since?
A. Yes, occasionally.

Q. To her face, I mean?
A. Yes.

Q. Often?
A. No sir.
Q. Seldom?
A. Seldom.

Q. Your usual address was Mrs. Borden?
A. Yes sir.

Q. Did your sister Emma call her mother?
A. She always called her Abby from the time she came into the family.

Q. Is your sister Emma older than you?
A. Yes sir.

Q. What is her age?
A. She is ten years older than I am. She was somewhere about fourteen when she came there.

Q. What was your stepmother's age?
A. I don't know. I asked her sister Saturday, and she said sixty-four. I told them sixty-seven; I did not know. I told as nearly as I knew. I did not know there was so much difference between she and father.

Q. Why did you leave off calling her mother?
A. Because I wanted to.

Q. Is that all the reason you have to give me?
A. I have not any other answer.

Q. Can't you give me any better reason than that?
A. I have not any reason to give, except that I did not want to.

Q. In what other respect were the relations between you and her not that of mother and daughter, besides not calling her mother?
A. I don't know that any of the relations were changed. I had never been

to her as a mother in many things. I always went to my sister, because she was older and had the care of me after my mother died.

Q. In what respects were the relations between you and her that of mother and daughter?
A. That is the same question you asked before; I can't answer you any better now than I did before.

Q. You did not say before you could not answer, but that you declined to answer.
A. I decline to answer because I do not know what to say.

Q. That is the only reason?
A. Yes sir.

Q. You called your father father?
A. Always.

Q. Were your father and mother happily united?
(Witness pauses a little before answering.)
A. Why, I don't know but that they were.

Q. Why do you hesitate?
A. Because I don't know but that they were, and I am telling the truth as nearly as I know it.

Q. Do you mean me to understand that they were happy entirely, or not?
A. So far as I know they were.

Q. Why did you hesitate then?
A. Because I did not know how to answer you any better than what came into my mind. I was trying to think if I was telling it as I should; that is all.

Q. Do you have any difficulty in telling it as you should, any difficulty in answering my questions?
A. Some of your questions I have difficulty in answering, because I don't know just how you mean them.

Q. Did you ever know of any difficulty between her and your father?
A. No, sir.

Q. Did he seem to be affectionate?
A. I think so.

Q. As man and woman who are married ought to be?
A. So far as I have ever had any chance of judging.

Q. They were?
A. Yes.

Q. What dress did you wear the day they were killed?
A. I had on a navy blue, sort of a bengaline or India silk skirt, with a navy blue blouse. In the afternoon they thought I had better change it. I put on a pink wrapper.

Q. Did you change your clothing before the afternoon?
A. No, sir.

Q. You dressed in the morning, as you have described, and kept that clothing on until afternoon?
A. Yes, sir.

Q. When did Morse come there first, I don't mean this visit, I mean as a visitor, John V. Morse?
A. Do you mean this day that he came and stayed all night?

Q. No. Was this visit his first to your house?
A. He has been in the east a year or more.

Q. Since he has been in the east has he been in the habit of coming to your house?
A. Yes; came in any time he wanted to.

Q. Before that had he been at your house, before he came east?
A. Yes, he has been here, if you remember the winter that the river was frozen over and they went across, he was here that winter, some 14 years ago, was it not?

Q. I am not answering questions, but asking them.
A. I don't remember the date. He was here that winter.

Q. Has he been here since?
A. He has been here once since; I don't know whether he has or not since.

Q. How many times this last year has he been at your house?
A. None at all to speak of; nothing more than a night or two at a time.

Q. How often did he come to spend a night or two?
A. Really I don't know; I am away so much myself.

Q. Your last answer is that you don't know how much he had been here, because you had been away yourself so much?
A. Yes.

Q. That is true the last year, or since he has been east?
A. I have not been away the last year so much, but other times I have been away when he has been here.

Q. Do I understand you to say that his last visit before this one was 14 years ago?
A. No, he has been here once between the two.

Q. How long did he stay then?
A. I don't know.

Q. How long ago was that?
A. I don't know.

Q. Give me your best remembrance.
A. Five or six years, perhaps six.

Q. How long has he been east this time?
A. I think over a year; I am not sure.

Q. During the last year how much of the time has he been at your house?
A. Very little that I know of.

Q. Your answer to that question before was, I don't know because I have been away so much myself.
A. I did not mean I had been away very much myself the last year.

Q. How much have you been away the last year?
A. I have been away a great deal in the daytime, occasionally at night.

Q. Where in the daytime, any particular place?
A. No, around town.

Q. When you go off nights, where?
A. Never unless I have been off on a visit?

Q. When was the last time when you have been away for more than a night or two before this affair?
A. I don't think I have been away to stay more than a night or two since I came from abroad, except about three or four weeks ago I was in New Bedford for three or four days.

Q. Where at New Bedford?
A. At 20 Madison street.

Q. How long ago were you abroad?
A. I was abroad in 1890.

Q. When did he come to the house the last time before your father and mother were killed?
A. He stayed there all night Wednesday night.

Q. My question is when he came there.
A. I don't know; I was not at home when he came; I was out.

Q. When did you first see him there?
A. I did not see him at all.

Q. How did you know he was there?
A. I heard his voice.

Q. You did not see him Wednesday evening?
A. I did not; I was out Wednesday evening.

Q. You did not see him Thursday morning?
A. I did not; he was out when I came down stairs.

Q. When was the first time you saw him?
A. Thursday noon.

Q. You had never seen him before that?
A. No sir.

Q. Where were you Wednesday evening?
A. I spent the evening with Miss Russell.

Q. As near as you can remember, when did you return?
A. About nine o'clock at night.

Q. The family had then retired?
A. I don't know whether they had or not. I went right to my room; I don't remember.

Q. You did not look to see?
A. No sir.

Q. Which door did you come in at?
A. The front door.

Q. Did you lock it?
A. Yes sir.

Q. For the night?
A. Yes sir.

Q. And went right up stairs to your room?
A. Yes sir.

Q. When was it that you heard the voice of Mr. Morse?
A. I heard him down there about supper time---no, it was earlier than that. I heard him down there somewhere about three o'clock, I think. I was in my room Wednesday, not feeling well, all day.

Q. Did you eat supper at home Wednesday night?
A. I was at home; I did not eat any supper, because I did not feel able to eat supper; I had been sick.

Q. You did not come down to supper?
A. No sir.

Q. Did you hear him eating supper?
A. No sir. I did not know whether he was there or not.

Q. You heard him in the afternoon?
A. Yes sir.

Q. Did you hear him go away?
A. I did not.

Q. You did not go down to see him?
A. No sir.

Q. Was you in bed?
A. No sir, I was on the lounge.

Q. Why did you not go down?
A. I did not care to go down, and I was not feeling well, and kept my room all day.

Q. You felt better in the evening?
A. Not very much better. I thought I would go out, and see if the air would make me feel any better.

Q. When you came back at nine o'clock, you did not look in to see if the family were up?
A. No sir.

Q. Why not?
A. I very rarely do when I come in.

Q. You go right to your room?
A. Yes sir.

Q. Did you have a night key?
A. Yes sir.

Q. How did you know it was right to lock the front door?
A. That was always my business.

Q. How many locks did you fasten?
A. The spring locks itself, and there is a key to turn, and you manipulate the bolt.

Q. You manipulated all those?
A. I used them all.

Q. Then you went to bed?
A. Yes, directly.

Q. When you got up the next morning, did you see Mr. Morse?
A. I did not.

Q. Had the family breakfasted when you came down?
A. Yes, sir.

Q. What time did you come down stairs?
A. As near as I can remember, it was a few minutes before nine.

Q. Who did you find down stairs when you came down?
A. Maggie and Mrs. Borden.

Q. Did you inquire for Mr. Morse?
A. No sir.

Q. Did you suppose he had gone?
A. I did not know whether he had or not; he was not there.

Q. Your father was there?
A. Yes sir.

Q. Then you found him?
A. Yes sir.

Q. Did you speak to either your father or Mrs. Borden?
A. I spoke to them all.

Q. About Mr. Morse?
A. I did not mention him.

Q. Did not inquire anything about him?
A. No sir.

Q. How long before that time had he been at the house?
A. I don't know.

Q. As near as you can tell?
A. I don't know. He was there in June sometime, I don't know whether he was there after that or not.

Q. Why did you not go to Marion with the party that went?
A. Because they went sooner than I could, and I was going Monday.

Q. Why did they go sooner than you could; what was there to keep you?
A. I had taken the secretaryship and treasurer of our C. E. society, had the charge, and the roll call was the first Sunday in August, and I felt I must be there and attend to that part of the business.

Q. Where was your sister Emma that day?
A. What day?

Q. The day your father and Mrs. Borden were killed?
A. She had been in Fairhaven.

Q. Had you written to her?
A. Yes sir.

Q. When was the last time you wrote to her?
A. Thursday morning, and my father mailed the letter for me.

Q. Did she get it at Fairhaven?
A. No sir, it was sent back. She did not get it at Fairhaven, for we telegraphed for her, and she got home here Thursday afternoon, and the letter was sent back to this post office.

Q. How long had she been in Fairhaven?
A. Just two weeks to a day.

Q. You did not visit in Fairhaven?
A. No sir.

Q. Had there been anybody else around the house that week, or premises?
A. No one that I know of, except the man that called to see him on this business about the store.

Q. Was that that week?
A. Yes sir.

Q. I misunderstood you probably, I thought you said a week or two before.
A. No, I said that week. There was a man came the week before and gave up some keys, and I took them.

Q. Do you remember of anybody else being then around the premises that week?
A. Nobody that I know of or saw.

Q. Nobody at work there?
A. No sir.

Q. Nobody doing any chores there?
A. No sir, not that I know of.

Q. Nobody had access to the house, so far as you know, during that time?
A. No sir.

Q. I ask you once more how it happened that, knowing Mr. Morse was at your house, you did not step in and greet him before you retired?
A. I have no reason, except that I was not feeling well Wednesday, and so did not come down.

Q. No, you were down. When you came in from out.
A. Do you mean Wednesday night?

Q. Yes.
A. Because I hardly ever do go in. I generally went right up to my room, and I did that night.

Q. Could you then get to your room from the back hall?
A. No sir.

Q. From the back stairs?
A. No sir.

Q. Why not? What would hinder?
A. Father's bedroom door was kept locked, and his door into my room was locked and hooked too I think, and I had no keys.

Q. That was the custom of the establishment?
A. It had always been so.

Q. It was so Wednesday, and so Thursday?
A. It was so Wednesday, but Thursday they broke the door open.

Q. That was after the crowd came; before the crowd came?
A. It was so.

Q. There was no access, except one had a key, and one would have to have
two keys?
A. They would have to have two keys if they went up the back way to get
into my room. If they were in my room, they would have to have a key to
get into his room, and another to get into the back stairs.

Q. Where did Mr. Morse sleep?
A. In the next room over the parlor in front of the stairs.

Q. Right up the same stairs that your room was?
A. Yes sir.

Q. How far from your room?
A. A door opened into it.

Q. The two rooms connected directly?
A. By one door, that is all.

Q. Not through the hall?
A. No sir.

Q. Was the door locked?
A. It has been locked and bolted, and a large writing desk in my room
kept up against it.

Q. Then it was not a practical opening?
A. No sir.

Q. How otherwise do you get from your room to the next room?
A. I have to go into the front hall.

Q. How far apart are the two doors?
A. Very near, I don't think more than so far (measuring.)

Q. Was it your habit when you were in your room to keep your door shut?
A. Yes sir.

Q. That time, that Wednesday afternoon?
A. My door was open part of the time, and part of the time I tried to

get a nap and their voices annoyed me, and I closed it. I kept it open in summer more or less, and closed in winter.

Q. Then, unless for some special reason, you kept your door open in the summer?
A. Yes sir, if it was a warm day. If it was a cool day, I should have closed it.

Q. Where was your father when you came down Thursday morning?
A. Sitting in the sitting room in his large chair, reading the Providence Journal.

Q. Where was your mother? Do you prefer me to call her Mrs. Borden?
A. I had as soon you called her mother. She was in the dining room with a feather duster dusting.

Q. When she dusted did she wear something over her head?
A. Sometimes when she swept, but not when dusting.

Q. Where was Maggie?
A. Just come in the back door with the long pole, brush, and put the brush on the handle, and getting her pail of water; she was going to wash the windows around the house. She said Mrs. Borden wanted her to.

Q. Did you get your breakfast that morning?
A. I did not eat any breakfast; I did not feel as though I wanted any.

Q. Did you get any breakfast that morning?
A. I don't know whether I ate half a banana; I don't think I did.

Q. You drank no tea or coffee that morning?
A. No sir.

Q. And ate no cookies?
A. I don't know whether I did or not. We had some molasses cookies; I don't know whether I ate any that morning or not.

Q. Were the breakfast things put away when you got down?
A. Everything except the coffee pot; I am not sure whether that was on the stove or not.

Q. You said nothing about Mr. Morse to your father or mother?
A. No sir.

Q. What was the next thing that happened after you got down?
A. Maggie went out of doors to wash the windows and father came out into the kitchen and said he did not know whether he would go down to the post office or not. And then I sprinkled some handkerchiefs to iron.

Q. Tell me again what time you came down stairs.
A. It was a little before nine, I should say about quarter; I don't know sure.

Q. Did your father go down town?
A. He went down later.

Q. What time did he start away?
A. I don't know.

Q. What were you doing when he started away?
A. I was in the dining room I think; yes, I had just commenced, I think, to iron.

Q. It may seem a foolish question. How much of an ironing did you have?
A. I only had about eight or ten of my best handkerchiefs.

Q. Did you let your father out?
A. No sir; he went out himself.

Q. Did you fasten the door after him?
A. No sir.

Q. Did Maggie?
A. I don't know. When she went up stairs she always locked the door; she had charge of the back door.

Q. Did she go out after a brush before your father went away?
A. I think so.

Q. Did you say anything to Maggie?
A. I did not.

Q. Did you say anything about washing the windows?
A. No sir.

Q. Did you speak to her?
A. I think I told her I did not want any breakfast.

Q. You do not remember of talking about washing the windows?
A. I don't remember whether I did or not; I don't remember it. Yes,
I remember; yes, I asked her to shut the parlor blinds when she got
through, because the sun was so hot.

Q. About what time do you think your father went down town?
A. I don't know; it must have been after nine o'clock. I don't know what
time it was.

Q. You think at that time you had begun to iron your handkerchiefs?
A. Yes sir.

Q. How long a job was that?
A. I did not finish them; my flats were not hot enough.

Q. How long a job would it have been if the flats had been right?
A. If they had been hot, not more than 20 minutes, perhaps.

Q. How long did you work on the job?
A. I don't know, sir.

Q. How long was your father gone?
A. I don't know that.

Q. Where were you when he returned?
A. I was down in the kitchen.

Q. What doing?
A. Reading an old magazine that had been left in the cupboard, an old
Harper's Magazine.

Q. Had you got through ironing?
A. No sir.

Q. Had you stopped ironing?
A. Stopped for the flats.

Q. Were you waiting for them to be hot?
A. Yes sir.

Q. Was there a fire in the stove?
A. Yes sir.

Q. When your father went away, you were ironing then?
A. I had not commenced, but I was getting the little ironing board and the flannel.

Q. Are you sure you were in the kitchen when your father returned?
A. I am not sure whether I was there or in the dining room.

Q. Did you go back to your room before your father returned?
A. I think I did carry up some clean clothes.

Q. Did you stay there?
A. No sir.

Q. Did you spend any time up the front stairs before your father returned?
A. No, sir.

Q. Or after he returned?
A. No, sir. I did stay in my room long enough when I went up to sew a little piece of tape on a garment.

Q. Was that the time when your father came home?
A. He came home after I came down stairs.

Q. You were not up stairs when he came home?
A. I was not up stairs when he came home; no, sir.

Q. What was Maggie doing when your father came home?
A. I don't know whether she was there or whether she had gone up stairs; I can't remember.

Q. Who let your father in?
A. I think he came to the front door and rang the bell, and I think Maggie let him in, and he said he had forgotten his key; so I think she must have been down stairs.

Q. His key would have done him no good if the locks were left as you left them?
A. But they were always unbolted in the morning.

Q. Who unbolted them that morning?
A. I don't think they had been unbolted; Maggie can tell you.

Q. If he had not forgotten his key it would have been no good?
A. No, he had his key and could not get in. I understood Maggie to say he said he had forgotten his key.

Q. You did not hear him say anything about it?
A. I heard his voice, but I don't know what he said.

Q. I understood you to say he said he had forgotten his key?
A. No, it was Maggie said he said he had forgotten the key.

Q. Where was Maggie when the bell rang?
A. I don't know, sir.

Q. Where were you when the bell rang?
A. I think in my room up stairs.

Q. Then you were up stairs when your father came home?
A. I don't know sure, but I think I was.

Q. What were you doing?
A. As I say, I took up these clean clothes, and stopped and basted a little piece of tape on a garment.

Q. Did you come down before your father was let in?
A. I was on the stairs coming down when she let him in.

Q. Then you were up stairs when your father came to the house on his return?
A. I think I was.

Q. How long had you been there?
A. I had only been upstairs just long enough to take the clothes up and baste the little loop on the sleeve. I don't think I had been up there over five minutes.

Q. Was Maggie still engaged in washing windows when your father got back?
A. I don't know.

Q. You remember, Miss Borden, I will call your attention to it so as to see if I have any misunderstanding, not for the purpose of confusing you; you remember that you told me several times that you were down stairs, and not up stairs when your father came home? You have forgotten, perhaps?
A. I don't know what I have said. I have answered so many questions and I am so confused I don't know one thing from another. I am telling you just as nearly as I know.

Q. Calling your attention to what you said about that a few minutes ago, and now again to the circumstance you have said you were up stairs when the bell rang, and were on the stairs when Maggie let your father in; which now is your recollection of the true statement of the matter, that you were down stairs when the bell rang and your father came?
A. I think I was down stairs in the kitchen.

Q. And then you were not up stairs?
A. I think I was not; because I went up almost immediately, as soon as I went down, and then came down again and stayed down.

Q. What had you in your mind when you said you were on the stairs as Maggie let your father in?
A. The other day somebody came there and she let them in and I was on the stairs; I don't know whether the morning before or when it was.

Q. You understood I was asking you exactly and explicitly about this fatal day?
A. Yes, sir.

Q. I now call your attention to the fact that you had specifically told me you had gone up stairs, and had been there about five minutes when the bell rang, and were on your way down, and were on the stairs when Maggie let your father in that day---
A. Yes, I said that, and then I said I did not know whether I was on the stairs or in the kitchen.

Q. Now how will you have it?

A. I think, as nearly as I know, I think I was in the kitchen.

Q. How long was your father gone?

A. I don't know, sir; not very long.

Q. An hour?

A. I should not think so.

Q. Will you give me the best story you can, so far as your recollection serves you, of your time while he was gone?

A. I sprinkled my handkerchiefs, and got my ironing board and took them in the dining room. I took the ironing board in the dining room and left the handkerchiefs in the kitchen on the table and whether I ate any cookies or not I don't remember. Then I sat down looking at the magazine, waiting for the flats to heat. Then I went in the sitting room and got the Providence Journal, and took that into the kitchen. I don't recollect of doing anything else.

Q. Which did you read first, the Journal or the magazine?

A. The magazine.

Q. You told me you were reading the magazine when your father came back?

A. I said in the kitchen, yes.

Q. Was that so?

A. Yes, I took the Journal out to read, and had not read it. I had it near me.

Q. You said a minute or two ago you read the magazine awhile, and then went and got the Journal and took it out to read?

A. I did, but I did not read it; I tried my flats then.

Q. And went back to reading the magazine?

A. I took the magazine up again, yes.

Q. When did you last see your mother?

A. I did not see her after when I went down in the morning and she was dusting the dining room.

Q. Where did you or she go then?
A. I don't know where she went. I know where I was.

Q. Did you or she leave the dining room first?
A. I think I did. I left her in the dining room.

Q. You never saw her or heard her afterwards?
A. No, sir.

Q. Did she say anything about making the bed?
A. She said she had been up and made the bed up fresh, and had dusted the room and left it all in order. She was going to put some fresh pillow slips on the small pillows at the foot of the bed, and was going to close the room, because she was going to have company Monday and she wanted everything in order.

Q. How long would it take to put on the pillow slips?
A. About two minutes.

Q. How long to do the rest of the things?
A. She had done that when I came down.

Q. All that was left was what?
A. To put on the pillow slips.

Q. Can you give me any suggestion as to what occupied her when she was up there, when she was struck dead?
A. I don't know of anything except she had some cotton cloth pillow cases up there, and she said she was going to commence to work on them. That is all I know. And the sewing machine was up there.

Q. Whereabouts was the sewing machine?
A. In the comer between the north and west side.

Q. Did you hear the sewing machine going?
A. I did not.

Q. Did you see anything to indicate that the sewing machine had been used that morning?
A. I had not. I did not go in there until after everybody had been in there, and the room had been overhauled.

Q. If she had remained down stairs, you would undoubtedly have seen her?
A. If she had remained down stairs, I should have; if she had remained in her room, I should not have. If she had remained down stairs, I should have. If she had gone to her room, I should not have.

Q. Where was that?
A. Over the kitchen.

Q. To get to that room she would have to go through the kitchen?
A. To get up the back stairs.

Q. That is the way she was in the habit of going?
A. Yes, sir, because the other doors were locked.

Q. If she had remained down stairs, or had gone to her own room, you undoubtedly would have seen her?
A. I should have seen her if she had stayed down stairs; if she had gone to her room, I would not have seen her.

Q. She was found a little after 11 in the spare room, if she had gone to her own room she must have gone through the kitchen and up the back stairs, and subsequently have gone down and gone back again?
A. Yes, sir.

Q. Have you any reason to suppose you would not have seen her if she had spent any portion of the time in her own room, or down stairs?
A. There is no reason why I should not have seen her if she had been down there, except when I first came down stairs, for two or three minutes I went down cellar to the water closet.

Q. After that you were where you practically commanded the view of the first story the rest of the time?
A. I think so.

Q. When you went up stairs for a short time, as you say you did, you then went in sight of the sewing machine?
A. No, I did not see the sewing machine, because she had shut that room up.

Q. What do you mean?
A. I mean the door was closed. She said she wanted it kept closed to keep the dust and everything out.

Q. Was it a room with a window?
A. It has three windows.

Q. A large room?
A. The size of the parlor; a pretty fair sized room.

Q. It is the guest room?
A. Yes, the spare room.

Q. Where the sewing machine was was the guest room?
A. Yes, sir.

Q. I ask again, perhaps you have answered all you care to, what explanation can you give, can you suggest, as to what she was doing from the time she said she had got the work all done in the spare room until 11 o'clock?
A. I suppose she went up and made her own bed.

Q. That would be in the back part?
A. Yes sir.

Q. She would have to go by you twice to do that?
A. Unless she went when I was in my room that few minutes.

Q. That would not be time enough for her to go and make her own bed and come back again?
A. Sometimes she stayed up longer and sometimes shorter; I don't know.

Q. Otherwise than that, she would have to go in your sight?
A. I should have to have seen her once; I don't know that I need to have seen her more than once.

Q. You did not see her at all?
A. No sir, not after the dining room.

Q. What explanation can you suggest as to the whereabouts of your mother from the time you saw her in the dining room, and she said her work in the spare room was all done, until 11 o'clock?
A. I don't know. I think she went back into the spare room, and whether she came back again or not I don't know; that has always been a mystery.

Q. Can you think of anything she could be doing in the spare room?
A. Yes sir. I know what she used to do sometimes. She kept her best cape she wore on the street in there, and she used occasionally to go up there to get it and to take it into her room. She kept a great deal in the guest room drawers; she used to go up there and get things and put things; she used those drawers for her own use.

Q. That connects her with her own room again, to reach which she had to go down stairs and come up again?
A. Yes.

Q. Assuming that she did not go into her own room, I understand you to say she could not have gone to her own room without your seeing her?
A. She could while I was down cellar.

Q. You went down immediately you came down, within a few minutes, and you did not see her when you came back?
A. No sir.

Q. After that time she must have remained in the guest chamber?
A. I don't know.

Q. So far as you can judge?
A. So far as I can judge she might have been out of the house, or in the house.

Q. Had you any knowledge of her going out of the house?
A. No sir.

Q. Had you any knowledge of her going out of the house?
A. She told me she had had a note, somebody was sick, and said "I am going to get the dinner on the way," and asked me what I wanted for dinner.

Q. Did you tell her?
A. Yes, I told her I did not want anything.

Q. Then why did you not suppose she had gone?
A. I supposed she had gone.

Q. Did you hear her come back?
A. I did not hear her go or come back, but I supposed she went.

Q. When you found your father dead you supposed your mother had gone?
A. I did not know. I said to the people who came in "I don't know whether Mrs. Borden is out or in; I wish you would see if she is in her room."

Q. You supposed she was out at the time?
A. I understood so; I did not suppose anything about it.

Q. Did she tell you where she was going?
A. No sir.

Q. Did she tell you who the note was from?
A. No sir.

Q. Did you ever see the note?
A. No sir.

Q. Do you know where it is now?
A. No sir.

Q. She said she was going out that morning?
A. Yes sir.

(Hearing continued [Wednesday] Aug. 10, 1892.)

Q. I shall have to ask you once more about that morning. Do you know what the family ate for breakfast?
A. No sir.

Q. Had the breakfast all been cleared away when you got down?
A. Yes sir.

Q. I want you to tell me just where you found the people when you got down that you did find there?
A. I found Mrs. Borden in the dining room. I found my father in the sitting room.

Q. And Maggie?
A. Maggie was coming in the back door with her pail and brush.

Q. Tell me what talk you had with your mother at that time?
A. She asked me how I felt. I said I felt better than I did Tuesday, but I did not want any breakfast. She asked me what I wanted for dinner. I told her nothing. I told her I did not want anything. She said she was going out, and would get the dinner. That is the last I saw her, or said anything to her.

Q. Where did you go then?
A. Into the kitchen.

Q. Where then?
A. Down cellar.

Q. Gone perhaps five minutes?
A. Perhaps. Not more than that; possibly a little bit more.

Q. When you came back did you see your mother?
A. I did not; I supposed she had gone out.

Q. She did not tell you where she was going?
A. No sir.

Q. When you came back was your father there?
A. Yes sir.

Q. What was he doing?
A. Reading the paper.

Q. Did you eat any breakfast?
A. No sir, I don't remember whether I ate a molasses cookie or not. I did not eat any regularly prepared breakfast.

Q. Was it usual for your mother to go out?
A. Yes sir, she went out every morning nearly, and did the marketing.

Q. Was it usual for her to be gone away from dinner?
A. Yes sir, sometimes, not very often.

Q. How often, say?
A. O, I should not think more than---well I don't know, more than once in three months, perhaps.

Q. Now I call your attention to the fact that twice yesterday you told me, with some explicitness, that when your father came in, you were just coming down stairs?
A. No, I did not, I beg your pardon.

Q. That you were on the stairs at the time your father was let in, you said with some explicitness. Do you now say you did not say so?
A. I said I thought first I was on the stairs; then I remembered I was in the kitchen when he came in.

Q. First you thought you were in the kitchen; afterwards you remembered you were on the stairs?
A. I said I thought I was on the stairs; then I said I knew I was in the kitchen. I still say that now. I was in the kitchen.

Q. Did you go into the front part of the house after your father came in?
A. After he came in from down street I was in the sitting room with him.

Q. Did you go into the front hall afterwards?
A. No sir.

Q. At no time?
A. No sir.

Q. Excepting the two or three minutes you were down cellar, were you away from the house until your father came in?
A. No sir.

Q. You were always in the kitchen or dining room, excepting when you went up stairs?
A. I went up stairs before he went out.

Q. You mean you went up there to sew a button on?
A. I basted a piece of tape on.

Q. Do you remember you did not say that yesterday?
A. I don't think you asked me. I told you yesterday I went up stairs directly after I came up from down cellar, with the clean clothes.

Q. You now say after your father went out, you did not go up stairs at all?
A. No sir, I did not.

Q. When Maggie came in there washing the windows, you did not appear from the front part of the house?
A. No sir.

Q. When your father was let in, you did not appear from up stairs?
A. No sir, I was in the kitchen.

Q. That is so?
A. Yes sir, to the best of my knowledge.

Q. After your father went out, you remained there either in the kitchen or dining room all the time?
A. I went in the sitting room long enough to direct some paper wrappers.

Q. One of the three rooms?
A. Yes sir.

Q. So it would have been extremely difficult for anybody to have gone through the kitchen and dining room and front hall, without your seeing them?
A. They could have gone from the kitchen into the sitting room while I was in the dining room, if there was anybody to go.

Q. Then into the front hall?
A. Yes sir.

Q. You were in the dining room ironing?
A. Yes sir, part of the time.

Q. You were in all of the three rooms?
A. Yes sir.

Q. A large portion of that time, the girl was out of doors?
A. I don't know where she was, I did not see her. I supposed she was out of doors, as she had the pail and brush.

Q. You knew she was washing windows?
A. She told me she was going to. I did not see her do it.

Q. For a large portion of the time you did not see the girl?
A. No sir.

Q. So far as you know you were alone in the lower part of the house, a large portion of the time, after your father went away, and before he came back?
A. My father did not go away I think until somewhere about 10, as near as I can remember; he was with me down stairs.

Q. A large portion of the time after your father went away, and before he came back, so far as you know, you were alone in the house?
A. Maggie had come in and gone up stairs.

Q. After he went out, and before he came back; a large portion of the time after your father went out, and before he came back, so far as you know, you were the only person in the house?
A. So far as I know, I was.

Q. And during that time, so far as you know, the front door was locked?
A. So far as I know.

Q. And never was unlocked at all?
A. I don't think it was.

Q. Even after your father came home, it was locked up again?
A. I don't know whether she locked it up again after that or not.

Q. It locks itself?
A. The spring lock opens.

Q. It fastens it so it cannot be opened from the outside?
A. Sometimes you can press it open.

Q. Have you any reason to suppose the spring lock was left so it could be pressed open from the outside?
A. I have no reason to suppose so.

Q. Nothing about the lock was changed before the people came?
A. Nothing that I know of.

Q. What were you doing in the kitchen when your father came home?
A. I think I was eating a pear when he came in.

Q. What had you been doing before that?
A. Been reading a magazine.

Q. Were you making preparations to iron again?
A. I had sprinkled my clothes, and was waiting for the flat. I sprinkled the clothes before he went out.

Q. Had you built up the fire again?
A. I put in a stick of wood. There was a few sparks. I put in a stick of wood to try to heat the flat.

Q. You had then started the fire?
A. Yes sir.

Q. The fire was burning when he came in?
A. No sir, but it was smoldering and smoking as though it would come up.

Q. Did it come up after he came in?
A. No sir.

Q. Did you do any more ironing?
A. I did not. I went in with him, and did not finish.

Q. You did not iron any more after your father came in?
A. No sir.

Q. Was the ironing board put away?
A. No sir, it was on the dining room table.

Q. When was it put away?
A. I don't know. Somebody put it away after the affair happened.

Q. You did not put it away?
A. No sir.

Q. Was it on the dining room table when you found your father killed?
A. I suppose so.

Q. You had not put it away then?
A. I had not touched it.

Q. How soon after your father came in, before Maggie went up stairs?
A. I don't know. I did not see her.

Q. Did you see her after your father came in?
A. Not after she let him in.

Q. How long was your father in the house before you found him killed?
A. I don't know exactly, because I went out to the barn. I don't know what time he came home. I don't think he had been home more than fifteen or twenty minutes; I am not sure.

Q. When you went out to the barn, where did you leave your father?
A. He had laid down on the sitting room lounge, taken off his shoes, and put on his slippers, and taken off his coat and put on the reefer. I asked him if he wanted the window left that way.

Q. Where did you leave him?
A. On the sofa.

Q. Was he asleep?
A. No sir.

Q. Was he reading?
A. No sir.

Q. What was the last thing you said to him?
A. I asked him if he wanted the window left that way. Then I went into the kitchen, and from there to the barn.

Q. Whereabouts in the barn did you go?
A. Up stairs.

Q. To the second story of the barn?
A. Yes sir.

Q. How long did you remain there?
A. I don't know, fifteen or twenty minutes.

Q. What doing?
A. Trying to find lead for a sinker.

Q. What made you think there would be lead for a sinker up there?
A. Because there was some there.

Q. Was there not some by the door?
A. Some pieces of lead by the open door, but there was a box full of old things up stairs.

Q. Did you bring any sinker back from the barn?
A. I found no sinker.

Q. Did you bring any sinker back from the barn?
A. Nothing but a piece of a chip I picked up on the floor.

Q. Where was that box you say was up stairs, containing lead?
A. There was a kind of a work bench.

Q. Is it there now?
A. I don't know sir.

Q. How long since have you seen it there?
A. I have not been out there since that day.

Q. Had you been in the barn before?
A. That day, no sir.

Q. How long since you had been in the barn before?
A. I don't think I had been into it, I don't know as I had in three months.

Q. When you went out did you unfasten the screen door?
A. I unhooked it to get out.

Q. It was hooked until you went out?
A. Yes sir.

Q. It had been left hooked by Bridget, if she was the last one in?
A. I suppose so; I don't know.

Q. Do you know when she did get through washing the outside?
A. I don't know.

Q. Did you know she washed the windows inside?
A. I don't know.

Q. Did you see her washing the windows inside?
A. I don't know.

Q. You don't know whether she washed the dining room and sitting room windows inside?
A. I did not see her.

Q. If she did would you not have seen her?
A. I don't know. She might be in one room and I in another.

Q. Do you think she might have gone to work and washed all the windows in the dining room and sitting room and you not know it?
A. I don't know, I am sure, whether I should or not. I might have seen her, and not know it.

Q. Miss Borden, I am trying in good faith to get all the doings that morning of yourself and Miss Sullivan, and I have not succeeded in doing it. Do you desire to give me any information or not?
A. I don't know it— I don't know what your name is.

Q. It is certain beyond reasonable doubt she was engaged in washing the windows in the dining room or sitting room when your father came home. Do you mean to say you know nothing of either of those operations?
A. I knew she washed the windows outside; that is, she told me so. She did not wash the windows in the kitchen, because I was in the kitchen most of the time.

Q. The dining room and sitting room, I said.
A. I don't know.

Q. It is reasonably certain she washed the windows in the dining room and sitting room inside while your father was out, and was engaged in that operation when your father came home; do you mean to say you know nothing of it?
A. I don't know whether she washed the windows in the sitting room and dining room or not.

Q. Can you give me any information how it happened at that particular time you should go into the chamber of the barn to find a sinker to go to Marion with to fish the next Monday?
A. I was going to finish my ironing; my flats were not hot; I said to myself "I will go and try and find that sinker; perhaps by the time I get back the flats will be hot." That is the only reason.

Q. How long had you been reading an old magazine before you went to the barn at all?
A. Perhaps half an hour.

Q. Had you got a fish line?
A. Not here; we had some at the farm.

Q. Had you got a fish hook?
A. No sir.

Q. Had you got any apparatus for fishing at all?
A. Yes, over there.

Q. Had you any sinkers over there?
A. I think there were some. It is so long since I have been there; I think there were some.

Q. You had no reason to suppose you were lacking sinkers?
A. I don't think there were any on my lines.

Q. Where were your lines?
A. My fish lines were at the farm here.

Q. What made you think there were no sinkers at the farm on your lines?
A. Because some time ago when I was there I had none.

Q. How long since you used the fish lines?
A. Five years, perhaps.

Q. You left them at the farm then?
A. Yes, sir.

Q. And you have not seen them since?
A. Yes, sir.

Q. It occurred to you after your father came in it would be a good time to go to the barn after sinkers, and you had no reason to suppose there was not abundance of sinkers at the farm and abundance of lines?
A. The last time I was there there were some lines.

Q. Did you not say before you presumed there were sinkers at the farm?
A. I don't think I said so.

Q. You did say so exactly. Do you now say you presume there were not sinkers at the farm?
A. I don't think there were any fish lines suitable to use at the farm; I don't think there were any sinkers on any line that had been mine.

Q. Do you remember telling me you presumed there were lines, and sinkers and hooks at the farm?
A. I said there were lines I thought, and perhaps hooks. I did not say I thought there were sinkers on my lines. There was another box of lines over there beside mine.

Q. You thought there were not sinkers?
A. Not on my lines.

Q. Not sinkers at the farm?
A. I don't think there were any sinkers at the farm. I don't know whether there were or not.

Q. Did you then think there were no sinkers at the farm?
A. I thought there were no sinkers anywhere, or I should not have been trying to find some.

Q. You thought there were no sinkers at the farm to be had?
A. I thought there were no sinkers at the farm to be had.

Q. That is the reason you went into the second story of the barn to look for a sinker?
A. Yes, sir.

Q. What made you think you would find sinkers there?
A. I heard father say, and I knew there was lead there.

Q. What made you think you would find sinkers there?
A. I went to see, because there was lead there.

Q. You thought there might be lead there made into sinkers?
A. I thought there might be lead with a hole in it.

Q. Did you examine the lead that was down stairs near the door?
A. No sir.

Q. Why not?
A. I don't know.

Q. You went straight to the upper story of the barn?
A. No, I went under the pear tree and got some pears first.

Q. Then went to the second story of the barn to look for sinkers for lines you had at the farm, as you supposed, as you had seen them there five years before that time?
A. I went up to get some sinkers, if I could find them. I did not intend to go to the farm for lines; I was going to buy some lines here.

Q. You then had no intention of using your own lines at Marion?
A. I could not get them.

Q. You had no intention of using your own line and hooks at the farm?
A. No sir.

Q. What was the use of telling me a little while ago you had no sinkers on your line at the farm?
A. I thought I made you understand that those lines at the farm were no good to use.

Q. Did you not mean for me to understand one of the reasons you were searching for sinkers was that the lines you had at the farm, as you remembered then, had no sinkers on them?
A. I said the lines at the farm had no sinkers.

Q. I did not ask you what you said. Did you not mean for me to understand that?
A. I meant for you to understand I wanted the sinkers, and was going to have new lines.

Q. You had not then bought your lines?
A. No sir, I was going out Thursday noon.

Q. You had not bought any apparatus for fishing?
A. No hooks.

Q. Had bought nothing connected with your fishing trip?
A. No sir.

Q. Was going to go fishing the next Monday, were you?
A. I don't know that we should go fishing Monday.

Q. Going to the place to go fishing Monday?
A. Yes sir.

Q. This was Thursday, and you had no idea of using any fishing apparatus before the next Monday?
A. No sir.

Q. You had no fishing apparatus you were proposing to use the next Monday until then?
A. No sir, not until I bought it.

Q. You had not bought anything?
A. No sir.

Q. Had not started to buy anything?
A. No sir.

Q. The first thing in preparation for your fishing trip the next Monday was to go to the loft of that barn to find some old sinkers to put on some hooks and lines that you had not then bought?
A. I thought if I found no sinkers I would have to buy the sinkers when I bought the lines.

Q. You thought you would be saving something by hunting in the loft of the barn before you went to see whether you should need them or not?
A. I thought I would find out whether there were any sinkers before I bought the lines; and if there was, I should not have to buy any sinkers. If there were some, I should only have to buy the lines and the hooks.

Q. You began the collection of your fishing apparatus by searching for the sinkers in the barn?
A. Yes sir.

Q. You were searching in a box of old stuff in the loft of the barn?
A. Yes sir, up stairs.

Q. That you had never looked at before?
A. I had seen them.

Q. Never examined them before?
A. No sir.

Q. All the reason you supposed there was sinkers there was your father had told you there was lead in the barn?
A. Yes, lead; and one day I wanted some old nails; he said there was some in the barn.

Q. All the reason that gave you to think there was sinkers was your father said there was old lead in the barn?
A. Yes sir.

Q. Did he mention the place in the barn?
A. I think he said up stairs; I am not sure.

Q. Where did you look up stairs?
A. On that work bench, like.

# Appendix A

Q. In anything?
A. Yes; it was a box, sort of a box, and then some things lying right on the side that was not in the box.

Q. How large a box was it?
A. I could not tell you. It was probably covered up with lumber, I think.

Q. Give me the best idea of the size of the box you can.
A. Well, I should say, I don't know, I have not any idea.

Q. Give me the best idea you have.
A. I have given you the best idea I have.

Q. What is the best idea you have?
A. About that large, (measuring with hands.)

Q. That long?
A. Yes.

Q. How wide?
A. I don't know.

Q. Give me the best idea you have.
A. Perhaps about as wide as it was long.

Q. How high?
A. It was not very high.

Q. About how high?
[A.] (Witness measures with her hands.)

Q. About twice the length of your forefinger?
A. I should think so. Not quite.

Q. What was in the box?
A. Nails, and some old locks, and I don't know but there was a door knob.

Q. Anything else?
A. I don't remember anything else.

Q. Any lead?
A. Yes, some pieces of tea lead, like.

Q. Foil, what we call tin foil, the same as you use on tea chests?
A. I don't remember seeing any tin foil; not as thin as that.

Q. Tea chest lead?
A. No, sir.

Q. What did you see in shape of lead?
A. Flat pieces of lead, a little bigger than that; some of them were doubled together.

Q. How many?
A. I could not tell you.

Q. Where else did you look beside in the box?
A. I did not look anywhere for lead except on the work bench.

Q. How full was the box?
A. It was not nearly as full as it could have been.

Q. You looked on the bench, beside that where else?
A. Nowhere except on the bench.

Q. Did you look for anything else beside lead?
A. No, sir.

Q. When you got through looking for lead did you come down?
A. No, sir, I went to the west window over the hay, to the west window, and the curtain was slanted a little. I pulled it down.

Q. What else?
A. Nothing.

Q. That is all you did?
A. Yes, sir.

Q. That is the second story of the barn?
A. Yes, sir.

Q. Was the window open?
A. I think not.

Q. Hot?
A. Very hot.

Q. How long do you think you were up there?
A. Not more than fifteen or twenty minutes, I should not think.

Q. Should you think what you have told me would occupy four minutes?
A. Yes, because I ate some pears up there.

Q. Do you think all you have told me would take you four minutes?
A. I ate some pears up there.

Q. I asked you to tell me all you did.
A. I told you all I did.

Q. Do you mean to say you stopped your work, and then, additional to that, sat still and ate some pears?
A. While I was looking out of the window, yes sir.

Q. Will you tell me all you did in the second story of the barn?
A. I think I told you all I did that I can remember.

Q. Is there anything else?
A. I told you I took some pears up from the ground when I went up; I stopped under the pear tree and took some pears up when I went up.

Q. Have you now told me everything you did up in the second story of the barn?
A. Yes sir.

Q. I now call your attention, and ask you to say whether all you have told me— I don't suppose you stayed there any longer than necessary?
A. No sir, because it was close.

Q. I suppose that was the hottest place there was on the premises?
A. I should think so.

Q. Can you give me any explanation why all you have told me would occupy more than three minutes?
A. Yes, it would take me more than three minutes.

Q. To look in that box that you have described the size of on the bench and put down the curtain and then get out as soon as you conveniently could; would you say you were occupied in that business twenty minutes?
A. I think so, because I did not look at the box when I first went up.

Q. What did you do?
A. I ate my pears.

Q. Stood there eating the pears, doing nothing?
A. I was looking out of the window.

Q. Stood there, looking out of the window, eating the pears?
A. I should think so.

Q. How many did you eat?
A. Three, I think.

Q. You were feeling better than you did in the morning?
A. Better than I did the night before.

Q. You were feeling better than you were in the morning?
A. I felt better in the morning than I did the night before.

Q. That is not what I asked you. You were then, when you were in that hot loft, looking out of the window and eating three pears, feeling better, were you not, than you were in the morning when you could not eat any breakfast?
A. I never eat any breakfast.

Q. You did not answer my question, and you will, if I have to put it all day. Were you then when you were eating those three pears in that hot loft, looking out of that closed window, feeling better than you were in the morning when you ate no breakfast?
A. I was feeling well enough to eat the pears.

Q. Were you feeling better than you were in the morning?
A. I don't think I felt very sick in the morning, only— Yes, I don't know but I did feel better. As I say, I don't know whether I ate any breakfast or not, or whether I ate a cookie.

Q. Were you then feeling better than you did in the morning?
A. I don't know how to answer you, because I told you I felt better in the morning anyway.

Q. Do you understand my question? My question is whether, when you were in the loft of that barn, you were feeling better than you were in the morning when you got up?
A. No, I felt about the same.

Q. Were you feeling better than you were when you told your mother you did not care for any dinner?
A. No sir, I felt about the same.

Q. Well enough to eat pears, but not well enough to eat anything for dinner?
A. She asked me if I wanted any meat.

Q. I ask you why you should select that place, which was the only place which would put you out of sight of the house, to eat those three pears in?
A. I cannot tell you any reason.

Q. You observe that fact, do you not? You have put yourself in the only place perhaps, where it would be impossible for you to see a person going into the house?
A. Yes sir, I should have seen them from the front window.

Q. From anywhere in the yard?
A. No sir, not unless from the end of the barn.

Q. Ordinarily in the yard you could see them, and in the kitchen where you had been, you could have seen them?
A. I don't think I understand.

Q. When you were in the kitchen, you could see persons who came in at the back door?
A. Yes sir.

Q. When you were in the yard, unless you were around the corner of the house, you could see them come in at the back door?
A. No sir, not unless I was at the corner of the barn; the minute I turned I could not.

Q. What was there?
A. A little jog like, the walk turns.

Q. I ask you again to explain to me why you took those pears from the pear tree?
A. I did not take them from the pear tree.

Q. From the ground, wherever you took them from. I thank you for correcting me; going into the barn, going up stairs into the hottest place in the barn, in the rear of the barn, the hottest place, and there standing and eating those pears that morning?
A. I beg your pardon, I was not in the rear of the barn. I was in the other end of the barn that faced the street.

Q. Where you could see anybody coming into the house?
A. Yes sir.

Q. Did you not tell me you could not?
A. Before I went into the barn, at the jog on the outside.

Q. You now say when you were eating the pears, you could see the back door?
A. Yes sir.

Q. So nobody could come in at that time without your seeing them?
A. I don't see how they could.

Q. After you got through eating your pears you began your search?
A. Yes sir.

Q. Then you did not see into the house?
A. No sir, because the bench is at the other end.

Q. Now I have asked you over and over again, and will continue the inquiry, whether anything you did at the bench would occupy more than three minutes?
A. Yes, I think it would, because I pulled over quite a lot of boards in looking.

Q. To get at the box?
A. Yes sir.

Q. Taking all that, what is the amount of time you think you occupied in looking for that piece of lead which you did not find?
A. Well, I should think perhaps I was ten minutes.

Q. Looking over those old things?
A. Yes sir, on the bench.

Q. Now can you explain why you were ten minutes doing it?
A. No, only that I can't do anything in a minute.

Q. When you came down from the barn, what did you do then?
A. Came into the kitchen.

Q. What did you do then?
A. I went into the dining room and laid down my hat.

Q. What did you do then?
A. Opened the sitting room door, and went into the sitting room, or pushed it open; it was not latched.

Q. What did you do then?
A. I found my father, and rushed to the foot of the stairs.

Q. What were you going into the sitting room for?
A. To go up stairs.

Q. What for?
A. To sit down.

Q. What had become of the ironing?
A. The fire had gone out.

Q. I thought you went out because the fire was not hot enough to heat the flats.
A. I thought it would burn, but the fire had not caught from the few sparks.

Q. So you gave up the ironing and was going up stairs?
A. Yes, sir, I thought I would wait till Maggie got dinner and heat the flats again.

Q. When you saw your father where was he?
A. On the sofa.

Q. What was his position?
A. Lying down.

Q. Describe anything else you noticed at that time.
A. I did not notice anything else, I was so frightened and horrified. I ran to the foot of the stairs and called Maggie.

Q. Did you notice that he had been cut?
A. Yes; that is what made me afraid.

Q. Did you notice that he was dead?
A. I did not know whether he was or not.

Q. Did you make any search for your mother?
A. No, sir.

Q. Why not?
A. I thought she was out of the house; I thought she had gone out. I called Maggie to go to Dr. Bowen's. When they came I said, "I don't know where Mrs. Borden is." I thought she had gone out.

Q. Did you tell Maggie you thought your mother had come in?
A. No, sir.

Q. That you thought you heard her come in?
A. No, sir.

Q. Did you say to anybody that you thought she was killed up stairs?
A. No, sir.

Q. To anybody?
A. No, sir.

Q. You made no effort to find your mother at all?
A. No, sir.

Q. Who did you send Maggie for?
A. Dr. Bowen. She came back and said Dr. Bowen was not there.

Q. What did you tell Maggie?
A. I told her he was hurt.

Q. When you first told her?
A. I says "Go for Dr. Bowen as soon as you can, I think father is hurt."

Q. Did you then know that he was dead?
A. No, sir.

Q. You saw him?
A. Yes sir.

Q. You went into the room?
A. No sir.

Q. Looked in at the door?
A. I opened the door and rushed back.

Q. Saw his face?
A. No, I did not see his face, because he was all covered with blood.

Q. You saw where the face was bleeding?
A. Yes sir.

Q. Did you see the blood on the floor?
A. No sir.

Q. You saw his face covered with blood?
A. Yes sir.

Q. Did you see his eye ball hanging out?
A. No sir.

Q. See the gashes where his face was laid open?
A. No sir.

Q. Nothing of that kind?
A. No sir. (Witness covers her face with her hand for a minute or two; then examination is resumed.)

Q. Do you know of any employment that would occupy your mother for the two hours between nine and eleven in the front room?
A. Not unless she was sewing.

Q. If she had been sewing you would have heard the machine?
A. She did not always use the machine.

Q. Did you see, or were there found, anything to indicate that she was sewing up there?
A. I don't know. She had given me a few weeks before some pillow cases to make.

Q. My question is not that. Did you see, or were there found, anything to indicate that she had done any sewing in that room that morning?
A. I don't know. I was not allowed in that room; I did not see it.

Q. Was that the room where she usually sewed?
A. No sir.

Q. Did you ever know her to use that room for sewing?
A. Yes sir.

Q. When?
A. Whenever she wanted to use the machine.

Q. When she did not want to use the machine, did you know she used that room for sewing?
A. Not unless she went up to sew a button on, or something.

Q. She did not use it as a sitting room?
A. No sir.

Q. Leaving out the sewing, do you know of anything else that would occupy her for two hours in that room?
A. No, not if she had made the bed up, and she said she had when I went down.

Q. Assuming the bed was made?
A. I don't know anything.

Q. Did she say she had done the work?
A. She said she had made the bed, and was going to put on the pillow cases, about 9 o'clock.

Q. I ask you now again, remembering that—
A. I told you that yesterday.

Q. Never mind about yesterday. Tell me all the talk you had with your
mother when you came down in the morning?
A. She asked me how I felt. I said I felt better, but did not want any breakfast. She said what kind of meat did I want for dinner. I said I did not
want any. She said she was going out, somebody was sick, and she would
get the dinner, get the meat, order the meat. And I think she said something about the weather being hotter, or something; and I don't remember
that she said anything else. I said to her: "Won't you change your dress
before you go out?" She had on an old one. She said: "No, this is good
enough." That is all I can remember.

Q. In this narrative you have not again said anything about her having
said that she had made the bed?
A. I told you that she said she made the bed.

Q. In this time saying, you did not put that in. I want that conversation
that you had with her that morning. I beg your pardon again, in this time
of telling me, you did not say anything about her having received a note.
A. I told you that before.

Q. Miss Borden, I want you now to tell me all the talk you had with your
mother, when you came down, and all the talk she had with you. Please
begin again.
A. She asked me how I felt. I told her. She asked me what I wanted for
dinner. I told her not anything, what kind of meat I wanted for dinner.
I told her not any. She said she had been up and made the spare bed,
and was going to take up some linen pillow cases for the small pillows at
the foot, and then the room was done. She says: "I have had a note from
somebody that is sick, and I am going out, and I will get the din- [sic]
at the same time." I think she said something about the weather, I don't
know. She also asked me if I would direct some paper wrappers for her,
which I did.

Q. She said she had had a note?
A. Yes sir.

Q. You told me yesterday you never saw the note?
A. No sir, I never did.

Q. You looked for it?
A. No sir, but the rest have.

Q. She did not say where she was going?
A. No sir.

Q. Does she usually tell you where she is going?
A. She does not generally tell me.

Q. Did she say when she was coming back?
A. No sir.

Q. Did you know that Mr. Morse was coming to dinner?
A. No sir, I knew nothing about him.

Q. Was he at dinner the day before?
A. Wednesday noon? I don't know. I had not seen him; I don't think he was.

Q. Were you at dinner?
A. I was in the house. I don't know whether I went down to dinner or not. I was not feeling well.

Q. Whether you ate dinner or not?
A. I don't remember.

Q. Do you remember who was at dinner the day before?
A. No sir, I don't remember, because I don't know whether I was down myself or not.

Q. Were you at tea Wednesday night?
A. I went down, but I think, I don't know, whether I had any tea or not.

Q. Did you sit down with the family?
A. I think I did, but I am not sure.

Q. Was Mr. Morse there?
A. No sir, I did not see him.

Q. Who were there to tea?
A. Nobody.

Q. The family were there, I suppose?
A. Yes, sir; I mean nobody but the family.

Q. Did you have an apron on Thursday?
A. Did I what?

Q. Have an apron on Thursday?
A. No sir, I don't think I did.

Q. Do you remember whether you did or not?
A. I don't remember sure, but I don't think I did.

Q. You had aprons, of course?
A. I had aprons, yes sir.

Q. Will you try and think whether you did or not?
A. I don't think I did.

Q. Will you try and remember?
A. I had no occasion for an apron on that morning.

Q. If you can remember I wish you would.
A. I don't remember.

Q. That is all the answer you can give me about that?
A. Yes sir.

Q. Did you have any occasion to use the axe or hatchet?
A. No sir.

Q. Did you know where they were?
A. I knew there was an old axe down cellar; that is all I knew.

Q. Did you know anything about a hatchet down cellar?
A. No sir.

Q. Where was the old axe down cellar?
A. The last time I saw it it was stuck in the old chopping block.

Q. Was that the only axe or hatchet down cellar?
A. It was all I knew about.

Q. When was the last you knew of it?
A. When our farmer came to chop wood.

Q. When was that?
A. I think a year ago last winter; I think there was so much wood on hand he did not come last winter.

Q. Do you know of anything that would occasion the use of an axe or hatchet?
A. No sir.

Q. Do you know of anything that would occasion the getting of blood on an axe or hatchet down cellar?
A. No sir.

Q. I do not say there was, but assuming an axe or hatchet was found down cellar with blood on it?
A. No sir.

Q. Do you know whether there was a hatchet down there before this murder?
A. I don't know.

Q. You are not able to say your father did not own a hatchet?
A. I don't know whether he did or not.

Q. Did you know there was found at the foot of the stairs a hatchet and axe?
A. No sir, I did not.

Q. Assume that is so, can you give me any explanation of how they came there?
A. No sir.

Q. Assume they had blood on them, can you give any occasion for there being blood on them?
A. No sir.

Q. Can you tell of any killing of an animal? or any other operation that would lead to their being cast there, with blood on them?
A. No sir, he killed some pigeons in the barn last May or June.

Q. What with?
A. I don't know, but I thought he wrung their necks.

Q. What made you think so?
A. I think he said so.

Q. Did anything else make you think so?
A. All but three or four had their heads on, that is what made me think so.

Q. Did all of them come into the house?
A. I think so.

Q. Those that came into the house were all headless?
A. Two or three had them on.

Q. Were any with their heads off?
A. Yes sir.

Q. Cut off or twisted off?
A. I don't know which.

Q. How did they look?
A. I don't know, their heads were gone, that is all.

Q. Did you tell anybody they looked as though they were twisted off?
A. I don't remember whether I did or not. The skin I think was very tender, I said why are these heads off? I think I remember of telling somebody that he said they twisted off.

Q. Did they look as if they were cut off?
A. I don't know, I did not look at that particularly.

Q. Is there anything else besides that that would lead, in your opinion so far as you can remember, to the finding of instruments in the cellar with blood on them?
A. I know of nothing else that was done.

(Judge Blaisdell)—Was there any effort made by the witness to notify Mrs. Borden of the fact that Mr. Borden was found?

Q. Did you make any effort to notify Mrs. Borden of your father being killed?

A. No sir, when I found him I rushed right to the foot of the stairs for Maggie. I supposed Mrs. Borden was out. I did not think anything about her at the time, I was so—

Q. At any time did you say anything about her to anybody?

A. No sir.

Q. To the effect that she was out?

A. I told father when he came in.

Q. After your father was killed?

A. No sir.

Q. Did you say you thought she was up stairs?

A. No sir.

Q. Did you ask them to look up stairs?

A. No sir.

Q. Did you suggest to anybody to search up stairs?

A. I said, "I don't know where Mrs. Borden is;" that is all I said.

Q. You did not suggest that any search be made for her?

A. No sir.

Q. You did not make any yourself?

A. No sir.

Q. I want you to give me all that you did, by way of word or deed, to see whether your mother was dead or not, when you found your father was dead.

A. I did not do anything, except what I said to Mrs. Churchill. I said to her: "I don't know where Mrs. Borden is. I think she is out, but I wish you would look."

Q. You did ask her to look?

A. I said that to Mrs. Churchill.

Q. Where did you intend for her to look?
A. In Mrs. Borden's room.

Q. When you went out to the barn did you leave the door shut, the screen door?
A. I left it shut.

Q. When you came back did you find it shut or open?
A. No, sir; I found it open.

Q. Can you tell me anything else that you did, that you have not told me, during your absence from the house?
A. No, sir.

Q. Can you tell me when it was that you came back from the barn, what time it was?
A. I don't know what time it was.

Q. Have you any idea when it was that your father came home?
A. I am not sure, but I think it must have been after 10, because I think he told me he did not think he should go out until about 10. When he went out I did not look at the clock to see what time it was. I think he did not go out until 10, or a little after. He was not gone so very long.

Q. Will you give me the best judgment you can as to the time your father got back? If you have not any, it is sufficient to say so.
A. No, sir, I have not any.

Q. Can you give me any judgment as to the length of time that elapsed after he came back, and before you went to the barn?
A. I went right out to the barn.

Q. How soon after he came back?
A. I should think not less than five minutes; I saw him taking off his shoes and lying down; it only took him two or three minutes to do it. I went right out.

Q. When he came into the house did he not go into the dining room first?
A. I don't know.

Q. And there sit down?
A. I don't know.

Q. Why don't you know?
A. Because I was in the kitchen.

Q. It might have happened, and you not have known it?
A. Yes sir.

Q. You heard the bell ring?
A. Yes sir.

Q. And you knew when he came in?
A. Yes sir.

Q. You did not see him?
A. No sir.

Q. When did you first see him?
A. I went into the sitting room, and he was there; I don't know whether he had been in the dining room before or not.

Q. What made you go into the sitting room?
A. Because I wanted to ask him a question.

Q. What question?
A. Whether there was any mail for me.

Q. Did you not ask him that question in the dining room?
A. No sir, I think not.

Q. Was he not in the dining room sitting down?
A. I don't remember his being in the dining room sitting down.

Q. At that time was not Maggie washing the windows in the sitting room?
A. I thought I asked him for the mail in the sitting room; I am not sure.

Q. Was not the reason he went in the dining room because she was in the sitting room washing windows?
A. I don't know.

Q. Did he not go up stairs to his own room before he sat down in the sitting room?
A. I did not see him go.

Q. He had the key to his room down there?
A. I don't know whether he had it; it was kept on the shelf.

Q. Don't you remember he took the key and went into his own room and then came back?
A. No, sir.

Q. You don't remember anything of that kind?
A. No, sir; I do not think he did go up stairs either.

Q. You will swear he did not?
A. I did not see him.

Q. You swear you did not see him?
A. Yes, sir.

Q. You were either in the kitchen or sitting room all the time?
A. Yes, sir.

Q. He could not have gone up without he had gone through the kitchen?
A. No, sir.

Q. When you did go into the sitting room to ask him a question, if it was the sitting room, what took place then?
A. I asked him if he had any mail. He said "none for you." He had a letter in his hand. I supposed it was for himself. I asked him how he felt. He said "About the same." He said he should lie down[.] I asked him if he thought he should have a nap. He said he should try to. I asked him if he wanted the window left the way it was or if he felt a draught. He said "No." That is all.

Q. Did you help him about lying down?
A. No, sir.

Q. Fix his pillows or head?
A. No, sir; I did not touch the sofa.

Q. Did he lie down before you left the room?
A. Yes, sir.

Q. Did anything else take place?
A. Not that I remember of.

Q. Was he then under medical treatment?
A. No, sir.

Q. The doctor had not given him any medicine that you know of?
A. No, sir; he took some medicine; it was not doctor's medicine; it was what we gave him.

Q. What was it?
A. We gave him castor oil first and then Garfield tea.

Q. When was that?
A. He took the castor oil some time Wednesday. I think some time Wednesday noon, and I think the tea Wednesday night; Mrs. Borden gave it to him. She went over to see the doctor.

Q. When did you first consult Mr. Jennings?
A. I can't tell you that; I think my sister sent for him; I don't know.

Q. Was it you or your sister?
A. My sister.

Q. You did not send for him?
A. I did not send for him. She said did we think we ought to have him. I said do as she thought best. I don't know when he came first.

Q. Now, tell me once more, if you please, the particulars of that trouble that you had with your mother four or five years ago.
A. Her father's house on Fourth street was for sale—

Q. Whose father's house?
A. Mrs. Borden's father's house. She had a stepmother and a half sister, Mrs. Borden did, and this house was left to the stepmother and a half sister, if I understood it right, and the house was for sale. The stepmother, Mrs. Oliver Gray, wanted to sell it, and my father brought [sic] out the Widow Gray's share. She did not tell me, and he did not tell me, but some

outsiders said that he gave it to her. Put it in her name. I said if he gave that to her, he ought to give us something. Told Mrs. Borden so. She did not care anything about the house herself. She wanted it so this half sister could have a home, because she had married a man that was not doing the best he could, and she thought her sister was having a very hard time and wanted her to have a home. And we always thought she persuaded father to buy it. At any rate he did buy it, and I am quite sure she did persuade him. I said what he did for her people he ought to do for his own children. So he gave us grandfather's house. That was all the trouble we ever had.

Q. You have not stated any trouble yet between you and her?
A. I said there was feeling four or five years ago when I stopped calling her mother. I told you that yesterday.

Q. That is all there is to it then?
A. Yes, sir.

Q. You had no words with your stepmother then?
A. I talked with her about it and said what he did for her he ought to do for us; that is all the words we had.

Q. That is the occasion of his giving you the house that you sold back to him?
A. Yes, sir.

Q. Did your mother leave any property?
A. I don't know.

Q. Your own mother?
A. No, sir; not that I ever knew of.

Q. Did you ever see that thing? (Wooden club.)
A. Yes, sir; I think I have.

Q. What is it?
A. My father used to keep something similar to this, that looked very much like it under his bed. He whittled it out himself at the farm one time.

Q. How long since you have seen it?
A. I have not seen it in years.

Q. How many years?
A. I could not tell you. I should think 10 or 15 years; not since I was quite a little girl, if that is the one. I can't swear that it is the one; it was about that size. (Marks it with a cross.)

Q. How many years, 10 or 15?
A. I was a little girl, it must be as much as that.

Q. When was the last time the windows were washed before that day?
A. I don't know.

Q. Why don't you know?
A. Because I had nothing to do with the work down stairs.

Q. When was the last time that you ate with the family, that you can swear to, before your mother was killed?
A. Well, I ate with them all day Tuesday, that is, what little we ate we sat down to the table; and I think I sat down to the table with them Wednesday night, but I am not sure.

Q. All day Tuesday?
A. I was down at the table.

Q. I understand you to say you did not come down to breakfast?
A. That was Wednesday morning.

Q. I understood you to say that you did not come down to breakfast?
A. I came down, but I did not eat breakfast with them. I did not eat any breakfast. Frequently I would go into the dining room and sit down to the table with them and not eat any breakfast.

Q. Did you give to the officer the same skirt you had on the day of the tragedy?
A. Yes, sir.

Q. Do you know whether there was any blood on the skirt?
A. No, sir.

Q. Assume that there was, do you know how it came there?
A. No, sir.

Q. Have you any explanation of how it might come there?
A. No, sir.

Q. Did you know there was any blood on the skirt you gave them?
A. No, sir.

Q. Assume that there was, can you give any explanation of how it came there, on the dress skirt?
A. No, sir.

Q. Assume that there was, can you suggest any reason how it came there?
A. No, sir.

Q. Have you offered any?
A. No, sir.

Q. Have you ever offered any?
A. No, sir.

Q. Have you said it came from flea bites?
A. On the petticoats I said there was a flea bite. I said it might have been. You siad [sic] you meant the dress skirt.

Q. I did. Have you offered any explanation how that came there?
A. I told those men that were at the house that I had had fleas; that is all.

Q. Did you offer that as an explanation?
A. I said that was the only explanation that I knew of.

Q. Assuming that the blood came from the outside, can you give any explanation of how it came there?
A. No, sir.

Q. You cannot now?
A. No, sir.

Q. What shoes did you have on that day?
A. A pair of ties.

Q. What color?
A. Black.

Q. Will you give them to the officer?
A. Yes.

Q. Where are they?
A. At home.

Q. What stockings did you have on that day?
A. Black.

Q. Where are they?
A. At home.

Q. Have they been washed?
A. I don't know.

Q. Will you give them to the officer?
A. Yes, sir.

Q. The window you was at is the window that is nearest the street in the barn?
A. Yes, sir; the west window.

Q. The pears you ate you got from under the tree in the yard?
A. Yes, sir.

Q. How long were you under the pear tree?
A. I think I was under there very nearly four or five minutes. I stood looking around. I looked up at the pigeon house that they have closed up. It was no more than five minutes, perhaps not as long. I can't say sure.

(Judge Blaisdell.) Was this witness on Thursday morning in the front hall or front stairs or front chamber, any part of the front part of the house at all?
Q. What do you say to that?
A. I had to come down the front stairs to get into the kitchen.

Q. When you came down first?
A. Yes, sir.

Q. Were you afterwards?
A. No, sir.

Q. Not at all?
A. Except the few minutes I went up with the clean clothes, and I had to come back again.

Q. That you now say was before Mr. Borden went away?
A. Yes, sir.

(Miss Borden recalled [Thursday] Aug. 11, 1892.)

Q. (Mr. Knowlton.) Is there anything you would like to correct in your previous testimony?
A. No, sir.

Q. Did you buy a dress pattern in New Bedford?
A. A dress pattern?

Q. Yes.
A. I think I did.

Q. Where is it?
A. It is at home.

Q. Where?
A. Where at home?

Q. Please.
A. It is in a trunk.

Q. In your room?
A. No, sir; in the attic.

Q. Not made up?
A. O, no, sir.

Q. Where did you buy it?
A. I don't know the name of the store.

Q. On the principal street there?
A. I think it was on the street that Hutchinson's book store is on. I am not positive.

Q. What kind of a one was it, please?
A. It was a pink stripe and a white stripe, and a blue stripe corded gingham.

Q. Your attention has already been called to the circumstance of going into the drug store of Smith's, on the corner of Columbia and Main streets, by some officer, has it not, on the day before the tragedy?
A. I don't know whether some officer has asked me, somebody has spoken of it to me; I don't know who it was.

Q. Did that take place?
A. I [sic] did not.

Q. Do you know where the drug store is?
A. I don't.

Q. Did you go into any drug store and inquire for prussic acid?
A. I did not.

Q. Where were you on Wednesday morning that you remember?
A. At home.

Q. All the time?
A. All day, until Wednesday night.

Q. Nobody there but your parents and yourself and the servant?
A. Why, Mr. Morse came sometime in the afternoon, or at noon time, I suppose, I did not see him.

Q. He did not come so to see you?
A. No, sir, I did not see him.

Q. He did not come until afternoon anyway, did he?
A. I don't think he did; I am not sure.

Q. Did you dine with the family that day?
A. I was down stairs, yes, sir. I did not eat any breakfast with them.

Q. Did you go into the drug store for any purpose whatever?
A. I did not.

Q. I think you said yesterday that you did not go into the room where your father lay, after he was killed, on the sofa, but only looked in at the door?
A. I looked in; I did not go in.

Q. You did not step into the room at all?
A. I did not.

Q. Did you ever, after your mother was found killed, go into that room?
A. No, sir.

Q. Did you afterwards go into the room where your father was found killed, any more than to go through it to go up stairs?
A. When they took me up stairs they took me through that room.

Q. Otherwise than that did you go into it?
A. No, sir.

Q. Let me refresh your memory. You came down in the night to get some water with Miss Russell, along towards night, or in the evening, to get some water with Miss Russell?
A. Thursday night? I don't remember it.

Q. Don't you remember coming down sometime to get some toilet water?
A. No, sir; there was no toilet water down stairs.

Q. Or to empty the slops?
A. I don't know whether I did Thursday evening or not. I am not sure.

Q. You think it may have been some other evening?
A. I don't remember coming down with her to do such a thing. I may have, I can't tell whether it was Thursday evening or any other evening.

Q. Other than that, if that did take place, you don't recollect going into that room for any purpose at any time?
A. No, sir.

Q. Was the dress that was given to the officers the same dress that you wore that morning?
A. Yes, sir.

Q. The India silk?
A. No, it is not an India silk, it is silk and linen; some call it bengaline silk.

Q. Something like that dress there? (Pongee.)
A. No, it was not like that.

Q. Did you give to the officer the same shoes and stockings that you wore?
A. I did, sir.

Q. Do you remember where you took them off?
A. I wore the shoes ever after that, all around the house Friday, and all day Thursday, and all day Friday and Saturday until I put on my shoes for the street.

Q. That is to say you wore them all that day, Thursday, until you took them off for the night?
A. Yes, sir.

Q. Did you tell us yesterday all the errand that you had at the barn?
A. Yes, sir.

Q. You have nothing to add to what you said?
A. No, sir.

Q. You had no other errand than what you have spoken of?
A. No, sir.

Q. Miss Borden, of course you appreciate the anxiety that everybody has to find the author of this tragedy, and the questions that I put to you have been in that direction; I now ask you if you can furnish any other fact, or give any other, even suspicion, that will assist the officers in any way in this matter?
A. About two weeks ago—

Q. Was you going to tell the occurrence about the man that called at the house?
A. No, sir. It was after my sister went away. I came home from Miss Russell's one night, and as I came up, I always glanced towards the side door as I came along by the carriage way, I saw a shadow on the side steps. I did not stop walking, but I walked slower. Somebody ran down the steps,

around the east end of the house. I thought it was a man, because I saw no skirts, and I was frightened, and of course I did not go around to see. I hurried in the front door as fast as I could and locked it.

Q. What time of night was that?
A. I think about quarter of 9; it was not after 9 o'clock, anyway.

Q. Do you remember what night that was?
A. No, sir; I don't. I saw somebody run around the house once before last winter.

Q. One thing at a time. Do you recollect about how long ago that last occurrence was?
A. It was after my sister went away. She has been away two weeks today, so it must have been within two weeks.

Q. Two weeks today? Or two weeks at the time of the murder?
A. Is not today Thursday?

Q. Yes, but I thought you said she was gone two weeks the day of the murder?
A. Is not today Thursday?

Q. Yes, but that would be three weeks. I thought you said the day your father was murdered she had been away just two weeks?
A. Yes, she had.

Q. Then it would be three weeks today your sister went away, a week has elapsed?
A. Yes, it would be three weeks.

Q. You mean it was sometime within the two weeks that your sister was away?
A. Yes. I had forgotten that a whole week had passed since the affair.

Q. Different from that you cannot state?
A. No, sir; I don't know what the date was.

Q. This form when you first saw it was on the steps of the backdoor?
A. Yes, sir.

Q. Went down the rear steps?
A. Went down towards the barn.

Q. Around the back side of the house?
A. Disappeared in the dark; I don't know where they went.

Q. Have you ever mentioned that before?
A. Yes, sir; I told Mr. Jennings.

Q. To any officer?
A. I don't think I have, unless I told Mr. Hanscomb.

Q. What was you going to say about last winter?
A. Last winter when I was coming home from church one Thursday evening I saw somebody run around the house again. I told my father of that.

Q. Did you tell your father of this last one?
A. No, sir.

Q. Of course you could not identify who it was either time?
A. No, I could not identify who it was, but it was not a very tall person.

Q. Have you sealskin sacks?
A. Yes, sir.

Q. Where are they?
A. Hanging in a large white bag in the attic, each one separate.

Q. Put away for the summer?
A. Yes, sir.

Q. Do you ever use prussic acid on your sacks?
A. Acid? No, sir; I don't use anything on them.

Q. Is there anything else that you can suggest that even amounts to anything whatever?
A. I know of nothing else except the man who came, and father ordered him out, that is all I know.

Q. That you told about the other day?
A. I think I did; yes, sir.

Q. You have not been able to find that man?
A. I have not; I don't know whether anybody else has or not.

Q. Have you caused search to be made for him?
A. Yes, sir.

Q. When was the offer of reward made for the detection of the criminals?
A. I think it was made Friday.

Q. Who suggested that?
A. We suggested it ourselves, and asked Mr. Buck if he did not think it was a good plan.

Q. Whose suggestion was it, yours or Emma's?
A. I don't remember. I think it was mine.

# APPENDIX B

The Sunday Standard

NEW BEDFORD, MASS., SUNDAY, JULY 20, 1924

---

## BORDEN CASE HAD NO PARALLEL IN COUNTRY

---

### Called "Most Interesting and Puzzling" Tragedy in Nation's History by Edmund Lester Pearson in New Book Discussing American Murders

---

### By Cooper Gaw

Nearly a third of a century has elapsed since the murder of Mr. and Mrs. Andrew J. Borden in Fall River in August, 1892. In that period of time, so rapidly do happenings crowd upon each other, the memory of events once sharply outlined grows dim, and details once clear in the mind become blurred. By many who were keenly interested in the Borden case the facts have been forgotten; and to a host of others who have grown up since that time the celebrated mystery is little more than a name. The appearance of Edmund Lester Pearson's "Studies in Murder," published by the MacMillan Company, in which the place of honor is given to the Fall River tragedy, is therefore timely as a means of refreshing the memory and as a summary of the salient facts in a case which still ranks among the most fascinating of murder mysteries.

"Without a parallel," Mr. Pearson says of it, the "most interesting and perhaps the most puzzling murder which has occurred in this country." It involved people of a type which it is almost impossible to associate with such dreadful deeds of violence as those which cost Andrew Borden and his wife their lives. It was not complicated by scandals of the kind which lead to the 'crime passionel.' "Hardly ever was a murder committed where the limits of time and space so closed in upon the act leaving such a narrow gap for the assassin to slip through to security."

### Creates Proper State of Mind

Mr. Pearson tells his story with a keen sense of its dramatic values. He has the gift of creating the atmosphere of mystery and dread which is appropriate in such a recital. From a study of records he caught what the late James D. O'Neil of the Fall River Globe, who had a newspaper man's intimate connection with the case, once stressed in a talk he gave before the members of The Standard staff—the sharp contrast between the drowsy, listless, hot summer afternoon and the shocking butchery accomplished in the house on Second street.

Yet if Mr. Pearson thus colors his story by deftly creating the proper state of mind, his treatment of the facts is in the main objective and impartial. He has no purpose but to present the essential circumstances. Inevitably, however, certain facts are emphasized, and this emphasis, even in the absence of arguments and opinions, gives a clue to what is in the writer's mind.

Mr. Pearson quotes from one of the series of annual articles written by Mr. O'Neil for the Globe in the ironic conclusion that the Bordens were not murdered, but that they died of the heat. In line with this is Mr. Pearson's suggestion that the tragedy was a fitting consequence of the breakfast of mutton broth and boiled mutton of which the Bordens partook that sultry August morning. Plainly he approves the belief always held by Mr. O'Neil and set forth by Edwin H. Porter, also of the Globe, in his book,

"The Fall River Tragedy"—a book now out of print and, according to Mr. Pearson, which the Fall River public library does not permit to circulate. The belief is one to be implied and not expressed; a belief to be inferred, as it were, from the fact that all other hypotheses are discarded as absurd. In what Porter wrote, in all that O'Neil wrote in that remarkable series of anniversary articles noted for their bitter irony, there is the unmistakable insistence that of all possible explanations of this crime there was one, and only one, that was not so absurd as to be beneath serious consideration.

## Setting the Crime

The setting of the Borden murders may be briefly recalled. The household consisted of Andrew J. Borden and his wife; of Mr. Borden's two daughters, Emma and Lizzie; and of a servant, Bridget Sullivan. On the day of the murders, Emma was visiting friends in Fairhaven; and John Vinnicum Morse of Dartmouth, a relative, was making one of his occasional visits to the Bordens. Mr. Borden, after the mutton broth breakfast, went to business. Mr. Morse left the house to make a call in another part of the city. Mrs. Borden was engaged in making the beds and setting the spare bedroom to rights. Bridget Sullivan, after her breakfast, became sick and vomited and went to her room to lie down. Lizzie Borden, as she said afterward, visited the barn and climbed into the loft; one explanation was that she wanted something to fix a screen, another that she was looking for lead to use as a sinker on a fish line. Mr. Borden returned at his usual time and Bridget Sullivan let him into the house. Sometime after that Lizzie called her and said her father had been killed. He lay, his face almost unrecognizable from blows of an axe or hatchet, on a couch in the sitting room; and shortly after a neighbor, going upstairs, found Mrs. Borden dead and similarly disfigured on the floor of the spare bedroom.

In speaking of Officer Allen, the first policeman to appear upon the scene after Lizzie Borden gave the alarm, Mr. Pearson says that it was his task to begin "an investigation which was to call down upon the police unlimited criticism and abuse—quite undeserved, as best I can judge." "There have been many to assert that a prompt and intelligent search of the house, will all that this implies, would have solved the mystery at once. This assertion seems to be based upon the knowledge gained after the fact and upon suppositions which may or may not be sound. It is not at all impossible that the police did, within 24 hours, discover nearly all the evidence which it was humanly possible to find. I think that it can even be put more strongly: it is probable that they did. This statement holds true, it seems to me, whatever view one takes of the commission of the crime. If one follows the opinion of those who hold that the murders were the work of a stranger, and outsider, then this assassin certainly carried with him, when he fled from the house, all the most important evidence. And while it is not possible to discuss other theories, except as one may speculate upon a mystery, it is not unreasonable to believe that the most telling clews as to guilt were suppressed, destroyed or removed before the alarm was given. Officer Allen did not act with composure nor acumen—but it may be that his omissions were less damaging than they have been considered."

## Then Suspected Lizzie

It was the conversation between Miss Borden and Officer Philip Harrington which, when repeated to City Marshal Hilliard, aroused suspicions "in the mind of the police that the daughter knew more of the circumstances of the tragedy than she cared to tell." The police, the author goes on, were to pay dearly for such suspicions, but it seems hard to understand … how they could have avoided them. And yet it was a monstrous thing to suspect. The crime, so brutal and savage, was not the kind to be associated with a woman of this sort. To quote from Porter again: "The author of that hideous slaughter had come and gone as gently as a south wind, but had fulfilled his mission as terrifically as a cyclone."

The spreading of the news of the murders brought out the usual crop of fantastic stories. There was one about a mysterious Portuguese who, says Mr. Pearson, was called a Portuguese because he was a Swede. There were "miscreants who turned up in lonely places … still brandishing axes or hatchets dripping with gore." There was the wild-eyed man testified to by Dr. Handy—a creature sometimes referred to as Mike the Soldier. The police showed no lack of energy in running down all rumors, however incredible. All of them, of course, sprang from an assumption that the crime had been committed by some one outside the Borden household.

Meanwhile the police found no reason to abandon their suspicions concerning Lizzie Borden. The funeral of her father and step-mother took place Saturday, August 6. That night Marshal Hilliard and the Mayor, Dr.

John W. Coughlin, called at the Borden house and the Mayor told Lizzie that she was under suspicion. The following Tuesday the inquest began before Judge Blaisdell and Lizzie was one of the witnesses. Her attorney, Andrew J. Jennings, asked for permission to be present "in the interests of the witnesses," but his request was denied. The inquest ended Thursday and that night Lizzie was arrested. August 25 she had her preliminary hearing in the District Court and was found probably guilty and held for the grand jury.

### Not Killed at Same Time

By this time it had been established that Mrs. Borden was killed first in the spare bedroom upstairs, and that her husband had been killed about an hour and a half later—a circumstance of vital importance as affecting the probability of some one's having come in from the outside to perpetrate these crimes. It was shown that Lizzie Borden, a few days before, in conversation with a neighbor, Alice Russell, had expressed a premonition of disaster, and had referred to unnamed enemies of her father and to a suspicion that the majority of the household had been poisoned. It was shown, on the testimony of Eli Bence, who afterward kept a drug store in New Bedford, that Lizzie had tried to purchase prussic acid of him. During the time when her father must have been killed, Lizzie said she was out in the barn up in the loft, searching for lead to use as a sinker on a fish line, but her testimony on this point was given at the inquest was contradictory and unsatisfactory. Again, Lizzie had said that her step-mother left the house that morning in response to a note asking her to come to a sick friend. The note was never found, nor did any one come forward to acknowledge having sent it. No one had seen Mrs. Borden outside the house that morning, and when her body was found she was not dressed in clothes she would have worn on the street. As against all this, Mr. Pearson cites "the glaring improbability of such murders being committed by a woman: combined with the failure to find any definitely determined weapon: and above everything, the absence of blood from the clothing or person of the accused. All these not only strengthened the faith of those who were sure of her innocence, but convinced the authorities that they were far from having a strong case."

Indeed, before the trial in the Superior Court in New Bedford, District Attorney Hosea M. Knowlton wrote to Attorney General Pillsbury a letter in which he said: "The case has proceeded so far and an indictment has been found by the grand inquest of the county that it does not seem to me that we ought to take the responsibility of discharging her without trial, even though there is every reasonable expectation of a verdict of not guilty. I am unable to concur fully in your views as to the probable result. I think it may well be that the jury might disagree upon the case. But even in my most sanguine moments I have scarcely expected a verdict of guilty."

When Mr. Knowlton wrote this, the case, in his mind, was stronger than that which he was actually able to present. In addition to the points cited above he knew that he could prove long-standing ill-feeling between Lizzie Borden and her step-mother, and ill feeling between father and daughters over money matters. He also had evidence that Lizzie had, after the murders, burned a dress which she said was covered with paint.

The trial opened June 5, 1893, before Chief Justice Albert Mason and Justices Caleb Blodgett and Justin Dewey. Mr. Knowlton and William H. Moody, afterward Attorney General in the Roosevelt cabinet, appeared for the government. Counsel for the defense were George D. Robinson, ex-governor of the state, Andrew J. Jennings of Fall River and Melvin O. Adams.

### Weakens Government Case

The first blow suffered by the government was the exclusion of the transcript of the testimony given by Miss Borden at the inquest. The ground taken was that she was practically under arrest at the time she gave this testimony. Another severe blow was the ruling which excluded all testimony as to Miss Borden's attempted purchase of poison from Eli Bence, the court holding that the evidence did not come up to the offer. These rulings did much to weaken a case that was, in the opinion of Mr. Knowlton himself, none too strong to begin with.

Apropos of the inquest testimony, Mr. Pearson, while his language is a bit ambiguous, apparently is under the mistaken impression that no transcript of Lizzie Borden's testimony is available today. "I am not sure," he says, "that it is in existence. It is to be found today only in the press reports of that date"—the date of the hearing in the District Court— "and in Mr. Porter's book." He quotes from the latter source, what looks like a newspaper report of Lizzie's testimony as Mr. Knowlton read it at the preliminary hearing before Judge Blaisdell. It is not in question and answer form, but a running story such as a reporter would write. If Mr. Pearson had consulted the files of The Standard he would have found, in the issue of Monday, June 12, the complete text of Lizzie's inquest testimony. It is in question and answer form and comprises 15 newspaper columns. It was on that date that the court excluded this evidence; and Mr. Knowlton furnished The Standard with a copy of it and The Standard printed it. If Mr. Pearson means that the original stenographic report is not in existence he may be right, but this in The Standard was a verbatim copy of it.

It may be noted, in passing, that a copy of the Lizzie Borden testimony was given to The Standard in advance by Mr. Knowlton, subject to release the moment is was admitted or excluded. The matter had been put into type and printed in the form of a supplement to the regular edition, these supplements being kept under lock and key. The release came at a time which permitted the rejected evidence to be distributed with the first edition of The Standard which was the only newspaper in the country to print it that day.

Of the summing up for the government Mr. Pearson writes: "Mr. Knowlton, in closing for the government, had a much harder problem (than Governor Robinson). He was asking for a conviction of a woman and a church member who was supported and buttressed by friends, and by a press which had almost ceased to do anything except palpitate to the sentimentalism of the nosier section of the public. He was a thickset man, with a tremendous manner, easily exaggerated by his detractors into the air of the inquisitor or tyrant. No prosecuting officer in Massachusetts ever had a less enviable task than his: none ever carried his work through with more ability or more courageous fulfillment of a public duty. His address was acknowledged, even in the hostile press, as far abler than that of his opponent. Mr. Robinson talked down to the whims and prejudices of the country jury; Mr. Knowlton talked straight to citizens whom he assumed had an eye to their duty."

What counted in favor of the defense, besides the exclusion of important parts of the government's case, was the absence of any weapon known to have been used in the commission of the crimes, and the [*illegible*] absence of bloodstains on the person and clothing of the prisoner. There were various theories to account for this, one of them being that some sort of a covering was used, the other that the murderer at the time the crimes were committed was naked. The charge to the jury was delivered by Judge Dewey, and was characterized by Joe Howard, most conspicuous but by no means the ablest of the out of town journalists who "alternately amused and were amused by New Bedford," as a "plea for the innocent." This was intended as a compliment but Mr. Pearson thinks it could hardly have been enjoyed by the learned and supposedly impartial judge.

## Unfair to Government

Judge Charles G. Davis of Plymouth, in letters to the Boston Advertiser afterward published under the title of "The Conduct of the Law in the Borden Case," severely condemned the rulings of the court. "It was not the prisoner but the Commonwealth which did not have a fair trial," he said. To which Mr. Pearson adds: "It is impracticable to quote more, but I am led to believe from conversations with lawyers, that the Superior Court of Massachusetts has never been subjected to such criticism as that resulting from the conduct of the justices in the Borden case. And in this criticism there was no hint or intimation of corruption, but of a mental infirmity or bias resulting from an unwillingness to believe that a woman could murder her father."

John H. Wigmore, in "The American Law Review," while implying that the evidence did not justify a conviction, assailed the rulings made by the judges as to the prussic acid evidence and the testimony at the inquest. "It is difficult to see," he says, "how the assailant could have avoided receiving blood-marks during the assaults; it is also difficult to understand what arrangements of the implements and clothing, and what combination of opportunity, suffered to allow the accused, if she was the assailant to remove the traces upon the weapon and clothes after each assault. But, first, these are difficulties of ignorance; in other words, there is no proved fact which is inconsistent with the things being so: we merely cannot find traces of the exact modus operandi; second, this difficulty is equally as great for any other person than the accused, and we may say greater: it is a difficulty that cannot change the balance of conviction. On the other hand, the conduct of the accused after the killing was such that no conceivable hypothesis except that of guilt will explain the inconsistencies and improbabilities that were asserted by her. The statements about the purpose of the barn visit, and about the discovery of the father's death, are frightfully inconsistent; while the story of the note requires for its truth a combination of circumstances almost inconceivable. We may add to this the inevitable query: Why did the accused not take the stand to explain these things? Of course, it was her legal right to remain silent; but the rule against self-incrimination is not one of logic or of relevancy; it is a rule of policy and fairness, based on broad considerations or average results desirable in the long run. It cannot prevent us as logical beings from drawing our inferences; and if we weigh in this case the confounding inconsistencies and improbabilities of these statements and then place with these the opportunity and the refusal to explain them, we cannot help feeling that she failed to explain them because she could not; and one side of the balance sinks heavily."

## Sympathy for Accused

It is worth while to speak of the national interest which this celebrated case aroused and of the unanimous sentiment in favor of the accused. Mr. Pearson related that if, in intruding upon a party, one heard such a remark as "I tell you, she never did it," there would be no need of asking the topic of conversation [*illegible*] the Borden case. With a few exceptions the out-of-town newspaper men openly took sides with the accused. They seemed to think, as Mr. Pearson says, that the murders should be forgotten and Miss Borden sent home amid a shower of roses. The police of Fall River and District Attorney Knowlton were assailed as persecutors of innocence. Miss Borden was always "that unfortunate girl." Having been active in church work, he had the support of [*illegible*], and such women as Mary A. Livermore and other equal rights champions seemed to think that devotion to their cause required them to assert the defendant's innocence. Mr. Pearson refers several times to the Rev. Mr. Buck and Rev. Mr. Jubb, Fall River pastors, who shared the honor of escorting the prisoner as she appeared in public, and whom he describes as the "Box and Cox of the Borden case."

The jury, it would appear in retrospect, rendered a verdict in accordance with the evidence submitted to them and the instructions of the court, but there were and are many who believed that there had been a miscarriage of justice. "There are," says Mr. Pearson, in concluding his narrative, "a dozen unanswered questions to ponder. What was the meaning of the laugh from the head of the stairs heard by Bridget Sullivan? What is the explanation of the burglary in 1891? What caused the mysterious illness in the family? Assuming the theory of an assassin from outside, where did he go? What was his motive? Why did he kill Mrs. Borden? Adopting the opinion of the prosecution, how could the departure of Bridget Sullivan, to her own room, be counted upon? Or the time of Mr. Morse's return? What was the truth about the poison story? Could anybody have made this attempt so openly? ... Were there any grounds for the suspicions entertained against two men, and at least one other woman, all of whom testified at the trial? (Suspicions, that is, of complicity). Will the whole truth ever come out?"

# *A*PPENDIX *C*

## Annotated Bibliography of Works by
## Edmund Lester Pearson by Publication Date

*The Old Librarian's Almanack: A very rare pamphlet first published in New Haven Connecticut in 1773 and now reprinted for the first time.* Vermont: Elm Tree Press, 1909.
A reprint of an a 1773 publication found in the library of Nathaniel Cutter, Esq. (1835-1907), a lawyer who practiced his profession in Newburyport, Massachusetts. Pamphlet.

*The Library and the Librarian: A Selection of Articles from the Boston Evening Transcript and Other Sources.* Vermont: The Elm Tree Press, 1910.
A collection of articles that appeared in "The Librarian" column of the *Boston Evening Transcript*. It also contains "The Children's Librarian versus Huckleberry Finn," first printed in *The Library Journal*, and "An Amateur's Notions of Boy's Books," a paper read at the convention of the American Library Association in 1908.

*The Librarian at Play.* Boston: Small, Maynard and Company, 1911.
A collection of twelve articles that appeared in "The Librarian" column of the *Boston Evening Transcript*. It also contains "The Crowded Hour" and "Mulch," printed in this collection for the first time.

*The Believing Years.* New York: The MacMillan Company, 1912.
A Bildungsroman account for a juvenile audience. Fiction.

*The Voyage of the Hoppergrass.* New York: The MacMillan Company, 1913.
Story set in the year before the outbreak of World War I and set on the New England coast. It is the fictional story of one young man and his friends and their adventures over the course of a few days going sailing.

*The Secret Book.* New York: The MacMillan Company, 1914.
A collection of library anecdotes. Pearson writes that "a large part of this book has been contributed, in different form, to the *Boston Evening Transcript.*

*Theodore Roosevelt.* New York: The MacMillan Company, 1920.
Biography of Theodore Roosevelt, published a year after the subject's death.

*Books in Black or Red.* New York. The MacMillan Company, 1923.
A book about book collecting.

*Studies in Murder.* New York. The MacMillan Company, 1924.
Contains: "The Borden Case," "The Twenty-Third Street Murder," "Mate Bram!" "The Hunting Knife," "Uncle Amos Dreams a Dream."

*Murder at Smutty Nose and Other Murders.* London: William Heinemann Limited, 1927.
Contains: "The Murder at Smutty Nose; or, The Crime of Louis Wagner"; "A Dimnition Body; or, The Embarrassments of Mr. Udderook"; America's Classic Murder; or, The Disappearance of Dr. Parkman"; "The People versus Molineux; or, Tow Tragedies and a Farce"; "Three Footnotes to De Quncey: Doctor Cream, Doctor Crippen, Mr. Smith"; "The Salem Conspiracy; or, Proof by Circumstantial Evidence"; "The Tiverton Tragedy; or, The Strange Case of Miss Cornell and Rev. Mr. Avery"; "Two Victorian Ladies: Miss Madeleine Smith, Miss Constance Kent"; "Hell Benders; or, The Story of a Wayside Tavern"; "The Bordens: A Postscript"; "Number 31 Bond Street; or, The Accomplishments of Mrs. Cunningham."

*Five Murders, With a Final Note on the Borden Case.* New York: The Crime Club by Doubleday, Doran & Company, 1928.
Contains: "The Man Who Was Too Clever," "The Mystery of Tenants Harbour," Aboard the 'Glendower,'" "The Doctor's Whisky," "The Firm of Patrick & Jones," "A Postscript: The End of the Borden Case."

*Queer Books.* New York: Doubleday, Doran and Company, 1928.
Contains these Edmund Pearson essays on a variety of topics: "Temperance Novels," "Making the Eagle Scream," "Alonzo and Melissa," "The Tribe of Gifted Hopkins," "The Unfortunate Lovers," "Genteel Behaviour, I," "Genteel Behaviour, II," "Crotchets," "Side-Whiskers

and Seduction," "The Baedeker of Banner Elk," "Lilies and Languors," "From Sudden Death I," "From Sudden Death II," "The Three Sisters—A Yankee Casanova."

*Dime Novels; or, Following an Old Trail in Popular Literature.* Boston: Little, Brown and Company, 1929.
Contains: Part I. "Innocent Youth: The Pioneer," "The Times—Books and Readers of the Day," "Afloat and Ashore; Success," "Beadle, the Founder; Propriety Rampant," "The Imitators," "A Personal Interlude," "Morals, Morals," "Beadle's Authors." Part II. "Wild Days: The 1880s," "The Detectives: Old Cap," "The Detectives: Old Sleuth," "Broadway Billy and Jack Harkaway," "Deadwood Dick." Part III. "Old Age: The Menace of Respectability," "Nick Carter," "Yale's Greatest Hero," "All the Manly Virtues."

*Instigation of the Devil.* New York: Charles Scribner's Sons, 1930.
Contains: "Mrs, Wharton's House-Party," "The Colt," "What Does A Murderer Look Like?" "The Wicked Duke," "Five Times Convicted of Murder," "For the Borgia Medae, Connecticut Presents," "What Makes a Good Murder?" "The Tichborne Case," "A Young Lady Named Perkins," "The First Butterfly of Broadway," "You Murdering Ministers," "That Damned Fellow Upstairs," "Precedents in the Hall-Mills Case," "Was Poe a Detective?" "The Occasionally Veiled Murderess," The Man Pays — Sometimes," "The Hanging of Hicks the Pirate," "The Mysterious Murder of Cecile Combettes," "Eight Professors from Yale," "The Tirrells of Weymouth," "The 'Learned' Murderer," "Accomplished Female Liars," "A Rather Mysterious Chancellor," "The Death of Gulielma Sands," "The Crime in the Sunday School," "Mr. Spooner's in the Well," "Rules for Murderesses."

*More Studies in Murder.* New York: Harrison Smith & Robert Haas, 1936.
Contains: "The Abominable Yelverton," "The Archdeacon's Pajamas," "Bertram and Burglar," "Birth of the Brainstorm," The Corpse on the Speak-easy Floor," "The Curious Druces," "The Death of Bella Wright," "The First Great Disappearer," "Four Infamous Names— Jack the Ripper, Charley Page, J.P. Watson, Peter Kurken," "The Great Chowder Murder," "Legends of Lizzie," "Malloy the Mighty," "Miss Holland's Elopement," "Mr. Bravo's Burgundy," "Mr Elwell," "Mrs. Costello Cleans the Boiler," "Murder in Greenwich Village," "Nineteen Dandelions," "Pronounced 'Stewky'," "Sarah Jane Robinson,"

"Scenery by Currier & Ives," "The Sleepy Hollow Massacre," "Sob Sisters Emerge," "A Thousand Pounds a Minute," "The Wicked Hansom," "Willie's Legs."

*Trial of Lizzie Borden, edited, with a history of the case.* New York, Doubleday, Doran and Company, 1937.
Close reading of the trial transcript of The Commonwealth vs Lizzie A. Borden.

*Masterpieces of Murder: An Edmund Person True Crime Reader Edited together with an original essay on the Borden Case by Gerald Gross.* Boston: Little, Brown and Company, 1963.
Contains: "What Makes a Good Murder?" "Rules for Murderesses," "Accomplished Female Liars," "Three Footnotes to De Quincy," "America's Classic Murder or the Disappearance of Doctor Parkman," "The Firm of Patrick & Jones," "Nineteen Dandelions," "The First Great Disappear," "Sob Sisters Emerge," "Mrs. Costello Cleans the Boiler," "The Hunting Knife," "The Sixth Capsule or Proof by Circumstantial Evidence," "You Murdering Minsters!" "Pronounced 'Stwekey'," "Mrs. Wharton's House Party," "The Death of Bella Wright," "Mr. Elwell," "Willie's Legs," "That Damned Fellow Upstairs," "Legends of Lizzie," "The End of the Borden Case: The Final Word," "The Pearson-Radin Controversy over the Guilt of Lizzie Borden—A Postscript to 'The Final Word'" (by Gerald Gross), "A Postscript to 'The Pearson-Radin Controversy' (by Mrs. Edmund Pearson).

*Murders that Baffled the Experts.* New York: Signet Books, 1967.
Contains: "The Blue Blood Mystery of Boston," The Case of Mr. Wainwright," "The Case of Tommy Tucker," "The Death of Bella Wright," "The Locked Room," "Miss Holland's Elopement," "The Mystery of the Cottage by the Lake," "The Mystery of the Dancing Shoes," "The Petal of the Red Geranium," "Scotland Yard's Strangest Case."

*The Adventure of the Lost Manuscripts.* 1911, reprinted by Aspen Books, 1974.
A parody of Sherlock Holmes novels.

*The Librarian: selections from the column of that name.* Metuchen, New Jersey: Scarecrow Pres, 1976.
From March, 1906 to May, 1920, Edmund Lester Pearson wrote a weekly column titled "The Librarian," appearing in the *Boston Evening*

*Transcript.* "Edited by Jane B. Durnell and Norman D. Stevens, this compilation contains some of the most perceptive comments upon the state of American libraries during the period."

# INDEX

by Stefani Koorey, PhD

Entries in this index are arranged in word-by-word order, using the *Chicago Manual of Style*, 17th Edition.

www.ingramcontent.com/pod-product-compliance
Lightning Source LLC
Chambersburg PA
CBHW060246100426
42742CB00011B/1655